THE RANGE

3/07

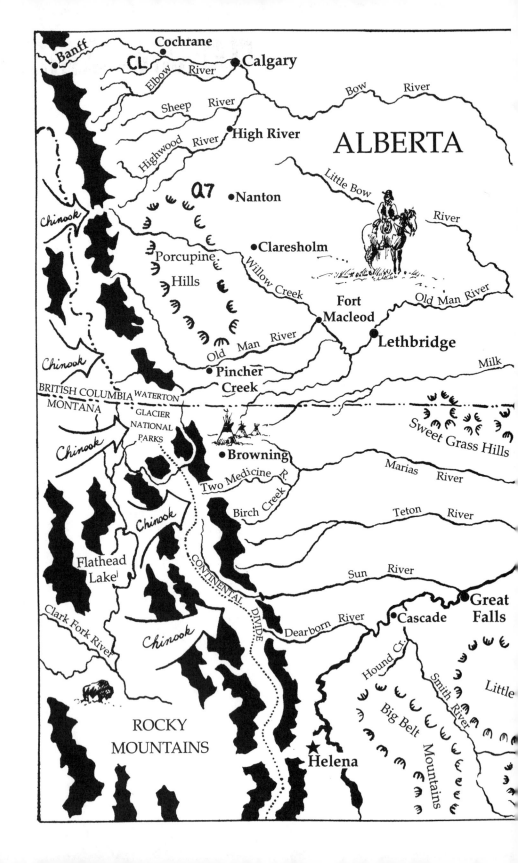

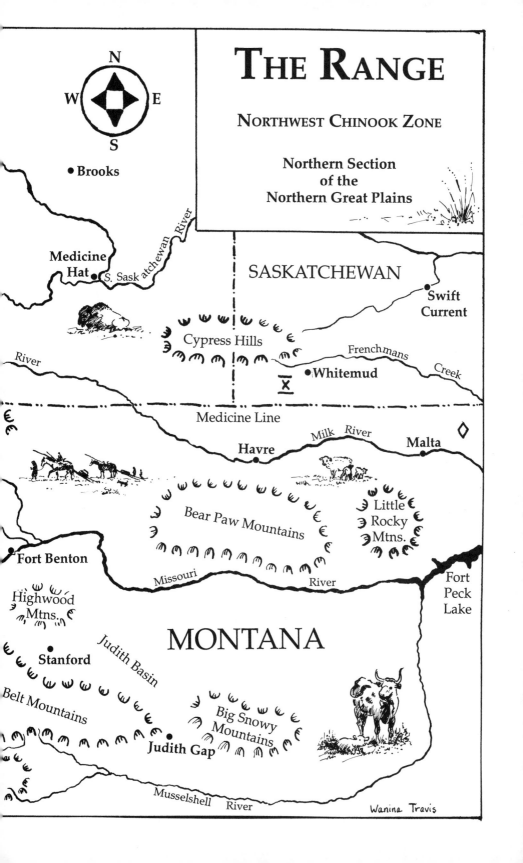

THE RANGE

NORTHWEST CHINOOK ZONE

Northern Section of the Northern Great Plains

N W E S

• Brooks

SASKATCHEWAN

Medicine Hat
S. Saskatchewan River

Swift Current

Cypress Hills

Frenchmans Creek

Whitemud

River

Medicine Line

Milk River

Havre

Malta

Bear Paw Mountains

Little Rocky Mtns.

Fort Benton

Missouri River

Fort Peck Lake

Highwood Mtns.

MONTANA

• Stanford

Judith Basin

Belt Mountains

Big Snowy Mountains

Judith Gap

Musselshell River

Wanina Travis

THE RANGE

Sherm Ewing

CLARKSTON CENTER

Mountain Press Publishing Company
Missoula, 1990

Cover painting and drawings
by Wanina Travis.

Second Printing
August 1991

Library of Congress Cataloging-in-Publication Data

Ewing, Sherm, 1926-
  The range / Sherm Ewing.
      p.   cm.
  Includes bibliographical references and index.
  ISBN 0-87842-274-9 : $25.00 — ISBN 0-87842-267-6 (pbk.) : $12.00
  1. Range management—Montana—History.   2. Range management—Alberta—History. 3. Ranch life—Montana—History.
  4. Ranch life—Alberta—History. 5. Rangelands—Montana—History.
  6. Rangelands—Alberta—History. 7. Livestock—Montana—History.
  8. Livestock—Alberta—History. 9. Ranchers—Montana—Interviews.
  10. Ranchers—Alberta—Interviews.   I. Title.
  SF85.35.M9E95   1990   90-45044
  636 ' .01 ' 09786—dc20   CIP

Mountain Press Publishing Company
P.O. Box 2399
Missoula, Montana 59806

And he gave it for his opinion, that whoever could make two ears of corn or two blades of grass to grow upon a spot of ground where only one grew before, would deserve better of mankind, and do more essential service to his country, than the whole race of politicians put together.

—Jonathan Swift (1726)

Contents

Foreword

Sherm Ewing came into the Cattlemen office one day twenty years ago holding an envelope in his hand. "Could you use a crossword puzzle in your magazine?" he asked. "All the words are about cows and ranches," he assured me. "Your readers would like it." It was a good crossword puzzle, too, and unique, of course, because you had to be a cowman to understand it. We published it in the next issue. Those readers who were smart enough to solve the puzzle loved it.

Up till then I had always thought of my friend Sherm as a top-notch manager of grass and cattle, but I had not realized how facile and lovely the English language was to him and how readily he was its master. Now you, too, can discover what a "good read" Sherm is when you turn the first pages of this book. But, before you do, I want to tell you something about the author and why *The Range* is important and why few others could have written it.

Sherm has always been a forerunner in devising and using good practices—in cattle breeding, in business and association affairs, and in range management. In 1955 he arrived in Alberta and bought a traditionally managed ranch and a herd of conventional cattle. Nothing much had changed in fifty years, except the cattle had grown smaller and the grass less productive.

In an industry where tradition was king, this energetic young man from Montana was one of those who introduced new concepts. By the seventies, he was known as a darned good cowman and grass-man, and his fellow ranchers elected him president of their most prestigious association, the Western Stock Growers.

The Range is mainly about people and grass. The people—great characters all—are Sherm's friends, and this is the measure of the man. Grass is the basic source of wealth in the ranching industry, and the people in this book acknowledge it. Long before ecology and its cousins became buzzwords, the Society for Range Management was promoting the application of scientific methods on rangeland, encompassing in a sort of holistic gestalt not just man and plants and animals, but also meteorology and all the earth sciences. And so it's not surprising that we find Sherm serving on the board of the Society, and as president of its International Mountain Section, which serves the plains and hills, mountains and streams, people, plants, and animals of Montana and Alberta.

The Society reveals rangeland as a fragile resource of great beauty which can be used by man in perpetuity if only he husbands it well. This is Sherm's belief and faith; though he does not come right out and say it, you seem to know as you turn the pages that he is writing of the handiwork of God.

Can you think of any one: Who progressed from the Ivy League— Yale, in economics, and Cornell, in agriculture—to become a ranch hand, manager, and owner? Who has been a successful cattle breeder and improver—first, with his own *Hightester* strain; later, as a member of the 10,000-cow *Beefbooster* group? Who has helped to found, and served as president of, a cattle performance-test association and a cattlemen's memorial foundation? Who, as a citizen of two countries, has advised governments on land-use planning? To whom writing has been a hobby for forty years...? Such a man should—and did—write this book.

The Range took a long time to write. When I visited Sherm in the summer of '87 the book was planned and its direction set. For two years he had been travelling North America, interviewing people, and tape recording stories about the range and ranching. He was writing seriously, but he needed two more years to piece together a cohesive manuscript from tales of land and weather, grass and cattle, adventure, hardship, and accomplishment—in the domain of the chinook.

David H. Breen, professor of history at the University of British Columbia, who is recognized as the ranking authority on the history of ranching in western Canada, praises *The Range*. He states that it is uniquely valuable because it contains what professional historians call "primary source" information: what was done, as told in their own words by the people who actually did it. Dr. Breen has said that this is the first time, to his knowledge, that the rangelands of both Alberta and Montana have been the subject of a single detailed study.

And so it is. But, quite apart from historical significance, this book is—as I said earlier—a great read. Enjoy it.

—Frank Jacobs

Preface

I am a writer by avocation only; that is, I enjoy words and have studied using them. But my business has been ranching. By the time this book was written, I had been in the ranching business—converting grass into useful human food—for over forty years. My wife Claire and I had raised our family on a ranch twenty miles from the little town of Claresholm, Alberta; we'd seen them marry and have children of their own. And when we judged the time was right, in 1982, we sold the ranch, outright, to our son, leaving to an experienced younger man full responsibility for growing grass and breeding efficient cattle. That was the great opportunity we ourselves had treasured; that was what we wanted for our kids.

The opportunity of a lifetime had come for us in 1955, when the SN Ranch came up for sale in Canada, just a hundred miles across the international boundary from the ranch we had been managing in Montana. The timing was perfect: the first of our three children had just turned three; we needed a home of our own. We had never thought of leaving the United States, but ranches that "pencil out" financially are always hard to find; it didn't take us long to decide to buy the SN in Alberta's Porcupine Hills when it was offered. Today Claire and I are citizens of both countries; it's been our great privilege to live on both sides of the border in this wonderful part of the world, in the shadow of Glacier Park and the Rocky Mountains, in the clean air of the northwest chinook zone, alongside wonderful neighbors who share a common heritage of freedom.

When we moved north we had just three friends in Canada, but they were good ones. Ranchers, Fletcher and Eleanor Bennett, introduced us to Alberta and, later, to Charolais cattle. Harry Hargrave, a director at the Lethbridge Research Station who seemed to know everyone in western North America, introduced us to a score of other ranchers, sponsored us at stock growers' conventions, welcomed us at range management meetings, and generally oversaw our higher education.

Because of the large number of acres required to support cattle in the West, ranching country is always sparsely settled. It takes a dozen acres or more to keep one cow alive; therefore, it takes perhaps 200 times that many to maintain a ranching family. Neighbors tend to be few and far between, but ours in the Trout Creek valley were the very best: the Alms, Arlts, Burtons, Eatons, McLeods, Rhodeses, Vances, and Vandervalks taught us much about Canada, and much more about living and ranching in the Porcupine Hills.

Centers of social life were, and still are, the little one-room schoolhouses that grace each coulee; ours was the "44." By the time our seventh-graders went to town, they'd heard six years of Grade One, five years of Grade Two, and so forth; they tended to be well grounded in the basics. Those schools are closed today, the victims of progress, but they continue as the sites of Christmas concerts, anniversary parties, and summer baseball games.

Technically, we think of range as home to "native" grasses, forbs, and shrubs. I have used the word here, loosely, to include land that has been plowed and farmed and eventually reseeded to "tame" grasses. It's important to understand that, however it may have been treated by civilized man, it has been home to grazing animals for many thousands of years; in turn, it relies upon them. As a rancher, I consider meat production to be the "best and highest use" for rangeland. As a citizen, I accept such broader uses as water storage, soil building, recreation, and wildlife habitat. As a writer I describe a remarkable *and* renewable resource, able to sustain a wide variety of uses. And, as master of ceremonies here, I introduce a wide variety of people who have lived their lives on rangeland. This book is about a way of life.

"What?" I hear you say; "no mention of Uncle Bill who homesteaded the Dry Fork in the thirties?"

Or, "What of my friend K— who survived the famous flood of '64? The way he told the story is as follows...."

Or, "Where's Professor E—? Or Dr. B—? They know everything about range grass from *Aveneae* to *Zea*; they should have been included."

I can only say that preparing a book like this has been great fun! You ought to try it. You ought to go interview your Uncle Bill, and Doctors B— and E— and all the rest while there's still time; a thousand books would not deplete the character supply. Meanwhile,

I have limited this collection to just some of the characters I've known and liked and trusted on The Range—those who had the fortune, good or bad (as time will tell), to cross my trail while taping was in session.

My old friend Harry Hargrave died before I began this book, and so the piece attributed to him is a contrivance. I wanted him present here with all his friends, so I "did" him with the help of material furnished by his wife Ruth and his brother Bert. Had I taped him "live," he would have added wit and many stories.

The "Farrington Carpenter" piece was not recorded by me. Claire and I did hear him tell his classic story of dividing up the U.S. public range one memorable night in Lethbridge, Alberta, in the mid-1960s. The occasion was a Western Stock Growers' convention. The location was a smoky, crowded motel room where President Gordon Burton entertained and Carpenter held us spellbound for five hours. Nobody interrupted. Ferry was a consummate storyteller, and the tale presented here is "vintage" Ferry, recorded during a speech at Bozeman in 1962 and printed in the Society for Range Management's publication, *Rangelands*. SRM has kindly granted permission to reprint it here, and I have edited and shortened it without—I hope—any loss of flavor.

With those two exceptions, every "piece" in this book results from a personal interview done by me, and I consider it a privilege and an honor that these real and wonderful characters have entrusted me with their personal life stories. In weaving these together into a history of our range, I have considered it my duty to stick as close as possible to the original transcriptions. I hope my characters, in reading what I've written, will say: "Yes, that's exactly what I said!" I hope other range people will agree: "Yeah, that's really the way it was!" My original tapes and unedited, phonetic transcripts will go to the archives of the Montana Historical Society in Helena, and the Stockmen's Foundation in Cochrane, Alberta, where they will be available to researchers. In that form, of course, they are tedious to read.

My objective throughout has been to produce an enjoyable book, so I have exercised some license in editing my sources. Some people rarely finish sentences. Some people are less organized than others. Some people's ideas come too fast for their vocal chords. Usually I—who ask the questions—have been reluctant to interrupt the flow, once started, and so have had to organize and clarify the results.

I have made it a practice to run technical and historical material back past my sources as a double or triple check on accuracy. Where I deemed it necessary, I have rearranged their statements into logical order; where appropriate, I have added a phrase or sentence to build a bridge between two characters or ideas; where it suited my—or my editor's—taste, I have refined grammar, rhythm, slang, and phonetics, but I have tried to keep such editing to a minimum. I hope I have not failed in my overall objectives: to record an accurate oral history of a given place and time with a string of continuity running through it; to produce an interesting book.

My friends, the range professors, have been interesting to work with. Although they owe much to the salty way they communicate their knowledge, they are sometimes horrified to see their words reproduced verbatim. One, who speaks the American language in all its richest color and beauty, got his red pencil out straight-away and marked the actual transcript of our interview like an English exam. The words were his, exactly. But, rather than go to my tapes as proof of innocence, I knuckled under, added "th"s, cut contractions, expurgated syntax to preserve professional pride, if not the spoken language.

"Where are the range women?" you might ask. I am aware that not many are featured in this book and the reason is quite simple. In the period I selected, few women were prominent in range management. A history of the years after 1980 can draw on the experiences of many women who have made the range their business and career. I am also well aware that the success of almost every ranch depends on at least one woman. Billy Big Spring made the point as we sat at his kitchen table drinking tea. "You should be talking to her," he said, nodding to his wife of many years. "If it hadn't been for Kathleen—keeping the books, feeding the crew, sometimes walking miles to feed the cows—I'm sure we would have gone broke long ago." As a happily married rancher I understood Bill's comment; as a writer I conceived another book.

I wish to thank Dr. Gordon Burton, economist, friend, and neighbor in the Porcupine Hills; Dr. Roy T. Berg, geneticist and professor of animal science at the University of Alberta, Edmonton; Dr. John R. Lacey, extension range management specialist at Montana State University, Bozeman; and Dr. David H. Breen, professor of history at the University of British Columbia, Vancouver, all of whom checked for errors and suggested many improvements.

Thanks also to my literary friends David Lavender of Ojai, California, and Frank Jacobs of Calgary, Alberta—established authors, both. They never even hinted that they could have written this better and they helped me to believe it would be published.

And, thanks to my favorite critics Claire Ewing, Nan Bull, Bill and Shirley Scott, Muriel Lavender, and Bette Weissman, who carefully read and commented on my manuscript and encouraged me a lot, even as other friends slept through my interminable readings.

I have used, with few exceptions, the common names for plants and have capitalized their first names (eg. Bluebunch wheatgrass), arbitrarily, in honor of their status as the primary producers on the range. Taxonomists will find a key to Latin names in an appendix preceding the Glossary.

Readers wishing to check credentials or statistics on the people of *The Range* will find a vital paragraph on each in the Register of Characters immediately following the Epilogue.

Sweet land of liberty, of thee I sing:

The Range

An Overview

There are two good ways, at least, to get to know a range: By saddle horse, explore each ridge and coulee, visit waterholes, smell the wind, feel the sod, and leave few tracks behind; or, from a Piper Cub get an overview of mountains, valleys, and pastures, check water levels, crops, and fences, see what's grazing where, and leave no tracks behind.

Tell you what let's do: let's fly this range. Don't worry, weather's fine; jump in the plane. I've flown a thousand sorties from this strip, and never lost or scratched a passenger yet. All kinds of friends have ridden in "Old Rags": ranchers, farmers, neighbors and their wives; MDs, MPs, bearded Hutterites; teachers, actors, preachers, black-robed priests; moms with screaming kids, a turbaned Sikh; Italians, Frenchmen, Englishmen, and Greeks.

As cargo, I've hauled baby pigs and packaged bees, and frozen sperm, and seedling trees, and groceries and mail a time or two, and—only once—a big Newfoundland dog; he wanted out—got airsick! How about you? Well, get in then; we'll climb 5,000 feet above The Range... give you a birds-eye view.

To the west, the Rocky Mountains form an L whose back retreats northwestward towards the Yukon, and whose base—the Yellowstone-Missouri river drainage—runs northeast across the plains. The angle of this L serves as a backstop for "The Range" of which I write. North, east, and south the Great Plains stretch away as far as you can see, scarred by rivers bound for the Gulf of Mexico and Hudson Bay. The real range—bluebunch, grama, fescue, needlegrass, and scores of other native plants—once made great feed for buffalo, and plenty still exists for cows today on hills and river breaks and unplowed land. But much native range is gone—plowed up to grow a world's supply of wheat. In the dry years of the twentieth century, the range "turned upside down" began to blow. I've flown this plane through clouds of dust at 15,000 feet.

This range of ours is windy. See that arch? That unmoving line of cloud stretched north and south across the sky along the mountains? A sign of wind! See those farms down there where strip-farming was born? This morning we'll see thousands of square miles of narrow strips, plowed and seeded across the wind to cut erosion. A breadbasket of nations: millions of acres of wheat, oats, barley, and oilseed crops grow here. Not wild range anymore, in the true sense of the word, but still The Range.

Center stage for stories spun out here is 60,000 square-mile sections of Alberta and Montana: three hundred miles between the Bow and Yellowstone rivers, north and south, and two hundred miles eastward from the Rocky Mountain Front. This stage, I think, needs just one common backdrop on which to paint the atmosphere and history and traditions of The Range. Notice old Chief Mountain, jutting from the Rockies to the west, scowling eastward down the valleys of the Milk. And, see the Sweet Grass Hills, away out east, just purple shadows ninety miles away. Between Chief and the Sweet Grass runs that vital line—the "49th"—the parallel of latitude picked by European statesmen long ago as the border between Rupert's Land and Louisiana. As civilization spread, that parallel—unseen, unmarked for many decades—remained an almost uncontested, never fortified, uniquely peaceful boundary between two sovereign, allied trading partners. Practically invisible, tremendously important, it was known to old-time Indians as the "Medicine Line."

Well we've checked the gates and waterholes and fences; we're getting low on fuel so let's go home. Let's go and meet some people of The Range.

The meat of the Buffalo tastes the same on both sides of The Border. —Sitting Bull

1

The Buffalo Range

FRANCIS V. GREENE

lieutenant, U.S. Army, a member of the International Boundary Commission surveying the "Medicine Line," he left camp just west of the Sweet Grass Hills, and rode a hundred miles across the prairie to Fort Shaw, Montana Territory. He wrote this letter home.[1]

September 13th, 1874
On the Missouri River

My Dear Parents:

I left the Three Buttes or the Sweet Grass Hills, and after traveling over a rather forlorn flat alkaline country,[2] it was a pleasing sight when I rode forward to the edge of a bluff before me and saw a broad green valley and the buildings and flag of Fort Shaw—the first building I had seen in a trail of little less than a thousand miles.

Sun River flows past the post through a fine valley already settled and joins the Missouri in about fifteen miles. Helena and its surrounding mines lie 80 miles to the South West through "the Gateway of the Mountains."

But it is not in mines that Northern Montana has her wealth, it is in her grazing land. It is destined to be the great stock raising region of the country; already it rivals Texas—both in numbers and quality, and the sheep that have been introduced have done splendidly and only a little more capital is required to introduce many herds of them. The day I reached this post, I saw 1000 or 1500 head of cattle running loose. I never ate more delicious beef than that on which we have been feasting for ten days.

The ground is covered both on hills & valleys with abundant growths of buffalo grass whose roots are green all seasons of the year, and no attention is ever given to the cattle beyond branding them in spring and driving them to market in the fall. They take care of themselves during the winter.

Your Affectionate Son;
Francis

Millions of antelope shared the range with the buffalo. —Museum of the Rockies

ALEX JOHNSTON

twentieth-century rangeman and historian, is a lifetime student
of the nature and the people of The Range. He speaks clear-cut
and rapid fire on the history of our land.

Any story about the ranching industry must start with land and
grass; I'll see if I can help to set the stage.

Our northern Great Plains, breadbasket to the world in recent
years, was range—all range—before the white man came. By "range"
I mean wild grassland—native fescues, wheatgrasses, ryes, gramas,
and many others—which developed under animals, grazing animals.
Grassland and grazing animals: Which came first? As a matter of
fact, they must have evolved together.

Grassland in general developed about thirty million years ago—
just suddenly developed all over the world. There's *prairies* here and
pampas in Argentina and *veldt* in South Africa, and they all seem to
have developed at about the same time. Climate would have been a
critical factor in determining whether the earth's crust became forest
or tundra or desert or steppe, and there must have been some sort of
radical climatic shift to cause the evolution of grassland to start so
suddenly. It's continued on a massive scale ever since.

7

Animals that had previously browsed forests and brushy vegetation kept adapting to new species. Their tooth structure and digestive systems changed tremendously, and they evolved right along with the various grasslands and prairies. The animal most associated with prairie is, of course, the buffalo—the American bison—descendant of a series of other primitive types. Perhaps Eurasian in origin, it certainly prospered here.

Most estimates of buffalo population go back to a zoologist by the name of Hornaday, active in the late 1800s.[3] He had access to people who had been familiar with the buffalo in their final days, so he studied their accounts and listened to their tales and came up with a general picture. He reported that the buffalo had ranged from the Peace River country of Alberta down into northern Mexico; and from the Continental Divide east into the deciduous forests of the Virginias: the most widely distributed land-based mammal in the world. His estimate of numbers at their peak was sixty million head, and he thought there were at least that many antelope.

Our range has always been subjected to heavy grazing by animals of one sort or another. I suspect there was periodic overgrazing during periods of drought; although the animals in those days would

Mule deer still roam the range. —Museum of the Rockies

With civilization, elk, once major herbivores of the plains, retreated to the mountains. —Museum of the Rockies

have responded very quickly by moving, or by dying off, or by not calving for a year or two, and numbers would have stayed in balance with available feed.

The eastern herds disappeared very quickly as settlement moved west of the Appalachians, and the period we tend to think of as "buffalo days" was the time when herds were relegated west of the Mississippi River. At that point the population on the Great Plains may still have been on the order of fifty or sixty million head. It's from about the 1840s that buffalo numbers began their precipitous decline.

The Indians living on buffalo made little impression on their numbers; the railways did, however. Contract hunters slaughtered them by hundreds to feed construction crews, and, more important, the buffalo range was cut as rails pushed west across the continent in the mid-1800s.

We read horror stories of European princes coming over here and killing two thousand head of buffalo a month, things like that—take a few trophies, leave the rest. Two thousand head a month! My God! That's seventy buffalo or so a day! What a waste! But even that had little impact on the total population. What really sealed the doom of the buffalo was the hide market. Industry boomed as a result of the Civil War, and water power drove the machines of industry. Factories and mills sprang up at every substantial waterfall in the East, and power had to be transmitted from water wheel to machinery by miles and miles and miles of belting. Buffalo hide was found to be ideal for industrial belting, and when the value of those hides was discovered, the final slaughter began. That's when we have this business of the Sharps rifle, and hunters able to drop fifty head from one stand. That's what killed off the buffalo.

The great southern herds of Texas and Oklahoma quickly vanished and attention turned to the north. I once tried to plot the number of hides purchased here in southern Alberta and transported south to the Missouri year by year. We have records left by the Whoop-up whiskey traders in the 1870s, and at first they were shipping 10,000 hides a year down to Fort Benton, then 5,000, then

Millions of buffalo hides went into the belt-and-pulley power-trains that ran 19th century industry.

Buffalo herd grazing The Big Open in northern Montana. —L.A. Huffman,
Museum of the Rockies

4,000—a very precipitous drop till, in a few years, none were left. The species *Bison bison* was virtually extinct on the Canadian prairies by 1879.[4]

The Montana herd was essentially last to go. In 1881 the Northern Pacific transported 50,000 hides and robes to market; by 1884 just one carload was shipped. By 1900 perhaps no more than three hundred buffalo survived in the United States—a few hundred more in Canada.

When the buffalo were gone, there was a gap of several years— several decades in western Canada, perhaps—during which there was very, very little grazing of The Range. As buffalo disappeared, the Indians' food supply declined and they turned to other animals, killed off the elk and antelope and deer; at one point they were down to eating gophers, so they say. The first large herds of cattle on the Canadian range were brought in to feed those starving Indians.[5]

Then followed a period of *underuse*—the years between the buffalo and cattle; that's the period we hear of from the earliest days of settlement, "when the prairie grass was ass-high to a tall Indian," as my father's generation used to say. That tradition is undoubtedly based on fact, but it was a very short period of transition, and totally, absolutely abnormal. Unfortunately, that's the era environmental extremists still "remember": an imagined, wishful, pristine state of things. My contention, based on a lifetime study of the land, is that our range today is in a damn sight better condition than it was in 1864 when the buffalo still roamed free.

SAVING A SPECIES

As demand for buffalo meat and hide began to grow in the early decades of the nineteenth century, perhaps the most efficient hunters on our range, and first to apply modern methods to the hunt, were the métis—French or Scottish mixed-bloods—from the Red River settlements in Manitoba. They shared the buffalo culture with the Indians, education and technology with the whites. They had the wheel. With their famous Red River carts, the annual métis hunting expeditions headed west; their settlements sprang up across the buffalo range, and métis names persist in northern Montana to this day.[6]

After the first year's hunt, about 1820, 500 carts of robes were delivered at Saint Paul. At the peak and towards the end, fifty years later, 500,000 robes a year were coming in by cart, train, and steamboat. Half a million hides would "impact" buffalo numbers!

The buffalo hunt was shared by métis, Indians, and whites; there was no way any individual or group could profit from restraint; Piegans themselves were in on the final slaughter. In the end, however, one individual Indian buffalo hunter deserves credit for preventing the extinction of the species.

Plains buffalo were not native to Montana's western valleys, so Samuel Walking-Coyote, a Pend d'Oreille Indian from the mountain valleys west of the divide, crossed the mountains every year to hunt buffalo on the plains. When he returned to the Flathead Valley in 1872, legend has it, he coaxed some calves to follow.[7] This sounds difficult, or impossible, considering the wildness of the species and the fact that this was years before railroads or even wagon roads crossed the northern Rockies. In fact, the only way of relocating buffalo from the plains to the Flathead Valley would have been to coax very young, unweaned, calves to follow at will. But how could they be fed and kept alive?

Walking-Coyote could have used foster mothers, like one a century later on the author's ranch in the Porcupine Hills. In 1975, a dry Welsh pony mare—never having had a foal herself—adopted a wild moose calf up in the hills one fine spring day and brought it to the barn, defending it against all comers while it butted and poked about in search of lunch. It must have been an orphan or a twin, and it was "rescued" by Department of Fish & Wildlife officers before it starved, but it certainly would have followed that Welsh mare to hell and gone, if only she'd had a little milk.

It's hard to imagine a Stone Age buffalo hunter deliberately setting out to save a species. But suppose a pack mare lost a foal and came across a newborn buffalo calf, its mother freshly killed; such a pair could easily have bonded. And the hunter, seeing the value of the accident, could easily have arranged a repeat performance.

However he accomplished it, by 1884 Walking-Coyote had thirteen head of buffalo for sale, and Flathead Indian ranchers Michel Pablo and Charles Allard bought them. In 1896, when Allard died, the herd had grown to at least 300 head. In 1906, when Pablo felt the time had come to liquidate his business, he had 600 head to offer, but his best prospect, the U. S. Government, turned him down. Thereupon, the Canadian Government offered $200,000 for the herd, f.o.b. Banff National Park, Alberta. The roundup took six years and must have been exciting: some renegades escaped and some were shot, but most were finally corralled and held for shipment. Eventually, 700 head of buffalo were delivered, first at Banff, later at Wainright, 200 miles to the east, where a sanctuary was set aside for buffalo and hybrid "cattalo" until needed as a military reserve in 1941.

In the United States, a National Bison Range was created in Montana's Flathead Valley in 1908; 18,500 acres were purchased for that purpose from the Salish, Kootenai, and Pend d'Oreille tribes for $40,000. Although most of the descendants of Walking-Coyote's orphans had gone to Canada, the American Bison Society—William Hornaday, president—was able to find thirty-seven remnants and scraped together $10,000 to buy them.

The species Bison bison—like the range it lived on—was the victim of free enterprise untempered by the restraints of private property; numbers declined from an estimated sixty million to, perhaps, 600 in three-quarters of a century. In the end, the market that had brought the species to near extinction played a major role in its salvation, as responsible owners like Pablo and Allard protected and multiplied their herds. In 1990 there are believed to be more than 100,000 buffalo on The Range, mostly on private farms and ranches. An excellent market for buffalo meat and hides, ironically, now guarantees their survival.

The Pablo herd was wild and fences were few when Charles Allard Jr. and his crew went out to gather buffalo. Here, they have been riding for two weeks and have coralled 100 buffalo. They averaged 57 miles a day.
— Norman K. Luxton, Montana Historical Society

Buffalo from the Pablo herd wait to be loaded onto Northern Pacific Railroad cars at Ravalli, Montana, for shipment to Banff, Alberta.
—Montana Historical Society

The Pablo buffalo were not "broke to load." Here cowboys on the off-side of a car use a snubbing post to draw animals up the loading chute and hold them while stall doors are closed. —Montana Historical Society

A shipment of buffalo on their way to Banff in 1908. Each car carried 15 to 20 animals. The last carload was shipped in 1912. —Montana Historical Society

SOI-TAINA—Rainy Chief

(a.k.a. Alex Johnston) is an honorary member of the Kainai Chieftainship of the Blood band of the Blackfoot Confederacy.

There's been much speculation on the prehistoric routes by which men and animals entered the Americas from Asia. No doubt, during parts of the ice age, a strip of land connected the two continents at what is now the Bering Strait, and much of Alaska was apparently quite warm back in those times. Furthermore, a dry corridor between enormous ice caps may have run down along the Rocky Mountain Front providing access to the south for wandering tribes. Although it takes considerable imagination to discern the so-called Old North Trail, there's little doubt some kind of centuries-old trade route passed this way, and various peoples have lived here from time to time. At any rate, when historic times began, three principle tribes inhabited our range.

As fur traders approached the mountains up the North Saskatchewan River, they met the *Siksika*, or Blackfoot, so-called because of moccasins black with soot of prairie fires. Then there were the *Kainai*, Many Chiefs, whom the Crees, to the north and east, called Bloods because they used so much red ocher in their paint. The third major tribe that claimed our range was the *Pekuni*, or Poor-Robed people—the name corrupted to *Piegan* or *Peigan*. Lewis and Clark had their only real Indian trouble with Piegans on the Marias River in northern Montana, and fur traders on the upper Missouri had difficulty penetrating their country. John Colter encountered them while trapping on the Gallatin in far southwestern Montana, and the story of his narrow escape became famous and enriched their reputation.

These three Algonquin-speaking tribes were allied in a so-called Blackfoot Confederacy. Spellings differ, by the way: South *Piegans* now live on the *Blackfeet* Reservation near Glacier Park and Browning, Montana, while North *Peigans* live at Brockett, between Pincher Creek and Fort Macleod, Alberta.[8]

However their names may be spelled today, the Blackfoot called themselves, collectively, *Nitsitapi*, Real People—a term now used for any Indian person—and they were real meat eaters, there's no doubt about that. The word for meat in Blackfoot is *natapi waksin*, real food (predating modern television commercials from the National Cattlemen's Association). They also used some vegetable matter, which they called *kistapi waksin*, nothing food.

The most important "nothing food" in those old-time diets was probably the saskatoon, or serviceberry. It was sweet—its name transliterated from the Cree *mis-sas-ka-too-mina*, sweet-growing berry—and in season, it was eaten in tremendous quantities and used in the manufacture of pemmican. Peter Fidler—the first white to report on our range—records the winnowing and cleaning of fifty bushels of saskatoons, an incredible amount. At other times the chokecherry, or *puk-keep* as the Blackfoot say, was used. These would all have been picked by the women, dried, then mashed in a rough stone mortar, seeds and all. The addition of a chokecherry mash to pemmican would have given it a nice, gritty texture, to say the least.[9]

There is some indication that there may have been as many as a million Indians in Canada when exploration first took place on our East Coast. Nobody knows; that's just an estimate. White men's diseases, of course, for which the Indians had absolutely no resistance or tolerance, killed them off at a tremendous rate. These included most of the viral diseases—common cold, measles, scarlet fever, small pox—and by the 1860s and '70s, when our western treaties were signed, the Indian population in all of Canada was down to 100,000, or something like that. A reduction of that magnitude had occurred! The Indian population in Alberta at the beginning of white settlement has been estimated at about 10,000; the densest concentration would have been in the southern foothills and grasslands of our range. Although we have to guess at numbers, the facts are plain: there weren't very many Indians around at the beginning of recorded history.[10]

The Europeans looked upon the Indian as the "vanishing American," a very familiar term back in the nineteenth century. It was thought the Indians would eventually die off, and a place was needed to put them, so they set up reservations. They took a Stone Age people—nomadic hunters, basically—and tried to make a sedentary farming population of them overnight. Some chiefs—Red Crow of the Blood band, Little Dog of the Piegans—set an example for their people by doing some actual farming with reasonable success. By and large, they didn't do too badly as long as they were using horses, and they adapted rather well to cattle raising.

For quite a few years Indian numbers decreased as expected, and then, sometime in the 1920s, the population suddenly turned around and has been climbing ever since. Apparently, simple health measures caught on: washing one's hands, for instance—still a new enough concept among the whites. The result has been almost a population explosion on these same reserves.

In the early decades of this century, political patronage was the order of the day, and Indians on both sides of the Medicine Line were subjected to the whims of Indian agents. A few odd ones stand out as doing their damnedest for their people, but the vast majority of them—in Canada, at least—were a bunch of politically appointed, useless ticks. Indian problems today are political, social, economic, and unique. Imagine any other racial group in North America accepting, even welcoming, segregation from the rest of society on reservations or reserves—a significant portion of our range, a portion plagued by chronic range mismanagement

DICK CASSUTT

blue-eyed Piegan rancher, was adopted by an Indian family and grew up among the old-time storytellers. Julia Wades-in-the-Water told him how the Real People got their names. As Dick speaks, his hands make signs understood by all the Indians on the plains. This is what Julia said:

Many cold snows ago our chief called his people together. He told them: "My people, my heart is heavy; it lays upon the ground. All of us are hungry. The old people are sick and they are dying; the children are crying, for they have no food. In the night, the Chief-who-lives-in-the-skies spoke to me; he said:

'Divide your people. Some will go to the mountains, some will go across the prairies; and in four suns-of-the-night they will return and meet at this place.' "

And this came to pass. And those who had gone to the mountains found many berries, and they ate, and they were full. In eating, the berries smeared across their faces and it looked the same as blood running from the nose. And they were forever afterwards called the Bloods.

And those who had gone across the prairies found buffalo and they killed them, and they ate, and they were full, and they made much dry meat. On their return, four months later, as the chief had ordered, they traveled across a vast area where a prairie fire had spread, and their moccasins were black, and they have ever since been known as the Blackfoot.

And that (Dick signs) is the end of the story.[11]

THE PLACE

As western ranching dawned in 1864, the Montana range was a big, empty, dangerous sort of place. Eastern Montana had just become a brand new U.S. territory, but it was Indian country still—the home of Blackfeet, Sioux, Assiniboin, and Crow—and not far east, the Sioux had recently massacred the farmers at New Ulm, Minnesota. The so-called Mullan Wagon Road connected Fort Walla Walla in Oregon Territory with Fort Benton, below the Falls of the Missouri; and steamboats provided seasonal communication with St. Louis and the East. To the north, across the unmarked British-American line, Rupert's Land had been the fief of the Hudson's Bay Company for many decades, but trading posts were few and far between. In 1862-64, placer miners fresh from creeks in California and British Columbia found gold in Montana's western valleys at Bannack, Virginia City, and Last Chance Gulch.

CHASE HIBBARD

Montana rancher, tells how his legendary great-grandfather established the ranch his family owns today.

My great-grandfather was a fellow by the name of Henry Sieben. Born in Germany in 1847, his family came to farm in Illinois when he was five years old; then, orphaned at seventeen, Henry and his older brother Leonard headed west to seek their fortunes. In June of '64, at Fort Laramie on the Platte, the army refused to let the boys continue west along the Oregon Trail, and so they joined a 100-wagon train headed north for the Montana gold fields under the leadership of John Bozeman.

Now, Bozeman had blazed a trail between the North Platte and Montana the year before. He'd come up across Wyoming, skirted the east slopes of the Big Horns, and cut across the Sioux and Cheyenne country moving fast with a pack string. Then, following west along the Yellowstone, he'd picked his way over the low pass that bears his name, and reached the mining camps at Alder Gulch. Betting that wagons could make the trail, he'd gone back to Fort Laramie next spring to wait for customers. That's where the Siebens joined him. As a sidelight, a couple of years later Nelson Story used John Bozeman's trail to bring the first Texas cattle into Montana from the south, but it was dangerous territory still; two years later Indians cut the route for almost another decade.[12]

19

Henry Sieben,
Chase Hibbard's
great-grandfather.
—Montana Historical Society

At any rate, the Sieben boys arrived on the Madison in the summer of '64, and hired out as ranch hands; then, next year, they went to freighting. For about four years Henry hauled freight in ox-drawn wagons from the steamboat landings at Fort Benton and the railhead at Corinne, Utah, to the gold camps in the mountains. And then he did something that changed his life.

One fall, after the freighting season was over, he took his savings and bought about ninety head of worn-out oxen for something like ten or twelve dollars a head, and he turned 'em out in the Chesnut River Valley south of the little town of Cascade, near the gap where the Missouri leaves the mountains. It happened to be one of Montana's good, mild winters with lots of grass, so next spring he found 'em fat and healthy, and he sold them for about twelve cents a pound to a butcher at Fort Benton. I figure they probably weighed 800 pounds; if so, he would have made about seventy bucks a head.

Well, Henry determined right then that there was more money in livestock and in livestock speculation than in freighting, so he sold his freighting outfit and sank his profits into 500 head of cattle down in northern Utah. He trailed those cattle back up to the Chesnut Valley, turned 'em out, and never looked back. Each year for several years, back in the early seventies, when Henry and his brother went to gather, they found their cattle strong and healthy in a little pocket they called the hole-in-the-wall. Way back then he said to himself: "This is the place! If ever I can afford to put a ranch together, this is where it's gonna be."

In the meantime, Henry got into the sheep business. He was a cattleman, but he was also a businessman, and he saw that sheep were going to be profitable in Montana. Another brother, Jacob, came west and joined the partnership, so one spring in the early seventies Jacob was sent to California where he purchased a band of 2,200 Merinos near Red Bluff, and hit the trail for the Montana range 1,500 miles away.

In December, on the Little Prickly Pear just north of Helena, in touch by then with his brothers, Jacob was stopped by a heck of a storm; with snow too deep to move, he had to send for hay to see him through. Then, after Christmas, scabies—a serious skin disease—hit the band and, understanding the damage it could do to their wool crop, the Siebens sent a wagon to Fort Benton for two hogsheads of trade tobacco—pretty strong stuff. Meanwhile they dug some dipping vats right there on the Little Prickly Pear, and the sheep were dipped in a solution of tobacco-juice which saved the day. We still use sheep, but quit tobacco years ago.

Well, with all the prospectors and miners moving in, the Helena-Cascade area was already getting crowded. Lots of people were running sheep and speculating in cattle—just turning them loose on the range with no fences of any kind—and Henry Sieben soon became aware that the range was deteriorating. I have it from my grandmother, his daughter, that as far back as the middle 1870s, he was concerned about overgrazing. So, he and his brothers split their partnership; Leonard moved away, Jacob took the sheep, and in 1882 Henry moved his cattle and horses onto Flatwillow Creek, a tributary of the Musselshell, near Winnett—fresh range, a few days ride to the east.

The 1880s were the legendary time on the Montana range depicted in so many Charlie Russell stories and paintings. Henry was active on those stockmens' committees that organized roundups, discouraged rustlers, decreed the number and age and type of bulls each

"Waiting for a Chinook" or *"The Last of 5,000."* —Montana Stockgrowers Association

owner would maintain, and that sort of thing. You have to remember that the Montana range was free, in every sense, with all associated advantages and problems: cattle were free to graze on millions of acres, most of which couldn't be bought or leased in any way. All you could do was tie up water holes, and use the grass before the next guy got it. As a result, the central Montana range was soon overgrazed, and when the famous winter of 1886-87 rolled around, there probably wasn't enough winter grass beneath the snow to have saved the herds, even if Charlie Russell's long-awaited chinook had actually arrived. Russell made his picture of the "Last of 5,000" Bar R cattle, and became famous; Henry Sieben lost three-quarters of his herd and learned a lesson that made his fortune.

My great-grandfather must have been a real survivor: instead of quitting after that terrible loss, he took the opportunity to buy up remnant herds from other ranchers who had had enough. He and Conrad Kohrs and others consolidated herds and found new ways to manage risk, and went on to become successful ranchers.

After the Indian treaties of 1887, more than fifteen million acres of range were opened to domestic livestock north of the Missouri.[13] The Blackfeet, Gros Ventres, Assiniboin, and Sioux were put on reservations; the buffalo were gone; the area went unused for several years. Henry moved his herds onto the old buffalo range in the far northeastern corner of Montana. As a base for winter feed, he bought several small ranches on the Missouri near the little town of Culbertson, and called the new spread the Diamond Ranch; by 1903

22

six or eight thousand head were carrying a big "diamond" on the rib. We still use the diamond as a horse brand today.

My great-grandad made his permanent home in Helena. He bought one ranch near Wolf Creek in the nineties; it's still owned by members of the family. And then, in 1903, he got the chance he'd wanted for so long; he bought the ranch on Hound Creek with the hole-in-the-wall, the place his cattle had selected long ago. My brothers and I have that ranch today, and with it we inherited a deep appreciation for the grass. Henry Sieben would not have liked to have seen the range abused.

JOHN CROSS

Alberta rancher, is a jovial man with piercing eyes; he's uncommonly serious as he speaks of a famous grandfather who made a lot of history on The Range.

My grandfather, Colonel James Macleod, came west in 1874 as assistant commissioner of the North West Mounted Police. They came to show the flag and bring the law to the Canadian range, and for several years my grandfather traveled constantly across the plains between Winnipeg and Bismark, North Dakota, and up the Missouri River to Fort Benton, and over the Whoop-up Trail to Fort Macleod, which became NWMP headquarters in 1876. In those days before the railroad he traveled by saddle horse, by team and cutter, by steamboat, occasionally by dog-sled, as police work called. He showed up at Wood Mountain, Assiniboia,[14] to confront Sitting Bull after the battle of Little Big Horn, he rode to Helena, Montana, to attend the extradition trials of border-jumping outlaws; it's amazing how much ground he covered.

My grandfather was on the scene through all the years when the buffalo were disappearing. He signed the famous Treaty Number Seven for the Queen at Blackfoot Crossing.[15] He was one of the first to understand that the Indians faced absolute starvation; his suggestion was that government should get right into the ranching business and produce the beef to feed them. I don't agree with him about the government in business, but there's no doubt that those were terrible times for Indians on The Range. My grandfather liked and admired many of them; they respected him, and he did what he could to help them.

My grandmother Macleod used to tell me about the Indian days. She was quite a pioneer, herself, and had grown up with Indians and uprisings and rebellions in the Red River settlements in Manitoba; her daughter—my mother—was the first white child born in southern Alberta, and they both remembered the Indians—Peigans and Bloods—at Fort Macleod as being terribly thin. In fact, they were in desperate condition and, of course, what the government actually did was to lease out large chunks of ground to big absentee eastern ranching companies, and give them contracts to produce the beef to feed 'em.

When my grandfather died in 1894, the governor general of Canada wrote:[16]

> It is not too much to say that Macleod's influence with his Indian friends has time and time again averted bloodshed.... Not in public capacity alone did this late government servant deserve well of his country; as guide, philosopher and friend to early settlers in Alberta, his experience, tact and judgment were of inestimable advantage.

Of course, by then the bureaucrats had taken over, and the colonel died quite disillusioned with politics, and—deserving well, or not—with eight dollars in savings. But, he had faithfully lived the motto of the Mounties: *Maintien le Droit.*

At the Blackfoot treaty of 1877 Chief Crowfoot, with an interpreter at his side, speaks to Lt. Colonel Macleod of the North West Mounted Police and Lt. Governor David Laird of the Canadian Northwest Territories seated under the canopy. —A. Bruce Stapleton, Glenbow Archives

Colonel James F. Macleod about 1880.
—Glenbow Archives

BILLY BIG SPRING

Piegan rancher, recalls the way a Stone Age people adapted to modern times.

My people, the *Pekuni* or Piegans, made only one real treaty with the U.S. Government: we call it Lame Bull's treaty of 1855. Under it, the Blackfoot Nation and the Gros Ventres agreed to stay north of a line from Medicine Rock or Hellgate Pass, near Helena, to the Musselshell; then north to the Missouri and along it to the mouth of Milk River, near present-day Glasgow. The Assiniboins and Sioux agreed to stay farther east than that, although they often broke their promise.[17]

The international border wasn't marked at that time, so I guess our northern cousins, the *Siksika* and *Kainai*, were included in the treaty. Anyway, they turned up to share the treaty payments of $20,000 in goods and services every year for the next ten years, and $15,000 in "benefits" of one kind or another.

After Lame Bull's treaty there was four amendments made by acts of Congress, or executive orders, you know. By 1874, our southern boundary had been moved north to Birch Creek and the Marias River; we lost the Sun and Smith river valleys and the Judith Basin, and the Highwoods, Little Belts, and Snowy mountains. No payment was received for all that country.

About 1874 the Medicine Line was surveyed to our north, so the Blackfoot Nation was split, and after that we Southern *Pekuni* or Piegans became known as the Montana Blackfeet, and agreed to stay down here in the United States with the Gros Ventres and hunt the buffalo. But the buffalo were disappearing fast; and then came what we call the "starvation winter" of 1883-84, when the last of the buffalo were gone and there was nothing left to eat. About 600 Montana Blackfeet starved that winter, and by 1885 there was fewer than 2,000 of our people left.

Then came White Calf's so-called treaty in 1887; that was what the old-time people called "the time we sold the Sweet Grass Hills." Well, they gave up a lot more land than that, but they didn't have a choice; that time they lost about four-fifths of the Lame Bull treaty land, maybe about fifteen million acres, everything from Cut Bank Creek east. That same year the Assiniboines gave up two or three million acres of their land, so most of northern Montana was opened up to cattlemen like Henry Sieben.

There was one more piece taken out of Blackfeet land; that was in 1896 when the Indian leaders agreed to sell, or cede, a strip along the east slope of the mountains. There'd been lots of pressure to open up that area to mining, but the government—remembering all the trouble after gold was discovered in the Black Hills just twenty years before—didn't want to let the prospectors in. This time they bought the land back from the Indians and then resold or leased it; and fifteen years later most of that "ceded strip" was included in Glacier National Park. After 1887 the Blackfeet stayed on their new, small reservation. There was nothing left to hunt, nothing to do but learn to raise cattle or draw rations.

In return for all those eastern hunting grounds, the tribe got $150,000—about one cent an acre—every year for ten years, which was issued out in machinery and seed and cattle, and they got the same for the sale of that "ceded strip" ten years later.

The Allotment Act of 1887 parceled out about half the reservation in 320-acre chunks of grazing land and an 80-acre homestead to each family. The allotted land was held in trust by the federal government, and the Indians had twenty years or so to make a success; at that point they got patents to their land.

My dad was *So-ko-yu-kris-cum*, Big Spring—my generation is the first to use Big Spring as a surname.[18] He was a big man—about 6'7" tall—and when he died in 1930, they estimated he was about sixty-four years of age. I thought he was a little older than that, but even that would have put his birth in 1866; so he was born just as the times began to change.

Somehow, my dad was able to adapt to the new ways very, very quick; he was one of the few who made a success with livestock in those early days. There were others, but they had to work very hard at it; they only went to town maybe once or twice a month, and a lot of them did their best at raising horses.

My dad had two, three hundred head of cows—the first Indian around here to have black cattle. And by the early 1900s, he had about a thousand head of horses. When the famous Eaton dude ranch pack trains came through Glacier National Park back in the teens, my dad furnished 150 broke saddle horses to 'em. He had two horse breakers workin' for him year-round.

In those days, the Great Northern Railroad hired Two-Guns-White-Calf, Wades-in-the-Water, and one or two others to advertise Glacier National Park; they had their portraits painted by Winold Reiss, and some of them did a lot of traveling back East to make appearances. They used to try to get my dad to go, but he made fun of all those people. "People just come to look at you," he said, and he didn't go for that. But, a lot of people did come to visit him out here; he had people come to his ranch just to train their hunting dogs. He put up tent frames where they stayed, and they brought their own cooks—colored cooks, you know—and they had a pretty good deal out here. For a while my dad was a very rich man.

But about the time I was born, in 1919, my dad and many others—red and white—went belly-up. That was the year they dipped all the range livestock for mange and it followed a couple of terrible dry years and a very hard winter when everybody lost a lot of cattle. They had to ship in hay from Minnesota, hay cut over the top of the ice, you know—cattails and muskrat houses at seventy-five dollars a ton. My dad lost everything.

27

A lot of the white homesteaders around Montana starved out then, too, and moved away. Our people had to stay. This was their only home. But a lot of them went hungry on very short government rations, so the agent at that time—there were ten different ones in fifteen years—got 'em started raising pigs and chickens and gardens so as to make it on their own. By the time I was a kid, we were living pretty well. I remember my dad getting several hogs and fattening them up. He made hams and bacon and salt-pork, mostly salt-pork, and we had a root cellar full of potatoes and rutabagas and carrots, and hams hanging down from the ceiling. He used to butcher about six to ten pigs a year.

Those old people lived in cabins scattered out along the river valleys in those days, but they sure loved to get together and camp and visit. About twice a year those people used to come from all

Big Spring,
ca. 1866-1930

directions to camp at our place. My dad would kill two beefs, and he'd go to town with five or six wagons, and bring back a lot of flour, potatoes, and bacon, and sometimes those people would stay for a week. Curly—General Custer's Crow Indian scout—came one time when I was a kid. Of course, my dad couldn't speak either Crow or English, so they talked in Indian sign-language while everybody sat around and watched.

The idea of all the government programs from 1887 on was to get the Indians off the government's back—help them support themselves so they could get along on their own. When I was about fourteen years old I was working on road crews with my dad's old friends, some of them seventy years old. Nowadays, you see some of these people; they're kinda five-by-five and walkin' spraddle-legged. You never saw a fat Indian in those days.

My dad worked hard and tried to learn, and caught on fast; he never went on rations like the others. Maybe that's why I don't believe in welfare programs today. When everything's free it ruins people. My dad was one of those old-time Indians who did a pretty good job adapting to a brand new world after the buffalo were gone. I'm very proud of him.

GERALD HUGHES

old-timer in Montana's Judith Basin, was raised on stories of the early days. He loves to tell about them.

I remember when I was a little kid—about 1908 or '09—the range 'round here was open, that is, unfenced. If your cattle got out, you had to ride and find 'em quick 'cuz if they got into the Missouri Breaks they were done for. Somebody—Indians, we thought—would surely get 'em. And there was lots and lots of horses. Oh, God, there was just hundreds and hundreds of horses. That was before the homesteaders came in.

My Uncle Ed Hamilton was out here pretty early; he spent the famous winter of '85-86 right over the hill, here, at the Skelton place. Uncle Ed and Ambrose Cheney, one of the real old-timers on this range and a friend of Charlie Russell, used to cross the Missouri River and ride up to the Bear Paw Mountains and help out on the roundups; Amby Cheney was a pretty good roper, so he'd get to rope and drag those calves to the brandin' fire.[19] You know, you had to find a calf followin' or suckin' a cow before you could rope it so as to be sure you had 'em paired; otherwise, you might get in trouble.

29

Like Dad used to say, "Those guys over on the other side of the river—them guys—they'd get short on meat for the cook, and butcher somebody else's steer; they'd never eat their own." [Gerald laughs]. Only them guys over 'cross the river in the Bear Paws ever did that.

BOB ROSS
a modern rangeman, grew up in central Montana when the range was free.

When I was a little kid we had a horse camp in the breaks—just a little lean-to built back into the hill, like an old wolfer's camp, was about all—and no fences in the country; that was before the Taylor act came along. And you didn't own the land, and you didn't lease it; you just turned your livestock loose and went down in there and branded whatever you could gather—hopefully your own.

I've read the history of grazing on the commons centuries ago in England, and the problems they encountered ring pretty true to me. When I was a kid out on the Musselshell, there was still a lot of unfenced range and, when you grazed the public domain, "whoever got there fustest, got the mostest" was the saying, and it was true. And it was terribly hard on rangeland.

The point is, without private ownership there's no incentive for any individual to conserve a resource because he has no rights to its future use. That goes for grass or almost anything. I've been a student of The Range—and human nature—from homestead days right through my long career; I've seen the care and attention people give to private property, time and time again. It's human nature. Of course there are millions of acres that nobody would ever want to own—land that would be hard pressed to return a tax assessment in these or any other days. That kind of land was never taken up, but at least it may be under lease today with some sort of security of tenure. And that would be a plus for the whole country.

The Roundup across the river, in the Bear Paw Mountains. Though Charlie Russell painted his pictures from memory many years later, real events, people, and horses were recognizable to old-timers who were there. One of the ropers here is Gerald's old friend, Amby Cheney. —Montana Historical Society

FRANK JACOBS

Canadian teacher, journalist, and rancher who outlines some
variety in the international history and background of The
Range.

The history of our range in western Canada got a different twist
when the government in Ottawa initiated a system of enormous
grazing leases in the early 1880s. Here's what happened:

In 1867, a new dominion of the British Empire was formed by
union of the provinces of Canada, Nova Scotia, and New Brunswick.
Next, the vast expanse of Rupert's Land was deeded to the British
Crown by the Hudson's Bay Company, and then in 1870 a huge
area—of which our range is part—was transferred to the new
Dominion of Canada as Northwest Territories.

To secure his wide domain, Prime Minister Sir John A. Macdonald
unveiled plans for a transcontinental railway, authorized western
homesteading with the Dominion Lands Act, and initiated a force of
North West Mounted Police to "maintien le droit" in the West, before
being thrown out of office, in disgrace, in 1873.[20]

Returning to power in 1878, he faced many matters calling for
immediate attention on The Range: Treaty Number Seven had been
signed with Chief Crowfoot just a year before at Blackfoot Crossing;
the buffalo were gone; Peigans and Bloods were starving and Police
Commissioner Macleod was calling for emergency beef supplies to
stave off famine; young Mounties were retiring early from the force
to take up homesteads and "cash in" on The Range. Across the Line,
American cattlemen were making fortunes on "free grass" and
looking north, while midwestern farmer-homesteaders starved on
quarter-section claims. Prime Minister Macdonald knew that land-
management mistakes had plagued the spread of civilization across
the West, and he wanted to avoid those errors. He was under
enormous pressure to take some sort of action very soon.

The prime minister had many friends, especially in the English-
speaking eastern townships of Quebec, and one was Matthew
Cochrane. Having made a fortune in the shoe-and-leather business
down in Boston, Cochrane had come home to Hillhurst Farm in
Compton County to become a full-time purebred cattle breeder. In
1868 he made a splash by paying a record price for a Shorthorn cow
in Britain; a decade later his *Hillhurst* line was back in Britain making
record sales. Shorthorn was the popular breed of the day, but
Hillhurst Farms branched out and won international acclaim with
Hereford and Aberdeen Angus breeding stock as well.

Matthew Cochrane liked the idea of large-scale beef production in the West; such a concept served his interests in many ways. And any enterprise that resulted in an orderly settlement of the Canadian West, with customers for the railroad and the East, served John Macdonald's government as well. And so, the two men cooked up a scheme for leasing out great tracts of western range.

Cochrane proposed units of 100,000 acres to be leased—to good Conservative Party members, like himself—for twenty-one-year periods at one cent per acre per year, and he recommended rights to purchase farmland and building sites within, or near, the leases. Macdonald approved the idea, and directed that Montana cattle be allowed to cross the border duty-free, for at least a couple of years, to stock the units. In 1881, Matthew Cochrane got the first of the big leases.[21]

Senator Matthew Henry Cochran (1823-1903) of Compton, Quebec.
—Glenbow Archives

There's a long history of struggle on The Range. No sooner were those giant leases granted than protest rose from early settlers against such elitist policies, and an important duty of the North West Mounted Police was keeping squatters off the grazing leases. By-and-large, however, bloodshed was avoided; I think it's safe to say we sidestepped many problems associated with free and public frontier grazing precisely through Macdonald's leasing system. Whatever other effect it may have had, his system brought a semblance of order, and it established *stocking rates*, which, while they may have been too high, provided a mechanism for controlling grazing. Consequently, the Canadian range was not abused to the same extent as some range south of the Line.

ALEX JOHNSTON

our range historian, emphasizes the importance of individual settlers or homesteaders in the permanent development of the West.

It's all very well to talk about tremendous grazing leases and the big, romantic cow outfits of the unfenced open range, but we should really honor the homesteaders who put down roots and stayed—the tough, resourceful men and women who came and toughed it out and lasted on this range.

By the early 1880s, this whole region had had its share of bad publicity: "... an extension of the Great American Desert, by no means suitable for agriculture," said Captain Palliser; at any rate, Sir John A.'s government in Ottawa foresaw little demand for homesteads on the plains.[22] In 1881, as Frank has said, Senator Cochrane got the first big grazing lease in Canada: 100,000 acres on the Bow River west of Calgary, near the town that bears his name. He didn't like it much, said it was too far north—too cold—for raising cattle. He reorganized, applied, and got another "ranche" down in the great grazing region southeast of Pincher Creek. He ended up with two of those giant ranches in his name, and other eastern interests joined him so that within a couple of years virtually all the grazing areas on our range were controlled by about ten companies. But not without a growing opposition.

American books with names like *The Beef Bonanza, or, How to Get Rich on the Plains* were widely read,[23] and even before Canadian grazing-lease regulations were completed, there was growing popular interest in western livestock raising. Meetings were held in

Calgary and Macleod, where prospectors, muleskinners, bullwhackers, and retired mounted policemen, as well as immigrants fresh off the boat, protested give-aways of western lands to eastern landlords. Resolutions urged the opening of the grazing lands to homesteading, and the adoption of the "American grazing system," whatever that might be.

Senator Cochrane fought for the right to "purchase" homestead sites within his grazing lease; he won the point, but few lessees took advantage of the feature. As far as I'm aware, not a single one of those big, early lease holders actually made the land his home. None, to the best of my knowledge, has left descendants on The Range.

On the other hand, many of our well-established, modern ranchers descended from squatters on those leases; examples are the many ranching members of the Copithorne family in the middle of Senator Cochrane's old domain, the Burton families in the Porcupine Hills, and the Hargrave/Gilchrist families in the shortgrass country. In fact, Alberta's successful, stable, world-class livestock industry has grown out of homesteads; I think the same thing's true across The Range.

AN EARLY SQUATTER

My great-great-grandfather George Ewing was a veteran of the Second Jersey Regiment; he sold the family farm in 1775, took bonds in payment, and—as those were redeemed in "continental" money—went broke as capital vanished through inflation. In 1781 a horse worth $150 "hard" was worth $150,000 "continental"—not worth a continental damn, in other words. But George had been at Valley Forge and General Washington's promise still rang in his ears: in victory, free land; in defeat, escape down the Ohio.

It wasn't quite that simple. For one thing, the new nation was in desperate need of cash, and saw in western land a most convenient source of revenue. So, after the war, George—victorious but broke with runaway inflation—uprooted his young family and worked his way west with what he hoped were "military rights" to new lands in the Ohio Valley. Over the next three decades he and several sons moved "westwards," as he said, down the river, squatting, "entering" new lands, scratching a living from the soil until he died in 1822. His sons and grandsons continued westward onto the plains.[24]

THE SURVEY

What has George's story got to do with western range? It marks a starting point for much of organized settlement. Thousands of Americans crossed the Appalachians in search of land. In Kentucky they blazed trees, built cairns, and hoped to hold their land claims in some legitimate fashion; many—Abraham Lincoln's family, among others—lost several hard-won, blood-soaked farms through the primitive filing process then available.

The federal lands of the old Northwest, north of the Ohio, fell under the jurisdiction of the Northwest Ordinance of 1787, which established a distribution pattern still in use today. Congress, following a New England precedent, adopted precise survey, rather than irregular metes and bounds defined by natural landmarks. The basic Northwest unit was the township: six-by-six miles square, surveyed into square-mile sections on a grid of north-south range and east-west township lines. Congress planned to auction off those wilderness sections—640 acres—as appropriate democratic units of a size a single family could clear. In fact, such units proved too large in forested areas; they were cut in half, and then in half again.

About 1796, George used his military rights to claim a parcel in one of the first townships surveyed from ceded Indian land west of the

Appalachians. He leaves no record of a so-called entry fee; he simply says there was no cash beyond the mountains. The medium of exchange was common salt derived from local springs, and that salt certainly would not have been legal tender at the General Land Office where Commissioner Josiah Meigs waxed enthusiastic: "So wise, beautiful, and perfect a system was never before adopted by any nation or government on earth," he wrote. Indeed, the system worked so well that it became the model for the western Canadian survey a century later, and is still the choice in most emerging nations of the world.[25]

THE HOMESTEAD ACTS

In 1862, President Lincoln signed the U.S. Homestead Act, which gave most adult citizens the right to claim a quarter-section of the surveyed public domain by simply paying a $10 entry-fee. Such a homestead was exempt from seizure for debt, and after five years residence and/or cultivation, a homesteader was eligible for patent upon payment of additional fees. In fact, after six months habitation, the land could be "preempted" by paying the preemption fee of, usually, $1.25 an acre. By the end of the Civil War, 15,000 homesteaders had claimed almost three million acres in homesteads and preemptions. In 1872, Canada passed her Dominion Lands (homestead) Act with similar exemptions and provision for a homesteader to preempt a second quarter.

While 160 acres may have seemed a lot to those in wetter regions, a quarter-section wouldn't support a family on the plains. But, if a man controlled some water and could graze the public land, then maybe—just maybe—he could make it. His chances would be better if—to boost capacity, ensure tenure, and ward off vicious neighbors— he could entice his cousins, brothers-in-law, and hired men to file on neighboring quarters. With the understanding—naturally—that, eventually, they would sell their land to him.

According to his letter, that's what old George had in mind in Indiana. That's how many a ranch—as you shall hear—was built up on The Range.

The following letter (italics added) was written many years before the Homestead Act of 1862 was passed. It illustrates the long-established tradition of having trusted relatives or friends secure adjoining claims to public land.

Perry County, Indiana
June 4th, 1818
My Dear Family:

Here we are all in good health and safely landed [in Indiana] after a tedious passage. We left the mouth of the Hockhocking May 4th, and arrived here on the 20th, our progress much delayed by high winds... for lack of room to sleep in her, our boat could not run after night.

We are of the opinion that J—, who last fall tricked us out of our intended "entry" here, eventually did us a great kindness. We have made an entry of 748 acres of excellent land at the mouth of Millstone Creek and fronting about 2 miles on the Ohio. There are on the Premises about 50 acres under cultivation, a hewn log house, several cabins, and a good Millseat. We are plentifully supplied with excellent fish by only throwing out our line in the evening and taking it up the next morning. We are comfortably accomodated, each family in a separate Cabin, and our neighbors appear to be generally honest, industrious and hospitable—with a few exceptions.

There is a Quarter Section adjoining our entry which we wish secured by some member of the family; and if not done soon will be too late. The land is excellent, and if you can spare and send on the entrance Money, *we will enter it in your name if you choose, or in our own and we will repay you with interest as soon as possible.* I am certain it is a Speculation should we wish to sell at a future day.

Another inducement is a family which both ourselves and all the civilized part of our Neighbours wish exiled from here, and who are making every effort to raise the money to make the entry which will place them immediately under our noses and dis-agreeable to the last degree. Should you send the Money it might be done soon, lest a vicious Neighbour be entailed upon us.

The weather has been mild. *Emigration to the Westwards continues very rapid.* Trade is dull. Specie scarce. Paper [money] of no account. No news worth relating.

Affectionately,
George

L.A. Huffman, the famous range photographer, entitled this picture, simply, "The Honyocker." Undated, it depicts an early twentieth century homesteader anywhere on The Range. —Montana Historical Society

I am told that you can come in on the morning train and start ploughing in the afternoon, but I am also told that some in this new country are not content. You know, ladies and gentlemen, some of us will not be content in heaven ... if we hear of a place farther west.

—Sir John A. Macdonald
Prime Minister of Canada
Brandon, Manitoba, 1881

2

Range Settlement

SOME ADVICE TO A YOUNG FELLOW

I say young man, I want to talk with you a minute. Get up and dust. Don't wait for something to turn up. Go at it and turn it up. Put the harness on and pull, no matter if the belly band chafes or the hames don't fit; pull, you'll soon get hardened to it. A collar spot here and there won't hurt long anyway. Don't try to begin where the old man left off. If you do, you'll quit where he began.

Get into the deal yourself, do as the old man did. If you cannot afford a thing, don't buy until you can. The old gentleman did that way, and that is how he got a credit.

A credit young fellow is worth more dollars than you can ever earn. No matter about money, get a credit and maintain it. It is the best asset anyone ever had.

Keep your appointments and be on time. Take time to think things out. Don't be stingy but be prudent. Don't get pessimistic. Shut your mouth and keep your eyes open. If a neighbor goes wrong, don't doubt the integrity of the neighbor over on the other corner.

Pessimism is a mountain that darkens the view. It is the obstruction to your vision, that makes it look so. Pull, and keep your faith in God and humanity. The world is just what we make it.

Opportunity is on all sides for the man who pulls steadily all the time, no matter what his station in life may be.

—by Anon

By "Anon." But couldn't a Sieben or Macleod or Big Spring have composed it? Such advice must have appealed to the men and women who settled and developed the West, for it appears among the archives of many a prairie family. My own grandfather carried it in his pocketbook along with other paeans to free enterprise. The above is how the Copithornes remember it.

MAYNARD SMITH

is a fourth generation rangeman who ranches in the southwest corner of Montana.

My great-grandfather went west to California by saddle horse in 1849 and started raising beef to feed the miners. Those early pioneer ranchers had a three-part goal: Survive! Survive the hostiles and the economy and the weather—all at once!

Sure, the country took a lot of abuse at first, and people often blame the pioneers. But who knew better? Those pioneer ranchers didn't really understand The Range. There was, likely, all kinds of feed where they came from, and all kinds of feed when they got here, and deterioration was a gradual thing. Eventually—if they survived— they came to understand that grass won't last forever. Remember Henry Sieben? He recognized range deterioration a century ago. But who knew what to do about it? Considering the lack of property-rights or, before the 1930s, tenure on public land, what could have been done about it?

As somebody once said, "there was no training school for pioneers; they just went out and *was* one."[1]

GORDON BURTON

owns a ranch northwest of Fort Macleod, Alberta, homesteaded by his father. Today, third-generation Burtons in the Porcupine Hills run cattle, buffalo, karakul sheep, quarter horses, and Brahma bucking bulls. Gordon tells us how it all began.

My mother's folks, the Furmans, came west from New York state across the Oregon Trail in the early 1850s. I suppose they thought of gold in California, but they settled in eastern Oregon and ran a stagecoach line and freight route between Baker City and Umatilla, on the Columbia River. They had lots of trouble with Indians, who killed their drivers and horses, but they ran that line till the railroad came and put them out of business. Then they came north to Montana.

Fort Benton was the "hub" of the freight lines of the day; in 1882 my Uncle John helped Grampa trail a bunch of horses from Oregon up to Benton, and then along the Whoop-up Trail for sale to the North West Mounted Police at Fort Macleod. In the spring of 1886, Grandma

Furman loaded her younger children and possessions into a wagon and headed up the Snake as far as Idaho Falls, then north over Monida Pass to meet her husband in Montana—a summer's trip of perhaps a thousand miles. In 1888, they homesteaded on Boundary Creek, Alberta, south of Fort Macleod. Later, Grampa returned to Augusta, Montana, to raise Thoroughbred horses, especially sprinters—*short horses*, he called them.[2] My mother, Minnie Furman, married and remained in Canada.

My father, Fred Burton, was a "grubber"—he started with nothing, came west from Elora, Ontario, in 1886, the younger son of a rather large, poverty-stricken family, and when he got to Fort Macleod he had five dollars in his pocket. He got a job on the Winder Ranche, and spent all summer walking behind a plow; eighteen years old, he was, and that was what he knew how to do.

In 1880 one of the Macdonald Government's very first leases had been granted to Superintendent Winder of the North West Mounted Police, who happened to be a native of Quebec and an acquaintance of Senator Cochrane. Winder had been responsible for the wonderful grazing area between Fort Macleod and Cardston, and he took advantage of what he saw and began acquiring livestock of his own, running them "on trust," while still on active duty. He may have been

Minnie and Edna Furman, well-mounted and stylishly turned out in habits their father purchased at a race meet, pose in front of their sod-roofed house on Boundary Creek, Alberta, about 1891. —Burton family

Frederick A. Burton in the mid-1890s, about the time he was courting Minnie Furman. —Glenbow Archives

responsible for arousing Cochrane's, and Sir John A.'s, interest; at any rate, he took retirement from the force and got a lease and established the Winder Ranche with headquarters a day's ride north along the Fort Macleod-Fort Calgary trail. In 1886 the Winder Ranche controlled 100,000 acres or so of rangeland in the Porcupine Hills.[3]

Well, my father soon went into business for himself. He simply built a cabin and squatted in a timbered well-grassed coulee on the Winder lease, and I have among his papers a letter from a federal civil servant—dated early 1890s—in which the writer scolds him for "... squatting, and hampering the efforts of serious ranchers..." and would my father "kindly advise the value of improvements and move off." The letter ends: "Your most Obedient Servant...."

Of course, I don't know the nature of my father's reply; he'd never heard of carbon paper, eh?—and wouldn't have used it if he had. But the department soon relented and accepted his homestead application, and it was all just part of the history of those days. The Canadian leasing program—while it allowed an industry to develop on the range—inhibited small, cash-starved, would-be ranchers like my dad. But he was tough. He got his homestead and then a preemption; then he bought out neighbors, one by one, as they went broke. And here we are today.

*Richard and Sophia
Copithorne married
when Sophia was
fourteen. They produced
seven children to help
populate the Jumping
Pound Valley.*
—Copithorne family

MARSHALL COPITHORNE

runs his CL ranch on part of the old buffalo range in the Bow
River Valley west of Calgary. A large extended family, the
Copithornes today are not so much pillars of the Jumping Pound
community—they are the community, and Marshall enjoys
recalling how they got there.

One day, way back in 1883, my grandfather and his brother, Uncle
John, were diggin' in a bog in County Cork in Ireland. Now, Uncle
John (as his sister wrote) was a "carefree scalawag"; one day he
tromped his spade into the bog—just left it quiverin' there—and,
"Dick," he says, "I've had it up to here with diggin' peat. I'm off for
Canada..." just like that. "So long."

So, he sailed for Montreal and took a train to Winnipeg before his
cash ran out; from there he got a job as muleskinner on the trail to
Calgary. In Saskatchewan, en route, he signed on with the army for

46

awhile, to live among the Cree and learn their language; he became a farm instructor; he met the Sioux chief Sitting Bull in his Wood Mountain refuge; and in 1885 he arrived in Blackfoot country.

In '86 and '87, John was whackin' bulls and haulin' government rations to the Stony Indian Reserve at Morley: a two-day trip by bull train west of Calgary across a major creek called Jumping Pound. The steep-banked Jumping Pound was used by old-time Indians as a buffalo jump—a likely place to spook small, peacefully grazing bands over the river bluffs, then finish off the cripples and collect the meat and hides down at the bottom—a common practice on the buffalo range. In fact, the early settlers collected tons of sun-bleached buffalo bones for shipment eastward on the railroads; many localities have a place still known as *Boneyard Coulee* or *Pile-o-bones Hill*.

Well, my grandfather, Richard Copithorne, caught up with John in 1887 and they took adjoining homesteads here on Jumping Pound. In those days, this land was well within the borders of Senator Cochrane's first big "ranche," so they were squatting on his lease, and they must have been involved in squabbles with the powerful absentee lease holders when they built any improvements on the range.[4]

But numbers soon won out as more and more hard-working, land-hungry immigrants streamed up along the rich and fertile valley. One of the most notorious of settlers along the Jumping Pound was a fellow called Frank Ricks. He claimed to be a cousin of Jesse James, and my grandad and his neighbors all believed him. He always wore

—Montana Historical Society

Richard Copithorne's homestead about 1900. —Copithorne family

a gun; he never talked too much; he sure did have a lot of cash; and he built a fancy house on a hill with a regular dance hall up on top—the scene of many a wild party. Legend says he buried his share of the James Gang gold somewhere on the place.

Meanwhile, my Uncle Sam had arrived from Ireland, and the brothers all soon married and started families. And then, as less determined settlers gave up, sold out, and moved, John, Dick, and Sam bought up many a scattered homestead quarter.

In 1911 local ranchers formed the Jumping Pound Stock Association to graze the public land. Generations have come and gone since then; brands and titles have swapped hands; public resources have passed from federal to provincial jurisdiction; politicians and civil servants have "recycled"; but our Jumping Pound association survives with third- and fourth-generation members—a dozen Copithornes among 'em. Few of us ever leave the country.

To this day, my mom believes a cache of Frank Rick's gold is buried here someplace; that's legend. And, someday, some Copithorne who don't mind "diggin' in a bog" may come along, and find old Frank Rick's cache out in the muskeg.

Until then, I guess we'll keep on runnin' cows.

JOHN CROSS

owns and operates the ⵕ7 Ranche with his family in Alberta's
Porcupine Hills. John, who's spent his life developing and
consolidating the ranch, chuckles as he tells how his father
originally built it up.

First of all, I'd better tell you that the ⵕ7 brand is actually put on
with a big, open *a*—like an O with a tail; that way it doesn't blotch.
It was recorded by my father over a century ago, and for many years
was "free," which meant that nobody—in Canada, at least—owned an
animal with an ⵕ7 brand, except ourselves, and we never sold a beast
except to slaughter.

My father, A. E. Cross, came out to work for Senator Cochrane on
the original Cochrane Ranche near Calgary in 1884; he worked for
him two years, which must have been quite an experience. He didn't
talk about it much, but one thing I remember was that, when the
Cochrane Ranche got sheep in 1886, a band drifted into a coulee in a
storm; they piled up dead—five deep—and my father was the one that
dug 'em out. Soon after that he quit, and he never had much use for
sheep again.

What they wanted on the Cochrane was somebody who could put
up lots of hay, and that meant keeping dozens of horses working. My
father was always quite a horseman, and he'd been trained as a
veterinarian at McGill, so he was a good man for the job. He didn't
have a doctorate—most vets didn't in those days—and he never had
a veterinary practice.

In those days, vets weren't called "doctor," but they were called
upon to practice many trades. One day a man came up and pointed
to a tooth, so Father got his dentist tools—we still have 'em somewhere—and took it out. The next day the man came back and said, "I
think I pointed to the wrong tooth." I guess my father hadn't practiced
dentistry hard enough.

One of Father's brothers left Montreal and went to Wyoming
before the Johnson County War; he wasn't in it, he just gave the
cattlemen moral support—supplied 'em with some liquor, an old
family custom [John laughs]. He believed that range was made for
rangemen, not for homesteaders.

But here in Canada, my father didn't go the route of Sir John
Macdonald's giant grazing leases; instead, he used the Lands Act,
and built a good-sized outfit up that way. After two years of working
on the Cochrane, he quit and took a saddle horse and pack horse, and
rode around to look the country over; he found a piece of land near

A.E. Cross, about 1912, when he started the Calgary Exhibition and Stampede.
—Cross family

where the town of Nanton is today, with lots of grass and a wonderful spring, and that's where he filed his homestead claim.

Soon, his brother Willie came along—kind of a lazy, smart, little guy, he was—and filed on a quarter-section fifteen miles back farther in the hills: a place my father wanted. What you did: you paid ten dollars—a month's wages—as a homestead fee, and then you had to fence it, and plow up forty acres, and put up some kind of house, and live in it awhile, and that was it; in time, you got your patent to the land. Well, Uncle Willie didn't spend much time up there, and so it took ten years to get his patent; when he did, he sold out to my father right away. It's the place that our son John lives on today.

A lot of the old homesteads on the ranch were bought from "neighbors" within a year of patent. In other words, a fellow working for the ranch would file a homestead claim on a useful piece of land— but much too small, itself, to make a living on—and as soon as he "proved up," he'd sell out right away, maybe doubling his wages for the year.

When my father first got started he made a decent living on his homestead raising horses for the mounted police; he'd get 'em going, ride 'em up to Calgary, sell one or two, and ride back home again. He loved the life, but it was tough—no cash for expansion, no way to build a ranch. Then something happened that might have killed him at an early age; instead, it led him straight to the opportunity of a lifetime. He got appendicitis.

My father's appendicitis was chronic, and all the riding he was doing made it worse, and, of course, they didn't operate in those days. So, on doctor's orders, he began to look around for something else to do, and with some other fellows got the idea of starting up a brewery; that's how the Calgary Brewing and Malting Company was born. Of course, making beer is just another part of agriculture, you know. Barley grows well here. The malting system paid the local farmers cash for barley, and the brewery brought in cash, with which my father built this ranch. He went on to start several other businesses, and was one of the "Big Four" who founded the Calgary Exhibition and Stampede in 1912. But he kept right on developing the C7 Ranche, which remained his greatest interest all his life.

Log house on the MacIntosh place, subsequently part of the C7. —Glenbow Archives

WES ALM

is another Alberta rancher who can tell about his father's youthful experience on the plains.

My father, Albert Alm, and his brothers—just kids, really, in their teens and early twenties—came west from Michigan in 1906, and began to farm the prairie about forty miles north of Swift Current, Saskatchewan. The Scotch-owned, giant Matador Land and Cattle Company of Alamositas, Texas, had recently obtained one of the enormous grazing leases in the nearby sand hills, and was fattening four- and five-year-old Texas steers for the Chicago market; the winter of 1906 and '07—one of the worst on record—very nearly put them out of business.

Well, my dad and his brothers bought a pair of oxen and they got a few acres plowed that summer. But before that terrible winter they were gone to British Columbia, hoping to earn enough at logging to see them through next summer. Those days, logging was all crosscut saws and horses—just what they were used to back in Michigan.

Those boys were certainly green at farming on the prairies; Dad used to tell of when they first hooked up those oxen. Along toward noon, first day, the oxen ran away—walking plow and all—over a hill, and into a big, old slough. All you could see was heads and horns above the water. Well, the boys were pretty worried; they figured

Breaking the sod with oxen was certainly slow business. One definition of an acre was the amount of land that can be plowed with one ox in one day.
—Glenbow Archives

their investment was gone—that they'd lost their oxen, plow, and everything. Then, along in the afternoon, some Matador cowboys come ridin' along, and they laughed when they heard what happened—just about fell off their horses laughin'.

Dad said: "What's there to laugh at? We've lost our whole damn outfit." He was mad!

"Hell," one of the cowboys said, "just wait till on toward sundown; them oxen'll come outa there themselves, plow and all. They're just gettin' away from the heel flies." Those greenhorn kids had never heard of heel flies.[5]

"From now on," the cowboy said, "you better start your plowin' about daybreak; turn 'em loose about ten, and start again about four, and plow till dark."

That's what they did, but oxen are awful slow. Dad told how, that summer, feelin' pretty lonely and hoping for letters from home, they hiked into Swift Current for the mail; they had the oxen, but drivin' them would have been much slower than walking. Well, tough luck, no letters; they were pretty disgusted, and walked the forty miles back home again, same day, packing a sack of flour on their backs. It's great to be young!

A year or two later they got rid of the oxen and got a team of horses, and after that they started tradin'. Every few weeks during the winter there'd be a horse sale in Swift Current; they had a big old Clydesdale that was pretty well broke, and they'd buy a bronc and

Then they added horsepower. —Glenbow Archives

hitch him with the Clyde. Of course the sleigh trails would be piled pretty high with snow, and if they wanted to run away, why, let 'em run! By the time they got back home, that new, soft horse would be tired and half broke. They'd work him awhile, then take him back to the next sale for a profit and hope the Quebec horse buyers would be there.

Those first few years they only got a few acres of the prairie broke with their walkin' plows. Each one of 'em had a quarter-section homestead, and each could get another quarter preemption. Well, the third or fourth year they mortgaged their preemptions and raised enough capital to line up a steam tractor with a fourteen-bottom plow; and with that, they were able to get their original homesteads broke. Dad said that was the difference between makin' it or not; it took so long to get the land worked with a walkin' plow, that anybody that tried it just missed out.

One of my uncles had apprenticed as a steam engineer, so the boys soon got started in the steam-traction business on their own. See that old tank-wagon sitting in my yard? Dad used that to haul water to his engines back in 1910 and '12. He said the only month that was any good for breaking prairie sod was June; land broke in August or September never did produce like land broke up in June—it never, ever did on the Canadian prairies.

With steampower you could break a lot of sod. — L.A. Huffman, Montana Historical Society

Dad stayed in Saskatchewan for about twenty years—through the years of good wheat prices and moisture around the First World War—and then he bought a farm near Olds, Alberta, in the fall of 1927. I remember goin' back with him to see his brother in Saskatchewan about 1935, and it was terrible! Nothing but tumbleweed and blow-dirt, terrible dry; it's amazing how that land is producing again today. That topsoil must have been terrible thick to start with, the way it blew.

In Alberta, Dad bought three quarters of good land, two of 'em solid willow; there's usually good land under willow brush, you know, if you ever get it cleared. Well, men were cheap them days, and it's a good thing they were because that land was cleared with pretty primitive stuff: an old steel-wheeled John Deere, and one of those side-cuttin' brush cutters like they used to have; and you had to have guys throwin' the brush in piles and burnin' it, or gettin' it out of the way for your next round. My uncle used to run that John Deere Model "D" and a 24-inch breakin' plow; if you got that "breaker" under a tough, old willow crown, why, it'd just dig her down. Then, pull the clutch, unhook, get out there on about twenty foot of chain and give-her-hell! Just hope it would jerk the plow clear through the stump; then, back up, hook on again, and sometimes go another twenty feet before you hit a stump. Real producin' land, once you got the roots out! But busting the sod and growing a crop, in those days, was a slow and tedious business.

JOE GILCHRIST

was raised in a sod-roofed homestead shack in the big, open southwest corner of Saskatchewan.

We arrived at Maple Creek, Assiniboia—as Saskatchewan was called—in April 1904, after a seven-day train ride from Nova Scotia. Father was a sea captain, born in Glasgow, Scotland, orphaned as a boy; he'd run away to sea, and sailed around the Horn and along the Atlantic coast for many years. When he came ashore for good, he took his family west; I was only four years old, but I remember.

From Maple Creek we took a wagon south across the prairie towards the Cypress Hills to find my oldest brother, Rube, who'd come west the year before to line things up. When we met him, he and Father filed on homesteads right away, and applied for water rights on Battle Creek, then hauled logs down out of the hills and built a

A colonist car that brought the homesteaders west. —Glenbow Archives

cabin of our own—three rooms, dirt roof, pine floors—and a little barn and corral. Trouble was, the survey wasn't finished, and they found out later that they'd put up their improvements on the wrong piece of land, and they had to move 'em all a couple of miles.

That spring we bought some cows and a dozen cayuse mares from a fellow across the border in Montana. The older boys built several miles of fence, dug ditches, cut wild hay, hauled firewood. I watched it all with interest.

Next year, with one whole section fenced, we kept a range-bull herd. In March, the boys took bulls from ranches fifty miles around—300 of 'em—pastured 'em at $2.50 a head till the end of June, and delivered 'em back home in time for breeding. Talk about crossbreeding today: there was lots of crossbred bulls in that bunch!

The next year was a wet one; I remember the mosquitoes. We made smudges for the stock: pits of burning straw with long clouds of thick smoke streaming across the prairie. But at least we had plenty of hay, and we bought our first mower and rake that year. And we needed every spear of hay we had because that winter of 1906 and '07 holds some records. We were lucky we had a corral to feed it in; without one, the range cattle would have cleaned us out of everything we had. I remember one old steer that drifted in around some buildings about

56

a mile away; I used to walk down there with Father and feed him hay and rosebush off the roof—that pulled him through.

It was a hard life for the older folks back then, and not all worry-free, either, for us kids; Mother had been a teacher in her younger days, and she decided to teach us all at home. You can imagine what it was like for her in that three-room house—three boys at school, cooking three squares a day for the men, and, always, riders stopping by for meals.

I remember one old Texas cowboy, Jack MacKenzie; he'd been caught out in a storm and froze his toes, and his boots turned up in front in a funny way that fascinated us kids. One cold spring day Jack corralled a bunch of horses at our place and stopped to eat. After dinner, he caught a fat, half-broke gelding, saddled up, and climbed aboard. That horse bucked all around the corral while Jack worked him over with his braided quirt; then, "Let 'em out," he says, and us kids swung the gate, and off they went across the frozen ground and out of sight. Many a modern cowboy would need just the right bit, breast collar, and tie-down strap, and maybe somebody to hunt his hat, and maybe wait till Monday when it wasn't windy, or next month when it wasn't slippery. Jack MacKenzie's outfit seemed to fit all horses, and he was ready for any ride that came his way.

The Gilchrist brothers in 1912: (left to right) Sandy, Joe, Ruben, Jack, and Chester (Chay). The camera was the first Joe ever saw. —Gilchrist family

For several years my brother Chay joined roundup crews—local outfits, or the "T Down" from Montana. He and Rube both gained a lot of experience on the range, and sank their wages into a few more cows at home. By 1910 or '12 we had about three hundred head, and three quarters of good homestead land to raise our winter feed. Each summer, we loose-herded on the range.

The year 1913 was good, with lots of grass, but farmers were moving in and breaking sod and taking up more range. Herd laws were in force—livestock "pounds" for holding strays, not many fences yet—and the farmers weren't much help; it was almost impossible to keep our livestock out of their crops. So, after paying a fair amount for crop damage and pound fees, we got ourselves a grazing lease— fourteen sections fenced into one block—and we moved our horses and cattle off the open range for good.

I was thirteen years old by then—a fair hay-raker, cowboy, and cook! I joined my older brothers in a family ranching company, and we ran our Bar X Bar cattle, along with sheep and horses, in that forgotten corner of Saskatchewan and across the shortgrass country of Alberta, for thirty years to come.

VIVIAN BRUNEAU ELLIS

saw range settlement through the eyes of a little girl.

My family moved to that same "forgotten corner" of Saskatchewan at about the same time as the Gilchrists; I remember all those boys very well from the early years, although I didn't stay in Saskatchewan very long.

I've lived in Montana most of my life, but I come from a very old Canadian family; the first Bruneau came from France as a settler in the seventeenth century and received a land-grant on the St. Lawrence River. Those old French-Canadians were a very adventurous lot; they saw the West as early as any whites. My great-grandfather came west with a Hudson's Bay Company fur brigade, and the Bruneau River in Idaho is named for him. My grandfather moved his family to a little French-Canadian community at Jefferson, South Dakota, in 1871, settled on a homestead there, and ran his cattle away out in the Sand Hills of western Nebraska.

Education always meant a great deal to the Bruneaus. The family stayed at Jefferson, where the kids could go to school, and that's where Dad grew up and met my mother; that's where they were married and went homesteading themselves, and that's where I was born in 1900. Soon after, my parents moved west to Montana in search of opportunity and—I'm sure—adequate education for their family. People were always on the move in those days, too.

We settled out on Smith River in a beautiful valley southwest of Great Falls. Our life may not have fitted the stereotype you think of now as homesteading, but, of course, like many others, we used our homestead as a starting point while we looked for better things. I remember that our first home was fitted with a simple tin chimney. One day Dad went to town and bought some brick because he thought the tin too dangerous, but—too late! Before he even got home the house burned down. After that sad experience, he built a beautiful frame house—one of the first big houses out along the Smith—but before we'd lived there very long we pulled up stakes and moved again, this time to a sod-roofed house in Canada.

Dad and his brother found they could raise wonderful grain-crops in this area of Montana, but the range was being fenced and plowed, so, leaving his brother behind to do the farming, Dad went north looking for cheaper grass. His cousin Bertha Zeigler and her husband had moved up onto Whitemud Creek in Saskatchewan, so Dad bought a neighboring ranch on Sucker Creek where we lived from the time I was five until I was ten years old.

Vivian (right) stands outside her home in 1903 with her sister Frances and their mother. The next year it burned. —Bruneau-Ellis family

Things were primitive, you might say. Our house was roofed with a layer of willow rods; they were covered with a layer of native hay and topped with about twenty-four inches of dirt from which grass and even a few wild flowers, grew. The summer of 1906 was very wet; every cloud we saw had a shower in it. And that roof leaked so badly that Mother pitched a tent in the living room, and she laid oil cloth over the kitchen table and piled our valuables under it to keep them dry. But that sod-roofed house had a good pine floor—the only dance floor for miles around. I remember wonderful parties in winter when people had the time to travel. Of course, most of the neighbors lived a long ways off; the nearest little girl my age lived five miles away. One family had a funny little sled; long and narrow, it looked like a canoe pulled by horses hitched in tandem. The passengers sat one behind another; they drove sixty miles to a dance one winter, over the frozen range. Of course, they stayed and visited for a spell.

I remember the wonderful day Dad went to Maple Creek and came home with a Victrola. It cost him fifty dollars. Mother was thrilled, but she said, "Fred! You shouldn't be so extravagant!" In those days fifty dollars was money! This will tell you something about my dad: he said, "No. You are living out here where you never see anybody, and you never have a chance to hear good music; this is a good thing for our family." That was the kind of man he was. He wanted us to have that Victrola, and it was a wonderful thing in those days before electricity and radios. But we were never allowed to play anything

Wild flowers grew on the sod roof of the house. —Bruneau-Ellis family

except "Red-Seals"—classical records and such—and, then, only when we had company, or on other special occasions.

There were just three girls in our family: I was the eldest, born in South Dakota; then there was Frances, born here in Montana; then Helen, born at Maple Creek, Saskatchewan. I know my family was concerned about education; there just weren't that many teachers in the range country in those days. My cousin Bertha started me out. I had to climb a little hill between our places; I was seven years old, and scared to death to go over by myself. Of course, everybody told me there was nothing to worry about. But there were coyotes there, and wolves. Of course, wolves don't attack people, but I wasn't sure of that, as a youngster.

Dad never went any place without a rifle fastened to his saddle or in the wagon box beside him; not that he was afraid of the wolves, but you could sometimes save livestock that way. A wolf killed a colt right outside our yard one night. Dad had thought it would be safe enough that close to the house, but it wasn't. It was a pitch-black night before the days of yardlights or flashlights, and we heard the dogs barking, so Dad got his gun and went out, but all he could do was shoot into the air. Usually, there'd be about five wolves in a pack; that night they got the colt. No wonder I was frightened!

Well, after a couple of winters of reading, writing, and"rithmetic under Cousin Bertha, my sister and I moved in to school at Maple Creek, and Dad's younger sister, my Aunt Jo, came up from Montana to live with us so that Mother wouldn't have to leave the ranch. Our teacher was named Miss Beckett; she was red-haired—and she had to be to handle that roomful of kids. In that one room she taught two classes—at least twenty kids in each. It was quite a job to handle forty kids who might do such interesting things as dip a girl's pigtail into the inkwell of the desk behind her. The boys were always whispering and giggling. Miss Beckett had a razor strop, and she'd fold it over, and then she'd just point to a guilty party and point to the cloakroom; you'd hear the sound effects as she'd spank their hands. I've since heard that you can injure nerves permanently by spanking a child on the hand, but I don't remember any damage being done, or the parents raising a fuss. Our Miss Beckett had to be pretty tough, under the circumstances.

At Christmas time Dad came for us in a sleigh for the two-day, forty-mile trip back to the ranch from Maple Creek. For winter travel we heated stones and wrapped them in old blankets and laid them in the bottom of the sleigh, being careful not to get the stones too hot! Then we covered them with hay, threw a canvass over the top, and we could cuddle down and stay warm most of the day. But you could still hear the howling of the wolves. It was dark before we reached home on the second day, and I remember the cold chills that ran up and down my spine when we heard the wolves around us. Dad told us not to be frightened because he had his gun right there, but the horses were spooky and nervous, all the same, when they heard those wolves.

The winter of 1906 was our first on the Saskatchewan range. That was one of the famous ones; the thermometer hit sixty degrees below zero and it wouldn't register lower. Our ranch produced quite a lot of hay and had some fences and sheds, so we didn't have it quite as bad as some of our neighbors who lost thirty to forty percent of their livestock. With a few fences you could keep cattle in for winter feeding, and you could keep the range cattle out of your hay stacks, but in those days you turned your cattle loose on the range after calving, and gathered them up in the fall. You did your branding out on the open range.

Dad didn't ride on the roundup, but he often kept the roundup crews supplied with fresh food and eggs and meat and sometimes fuel, although they used old buffalo chips for fuel when they could find them. I remember, once, they sent word they'd be camped at a certain place, and Dad set out in his buckboard and took his younger sister, Jo, along. Jo had some cattle of her own out on the range and she said, "Let's take Vivian with us"; so I got to visit one of the old-time roundups.

I remember they had this great big tent where all the men slept and a cook tent where everybody ate. Aunt Jo had been widowed at twenty-four and was very pretty and popular with the cowboys, although she never did marry again; but at that time she was going with Johnny Whitcomb, a partner in the Whitemud Ranch, later bought by the Gilchrists.

Well, while we were at the roundup, Johnny went to town to get a cattle buyer to come and look at the cattle and make a price, and we kept waiting for them to get back to camp. It got later and later, and we had a terrible lightning storm with heavy, heavy rain, and the tent leaked a little so that Aunt Jo put up her umbrella to keep dry in the tent. Of course, that was thought to be terribly bad luck, and the men kept kidding her about how bad it was to open an umbrella under cover. They said, "We don't think Johnny will ever come back now"; and he didn't get there for the longest time. It was very late when he got to camp, and we learned that one of his horses had been struck and killed by lightning. It was all Aunt Jo's fault!

Roundup camp on the Milk River in 1912. —Glenbow Archives

Our ranch was in a valley bottom with hills all around and all covered with grass. Each ranch had its own fire department, you might say. We kept three big barrels filled with water all ready on a wagon and plenty of gunny sacks; and we'd keep a look-out, especially after a lightning storm, and there was always a team kept in and ready. I remember one stormy night we saw five different fires start around us; you could see wagons coming from all directions and men working against the skyline. There'd be someone on each wagon to dip the sacks in water, and then he'd throw the wet sacks to a man down on the fire line who would go on beating out the fire. There were terrific lightning storms every summer up in that part of Saskatchewan, and you just expected to have cattle killed by lightning, as well as fires.

Meanwhile, things weren't going smoothly for the family back in Montana; my uncle had married and wanted a place of his own, and Dad had a chance to buy him out. So, in 1910 we moved back across the Line, and this time we shipped the cattle and equipment down by rail, while we came crosscountry in a buckboard—our camping things and household equipment packed in hay on a tarp-covered wagon. And so, we came home to our nice new house on Smith River.

I mentioned how dark it was at night before the days of yardlights. In those early times I especially remember the coal oil lamps and how I used to hate 'em; you filled those lamps every day, and, if you weren't careful, they'd smoke and blacken the chimney and you had to wad up newspaper and clean the soot before you could see again. Gaslights that had to be pumped up—they came later, and they were a

63

Men beating out a fire. —Glenbow Archives

wonderful invention! When I was a teenager, my parents put in a carbide lighting system. Carbide was used in the mines for miners' lamps and for headlights on the early cars; for indoor lighting, you had carbide gas piped through your house from a tank where carbide "rocks" were soaked in water.

Later, after I married Richard and moved to our ranch on MacDonald Creek near Choteau, an engineer friend noticed the fall between two beaver dams and suggested we build our own hydro-electric plant. Well, the more we thought about it the better it sounded, so we put in a miniature "Montana Power" set-up wired to the house and sheds and barn. The only trouble was there were so many beaver! Those beaver would cut sticks and twigs, and stuff them into the generator intake, and stop the water. Or, sometimes, twigs would get right through into the turbine and plug it up; then, guess who'd have to jump in the car and drive down to the creek in the dark to fish twigs and sticks out of the system, so we could have electric power again?

I'm sure lots of women used to suffer from the isolation that went with ranch life. I lived on a ranch all my life until we moved to town in 1954, and I can live without people around me all the time. But, of course, I had a different upbringing. I was very fortunate in the way my father treated my mother and my sisters and me. Every time there was anything important to decide, Dad would call us in and say, "Now, sit down here a minute; we've got to talk this over." When we

64

got those carbide lights, for instance, I was visiting a neighboring ranch—I was going with a young man, there—and Dad called on the phone to ask when I'd be home.

"Well," I said, "What's happening?" You had to yell on those old phones. Dad said, "We're trying to decide about putting in carbide lights," and we talked about the cost of it, and all.

After I hung up, my young man said, "Does your father always call you for an okay before he makes decisions?" I said, "No, but he always wants us to know about everything. One of these days he could have an accident and he wants us to be able to make decisions and carry on."

That seemed to put an end to my romance with that young man, and, looking back, I'm glad it did. Later, I married Dick Ellis and we ran our ranch together as a team; if Dick went to move cattle or tend sheep-camp or anything like that, why, I always went along. So, I always knew what was happening on The Range.

GERALD HUGHES

still lives on the ranch his father started in Montana's Judith Basin. The Hughes family was well established by the time real homestead days began, a time Gerald remembers very well.

Pa got started on his forty-acre homestead here in 1894, but he didn't stay on forty acres long. There was lots of opportunity. By the time he'd been here ten or fifteen years, he'd built up quite a farm where he raised hogs and cows, for milk and beef, and grain and vegetables, and put out teams on contract to construction crews, and worked a little coal mine on his land.

The railroad came in '07, and the whole town of Stanford was moved a mile or so, to where you'd get off the train right in front of the hotel. The homesteaders flooded in about 1910 or '12; they'd come to Stanford on two, three railroad cars: furniture in one; the family in one; a milk cow, a few horses, and some pigs in a third. They just kept comin' and comin', and lots of settlements sprang up with new businesses and stores, and Pa supplied a lot of 'em with coal out of his mine; and some forgot to pay—I've still got 'em on the books [Gerald chuckles].

And those homesteaders put up fences and made it awful hard on livestock when they couldn't steal grass anymore; you had to cut your numbers down and keep 'em home. The popular breed was Shorthorn. Pa got Shorthorn bulls from somebody in Canada: I particularly remember two red bulls and a beautiful roan, and we used that breed for years, until they kind of faded out.

And then, about 1915 or '16, Pa and Amby Cheney bought some longhorn cattle—one horn up, like this, and the other down, like that—so wild, they'd go through fences anywhere they liked. Mother says, "You kids stay in the yard! They'll getcha!" Dad said he never made a dollar from the bastards.

We shipped our cattle east by rail for almost fifty years—for thirty years, consecutive, to Chicago. Here's an old sale ticket: thirty-nine steers at twelve hundred pounds—big cattle, partly Shorthorn—at $3.86 a hundred; the whole lot brought eighteen hundred bucks. At times, they weren't worth nothin', and we never spent a nickel doctorin'; if a cow got sick, she died. A calf-bed out? Why, most people'd just go shoot her.[6]

They went to a lot more trouble over horses. All the transportation was by horse—you rode, or had a team and wagon—otherwise you walked. The only veterinarian I remember was a big old, tall, red-headed guy named Murphy—had a barn here where he doctored horses, people, too; he set my brother Curt's arm one time. He didn't sell much vaccine or anything like that, and he didn't get much calvin' work, I'll tell ya.

Pa used a lot of mules as well as horses—got 'em from the mines when they was through. They kept those mules right down in the pit—fed 'em oats, and hay, and shod 'em; had a vet look after 'em down there until they got too tall. Those long ears would touch the open power lines strung on the ceiling, and that was it—electrocute 'em; get another mule and drag 'em out. And mules that stayed below too long, why, they'd go blind, so when they brought 'em up they'd keep 'em in a barn for two, three weeks till they was used to light and then they'd sell 'em.

I remember Pa bought one black team for $400—great big brutes they got to be; Pa'd hafta put the collars on 'em for us kids. They were good mules, too—wouldn't kick or nothin'. I used 'em several years, and they'd just walk away from a team of horses. "Jim" and "Joe," we called 'em; my brother Harley worked 'em on the bull-rake. Joe was iron gray, but turned snow white, and Jim was a great big sorrel. Gawd, but they could pull! Feed the sheep, plow, cut hay, do everything.

All us kids went to school up at the mines, battlin' bohunks—miners' kids. Mother'd been a teacher, and she saw to it we all finished school and even went to college; so I was down at Bozeman

66

when the Great Depression hit, and I came home and helped around the ranch and took a quarter-section of my own. Proved up by putting in a dam with a four-mule team and plow and scraper—real small dam, but it still holds water, and I've still got the land.

As long as I've got that homestead, I'm not destitute. If hard times come again, we'll just move a sheep wagon over there, and set up camp again [and Gerald laughs].

The letter below was written by Gerald's father, William, to a brother in Vermont just fourteen years after he came west. It illustrates how quickly an industrious young homesteader could build a booming business on The Range.

March 22, 1908
Stanford, Montana

Dear Brother,

We've had a nice winter here, the best one I ever put in Montana. It has not snowed over six inches this winter. I did not get my grain thrashed until November 21st. We had six and one-half days of thrashing, 2890 bushels of oats, 1100 and more of rye, wheat and barley. It was a wonderful season here. I had five acres of spuds, over six hundred sacks, and five or six tons of cabbage, carrots, beets and rutabagas, and a wagon load of turnips.

I rented the B. E. Stack place last season and had a wonderful crop there, over 300 tons of hay and it is all gone now. Hay is good property: worth about $10 a ton in the stack. Last spring it was worth from $18 to $22. Since the railroad commenced to build, everything here is high.

William Hughes' freight outfit at Great Falls, ca. 1915. —Hughes family

Mr. Stack sold his ranch to the John G. Williams Coal Exploration Company for $10 per acre, now they have bought all of the Sage Creek Sheep Company—over 25,000 acres— at $10. They offered me $10, but I would not sell for that.

I have been getting out quite a lot of coal from our own mine here, and sold more than 200 ton to J. G. Williams in February. I have just got my check today, and it is for $1,485.98 for one month. Now the Company is sinking a shaft of their own on the bench about two miles from here that will be 460 feet deep when they get to the coal. The railroad company is going to build a road right up here to it, and I have traded them some forty-acre tracts of land on the bench for 27 'forties' down on Willow Creek. I've heard that the coal mine here will be the largest one in the State in two or three years.

I bought three teams this winter and had four teams before. I did not ship any beef last fall, and have been feeding some all winter. We use one beef and sometimes two a week, and one hog. I have over fifty steers that are good beef, and 16 big hogs and over 300 hens and 1 turkey. We get 12 to 13 dozen eggs in a day now. I bought the Cook Ranch last June and cattle and horses. I bought Mr. Parkins Ranch in October 1906, and have the offer of all the land on Willow Creek below here. The Stack Ranch I will rent for the same as last year for $500 cash the 1st of November, 1908 and the rest of it on halves.

There's been a great change here since you left. We've got a man cook, and he feeds from 15 to 25 at a meal.

Hoping this finds you on the gain.

Will I. Hughes

JIM LITTLE

describes the way his grandad built a business based on home-steads and public range. Although his range is across the mountains from our own, his story's typical of many parts of the West.

My grandfather, Andrew Little, came from Scotland in 1890; he got off the stage near Boise with three bucks in his pocket, hiked out to a ranch, and went to work herding sheep.

He took his wages in sheep for several years, and one thing led to another, and before he finished, they tell me he was the biggest sheep producer in the world. Some companies were bigger, but Grandad had in excess of 100 bands himself—between 110 and 120 thousand sheep—scattered around the range between eastern Oregon and western Montana. He didn't own much land, of course, just sheep; the land was public domain and couldn't be bought. The only way to get some land was to homestead it—a quarter-section to a family; you used the dry old range for free.

The thing about those old-time range outfits, from what I hear, the cattleman was king. He told the old sheep man, said, "If you want water, you buy water. You're not usin' places where we water cattle."

And so sheepmen like my grandfather went around and bought up homesteads because, of course, homesteads were all settled on water. So when the Taylor Grazing Act came along in 1934, dividing up the public domain into grazing districts and allocating permits for its use, why, the cattlemen looked up and found that the sheepmen owned most of the deeded land and controlled lots of water, and got most of the grazing. That was the way it was around here, anyway.

At that, there wasn't much land worth owning, just homesteads checkerboarded here and there. There's lots of Taylor land around that has no value by itself because it's just dry range. If the Bureau of Land Management, which manages it today, came to us and said, "Here, we'd like to *give* you this Taylor land," we probably wouldn't take it. It wouldn't pay the taxes; that's the kind of ground it is. And, by the time the Great Depression hit, my grandfather was broke, and the bank would have taken the whole "empire." There was just one thing that stopped 'em: they knew they couldn't run it any cheaper. My grandad sure knew how to run things tight!

FARRINGTON CARPENTER
cattleman and lawyer who organized grazing districts following passage of the Taylor act, which ended the free use of the public domain but gave security and tenure to its users and made range management possible. He tells how it came to pass.

As the tide of settlement went west, it went very slowly. The real rush began in 1849 when gold was discovered in California—that's been a lure for mankind since the beginning of the world—and people began to cross the plains by thousands. It opened up the continent;

some of the first cattle to reach our northern ranges came east from Oregon or the gold fields of B.C.

Now, this country goes by rainfall. In the East you get thirty to forty inches a year, and down in the South you get fifty to sixty inches, and so it goes until, west of the 100th meridian, the rainfall drops to less than twenty inches. Rainfall is the outstanding physical fact of this continent.

The homesteads and railroad grants and state lands and Indian reservations and national forests, parks, and monuments took up little bits of western land—the public domain—but two-thirds of it was left. Well, the public domain was mostly natural pasture—nothing there but grass, a little sagebrush, a little browse—and people began using it.

Now, the people who wanted free land weren't wealthy people. They were hard-up people that had been closed out by the sheriff somewhere else and were trying to get a new start; the only way they could do it was with the Homestead Act. But most of the homestead land wouldn't make a living. So, around Christmas time of 1916, Congress got generous and passed the Stock-Raising Homestead Act; under it you could get a whole section—640 acres—but, still, the homesteaders couldn't make a living; so they grazed the public domain.

Most successful were the sheep people who were nomads. They'd get a loan on a bunch of sheep and start off with a wagon or a battered old jalopy, and just wander. There was no regulation on the public domain. The reason there wasn't is that Congress had embarked on a policy of "disposition"—they wanted to get the land off their hands. Now, back East they hadn't had to regulate the pastureland because it wasn't long till somebody farmed it up or homesteaded it; before the government acted, it had disappeared from public ownership. The majority of legislators came from that side of the meridian and didn't understand western conditions. It was the historical thing to do.

It wasn't until 1934 that the western states faced a crisis, and the crisis came on pretty much in the conflict between the sheep and cattle interests: there was no way to keep the sheepman off the cowman's range. He could move in and settle on the water with all his dogs and his wagon, and the cows wouldn't go near it. The cattleman had to move out.

Well, we didn't move out peaceably; we had range wars all over, and the law officers said nothing. Nearly every western state tried some kind of a law to regulate range use, but they couldn't do much about a situation where the federal government had already doled

70

out legal title to 640 acres under the homestead laws. This was what led to the Taylor Grazing Act.

The Taylor act was a tremendous turn in policy whereby the federal government said, "No longer will we try to dispose of all this land. Nobody wants it because it's too dry and too worthless to pay taxes on. We're going to do three things: first, we're going to sell isolated tracts; second, we'll sell any little pieces that don't fall into natural grazing districts; and third, we'll form grazing districts and supervise their use.

Well, the Taylor Grazing Act was a tremendous surprise and was very antagonistically received in the West, except in Utah, where the people—by training, religion, and practice—are more cooperatively minded. But the act also followed the example of something that had happened in the far southeastern corner of Montana. In 1928 stockmen out on Pumpkin Creek, between the Powder and Tongue rivers, got tired of squabbling and formed their own association to administer private, state, and federal grazing land in a cooperative way.[7] It was quite a remarkable thing to do. It set the stage for the Taylor grazing districts.

The most successful users of the public range were the sheepmen who were able to control some water. —L.A. Huffman photo, Montana Historical Society

HENRY WALLACE

secretary of agriculture from 1933 to 1940, wrote as follows (excerpted, italics added) to the U. S. Congress concerning western range conditions in 1936—during the Dirty Thirties.[8] Wallace's recommendations illustrate the thinking of the day: range depletion is caused by excessive stocking—just too many animals on the land. This sounds logical—so logical it has been the basis for public policy for well over sixty years. As the reader will discover, there is sound reason to question its validity.

April 24, 1936

Gentlemen:

In response to Senate Resolution No. 289, I am pleased to send you this report on the western range area of these United States—a great but neglected natural resource.

1. The range area of 728 million acres is nearly 40 percent of the total land area of the continental United States; more than 99 percent is available for livestock grazing.

2. About half that area, or 376 million acres, is in private ownership. One-third, or 239 million acres, is Federal range, divided among national forests, grazing districts, public domain, and other withdrawals and reservations.

3. Forage depletion averages more than half; the result of a few decades of livestock grazing.

4. Range depletion on the public domain and grazing districts averages 67 percent, on private, Indian, and State and County lands about half, and on national forests 30 percent.

8. *An outstanding cause of range depletion has been excessive stocking.* Some 17.3 million animal units are now grazed on ranges which it is estimated can carry only 10.8 million. *The removal of the surplus is the most effective way to stop depletion and start the range on the upgrade.*

9. About seven-tenths, or 523 million acres, of the range area is still subject to practically unrestricted grazing.

10. Precipitation in the range country averages less than one-third that of the Middle West and East. One to 4 drought years out of 10 characterize practically all of the range area.

The failure to recognize the fluctuation of forage production with precipitation has been one primary cause of depletion.

13. Unsuitable land laws and policies have made the range a bewildering mosaic of different kinds of ownership. and of uneconomic units, which together constitute a serious obstacle to range management and profitable livestock production.

16. Most spectacular among the maladjustments of rangeland use has been the attempt to use more that 50 million acres for dry-land farming. About half, ruined for forage production for years to come, has already been abandoned for cultivation, much of it even before going to patent.

17. A more serious, but much less spectacular maladjustment has been the private acquisition of many million acres, either submarginal for private ownership as shown by high tax delinquency and relief rolls, abandonment, etc., or having high public values for watershed protection which private owners cannot maintain, or both.

18. Four-fifths of the 232 million acres which yield 85 percent of the water of the major western streams is range, and low precipitation makes water the limiting factor.

19. 589 million acres of range land is eroding more or less seriously, reducing soil productivity and impairing watershed services. Three-fifths of this area is adding to the silt load of major western streams.

20. *It will probably require more than 50 years of management to restore the depleted range sufficiently to carry even the 17.3 million livestock units now grazed, and probably an additional 50 years to restore it to the nearest possible approach to its original grazing capacity of 22.5 million units.*

21. Action of the greatest immediate urgency and im-portance is required to:

- Stop soil and forage depletion, and start both on the upgrade;

- Reduce excessive stocking, place all range lands under management, and restore cheap range feed;

- Rectify ownership and use maladjustments, and obtain a sound distribution of ownership between private and public agencies;
- Build up economic private and public units;
- Balance and integrate crop and range use;
- Correlate the livestock, watershed, forest, wildlife, and recreation forms of range-land uses and services;
- Obtain a recognition of the responsibility of stewardship by private owners;
- Minimize or remove various financial handicaps of stock producers;
- Reconcile range conservation and financial needs of State institutions;
- Solve the tax delinquency problem;
- Place public lands under the supervision of agricultural agencies as a step toward unification of public responsibility for the entire range. Provide on such lands for a sound distribution of grazing privileges, and prevent the establishment of prescriptive rights;
- Obtain and apply the information necessary for the conservation and wise use of the range resource;
- Prevent human wastage and insure social and economic security.

Henry Wallace's social theories cut a swath in the halls of Congress where, as Farrington Carpenter liked to say: "Those people don't know which end of a cow gets up first."

This wonderful old L.A. Huffman photograph, entitled "Throwing Rangers Out," shows cattle moving north up one of the many coulees that drain our range, bringing with them the promise of a useful way of life for the Indians and for thousands of hard-pressed people who would come from around the world seeking their fortunes on the plains. —Montana Historical Society

Can anyone remember when times were not hard, and money not scarce?

—Ralph Waldo Emerson

3

Hard Times and Range Horses

As our characters have told us, the early 1900s brought good moisture and floods of immigrants to the plains. They weren't all graziers, of course, as we have seen; the great demand for wheat brought on by World War One drew farmers to The Range and dictated "busting" virgin sod on both sides of the border. It was mighty slow work; not even twelve-horse hitches, not even steam-powered tractors seemed to threaten The Range. But then, the climate changed and dry years came—again—and the drought, dust, and depression of the thirties drew waves of public interest as settlers left The Range. Nineteen nineteen, they say, was the driest year on record in Montana, and another cycle of drought began in 1929 and lasted for ten years. Prices collapsed worldwide: cattle worth nine dollars a hundredweight in 1929 brought three dollars five years later. "Dollar" wheat brought twenty-five cents a bushel. In Montana, 350,000 head of cattle were sold through government programs; in Alberta and Saskatchewan, things were just as bad—or worse.

Horses were worthless. As half a million people left the northern plains by train and Model T, on foot and horseback, they turned 100,000 head of horsepower loose to run wild and feed themselves out on The Range. It remains to be seen whether well-remembered conditions of the thirties were exceptional; tree rings indicate our range has suffered fifty-year periods of drought; the tragedy of the 1930s was that dry years and depression came together. As the Great Depression was the breeding ground where lasting social programs were conceived, so it was the burial ground where the age of horsepower expired.

JONATHAN FOX III

is a cigar-chewing, yarn-spinning, world-class livestock judge and breeder. He recalls the way his father sold horsepower.

It took a lot of power to break that prairie sod, and cultivate and seed and run the binders and haul in all those bundles to be thrashed. Even a family farm like ours would put two twelve-horse outfits in the field, at times a six-horse hitch or two, and need an extra team now and then as well. The world was run on horsepower in those days.

My dad raised Percheron horses, Shorthorn cattle, Shropshire sheep, and Poland-China hogs on a farm at Rochester, Minnesota. In those days before the First World War, with all the settlers heading west, those lard-type hogs and farmyard sheep were still in style.

—Glenbow Archives

Shorthorns made good dual-purpose cows for homesteaders, and were in great demand for upgrading range cattle. And Percherons were all the rage for horsepower—the most popular breed, by far, in North America. In 1917, I think it was, Dad made a trip out west to visit friends and, he hoped, to make some sales along the way. At Drumheller, Alberta, he sold four big, Percheron stallions to an old Minnesota friend, George Kennedy, who'd known our stock for years.

"I'll tell ya what," George said. "When you ship those horses, make the carload up with Shorthorns." So he did. Well, Dad had asthma pretty bad—he seldom ever got a good night's sleep in Minnesota; but at Drumheller, he went to bed and slept the whole night through. When he came west again a few months later, same thing happened. Dad said, "George, if I can sleep like this, I'm movin' here for good," and he went and got his family and they moved. When their immigrant car arrived, Mrs. Kennedy said, "George, there's something queer about these friends of yours. I was looking at the stuff come off that car and they brought along a bathtub; something's wrong!" But Dad didn't put down roots at Drum; he hitched up and drove northeast across two hundred miles of that incredible prairie wool. He settled down at Blackfoot, where our Justamere Farm is now, and went back to putting stallions on the road.

In Minnesota, in his younger days, Dad had traveled with his stallions every spring. Those farms were close together and all of them raised horses, so he'd set out on the road, drive one stallion on his cart and lead another and breed mares wherever he could find

Four Percheron stallions were sold to the Kennedy-Davis Ranch at Rosemary, Alberta, in 1917. Jonathan Fox II is second from right, holding the up-headed black. —Fox family

'em; it had been a nice substantial business. But, here in western Canada: new conditions, eh? Sparsely settled, fillin' fast with great demand for horses. Here's how it worked.

A community would form a stallion club. We'd provide them with a stallion and a groom. The groom would lead the stud around a circuit every week, broken into noon and evening stands; he'd go out Monday morning on a route of fifty miles, and be back in town by Saturday: same route each week, same stands each day. That way, a farmer knew to bring his mare to get her "tried," and to find out when she cycled; then, later, he'd bring her back to get her bred. In time we had thirty stallions on the road, right down the line, clear into Manitoba—mostly Percherons, one Belgian, and a Clyde.

I was born in 1920. When I was old enough—fifteen or sixteen—Dad had me training grooms and breaking ponies; there was always a shortage of reliable cart ponies. Each groom would lead his stallion tied behind a cart in which he carried his kit—a groomin' outfit: brush and comb, bit of first-aid for the stallion, water bucket—that was it. But, when you drove across that unfenced open country, there'd be range horses comin' up, and there'd often be a stud among 'em, eh? And then you'd have to turn your pony loose and look after your stallion.

We was always scoutin' around for quiet ponies. We found out we could use our risin' two-year-old Percheron fillies; they were the most reliable and easiest to break of all. Hell, I broke seventeen while I was goin' to school one winter. I'd drive 'em every weekend on some old breakin' cart, stoneboat, or somethin', and, when I got 'em goin', why, I'd hook 'em on the buggy, and my sister and I would drive 'em to school. All seventeen was ready by the first of May, when they went out on the circuit with the grooms.

The bugbear in the stallion business always used to be collectin' fees; that's why these little clubs were formed, each with its own council of president, vice president, and secretary-treasurer. They'd handle the arrangements, fix the route, and collect the fees—one-third at time of service, balance due when safe-in-foal. The clubs kept good records and kept a commission on collections, but what really made things work was that the government sent inspectors out to grade the stallions, and it subsidized the one-third service fee. That helped us stay afloat right through the Dirty Thirties, right up to World War Two, when the golden age of horsepower finally ended.

JOE GILCHRIST

the thirteen-year-old Saskatchewan cowboy introduced in Chapter Two, is, at eighty-nine, a slim, straight, silver-haired old rancher, sharp of mind and full of interest and good humor. In 1914 he and brothers Rube, Chay, Jack, and Sandy formed a partnership that spread across the southern Alberta range, surviving two world wars, two droughts, and the Great Depression.

In June of 1914, ten years after we came west and built our homestead base and learned the ropes, we bought the Whitemud Ranch on Frenchman's Creek from a couple of Montanans: Johnny Whitcomb and Park Zeigler. With the Whitemud we got several hundred acres of deeded land, eight sections of lease, about 700 cattle branded Q7 on the left hip, over twenty head of horses, and a hayin' outfit. Everything was done by horses in those days: we put up hay with horsepowered mowers, dump rakes, bull rakes, overshot stackers, and a lot of men.

We tried to build a good reserve of hay and keep a year's supply ahead, which is why we stayed in business for so long through all the ups and downs of many years—more ups than downs, but plenty of things went wrong. One fall, for instance, we bought some Manitoba

Joe Gilchrist about 1927. —Glenbow Museum

cattle—300 head of two-year-olds: heifers, steers, some Shorthorn in 'em—pretty good stock I think. The good part was we bought 'em right; the bad part was we brought home Bangs disease.[1] That almost put us out of business there and then. No vaccine in them days, of course; the only thing to do was to live with it and sell cows that were dry. I've seen as many as twenty-five slunk calves on the feed ground at the Whitemud in a morning. The old saying goes: "Buy trouble in the cow, and drive it home."

Mange was another problem; we had to dip our cattle every June. An animal with mange would lose its hair; you'd see 'em with big, bloody scabs on their backs and hips. Untreated animals wouldn't winter. First we built a cage vat and lowered 'em one by one in a crate hitched to a team—a real slow job. Later we built a swimming vat, which was a whole lot faster if you knew what you were doing. With a swimming vat, there's a hard way and an easy way to put the cattle through. The hard way is to corral 'em and try to push 'em through right now; they're full and don't handle easy. To do it right, you pen 'em up at noon and let 'em stand all night; at five o'clock next morning you have to slow 'em down. But you better brand your calves before you dip; it's almost impossible to brand a hide that's full of lime and sulfur, and it took a lot of lime and sulfur to charge that vat. The mixture cooked eight hours, and then we got the district mange inspector to make sure it was to strength. It's almost forgotten now, but mange was a serious problem on the range.

Another constant threat was prairie fire. Many were started by lightning; others by fearless greenhorns who threw their ashes out in the dry grass. Hundreds of homesteaders moved in around 1910, and a lot of country burned. About that time my brother Ruben got a contract to plow fireguards; he camped in an old house out on the prairie and when he brought his bed and camp gear home he brought bedbugs with him. Mother cleaned and scraped and used coal oil for years and years to keep those bugs in check.

Through the dry years following the First World War, our herd kept growing. The summer of 1919 was one of the driest I remember—almost as dry as 1988—and with 900 cattle to look after, we had to look outside the Whitemud Ranch for grass. Another kid and I loose-herded, living in a tent clear through November. We were always short of grass, and I got lots of practice camping on the range. I guess that's why I don't care much for camping anymore; it took me forty years to get up off the ground and sleep inside.

Back in 1912, the firm of J. H. Wallace had taken up a 300,000-acre lease quite near us in our corner of Saskatchewan. The next few years Jim Wallace and his partner Walter Ross picked up smaller leases for about a hundred miles along Milk River in Alberta: the Q, Cross Z, Blacktail, Lost River, Lower Spencer, and several others—each headquarters for a grazing lease. By 1924, Wallace and Ross controlled a half-million acres under fence, and they were broke. The partnership dissolved; the Royal Bank took the leases; young George,

The dipping vat used by Gilchrists and their neighbors. —Glenbow Archives

Walter's son, stayed on to run it while they got things sorted out. Ross owned outright, and kept, the old Milk River Ranch, but other pieces had to be dispersed; one lease became community pasture—a taste of things to come.

Well, by 1926, our Gilchrist Brothers' Bar X Bar herds had reached 3,000 head, so we went to see George Ross and took six townships of grazing leases off his hands. There were several different units—all of them grazed bare—so we only moved 500 head west to our new Alberta range that fall.

In Saskatchewan we'd always had a good backlog of hay close to our winter ground, and we decided to follow the same plan in Alberta. We found a place near Manyberries with a lot of hay to cut, and rented it, and that was the easy part; we found ourselves a hundred miles from home with no haying outfit. Around September first, when Sandy finished haying at the Whitemud, he loaded his outfit at a nearby railroad spur and shipped it on two flatcars up to Manyberries. Then, while a man trailed the teams across, Chay and I rented a railroad cook-car and a bunk-car, hired a cook and ten or twelve men, and got ready to go to work.

Putting together a hay outfit that somebody else has taken apart is quite a job, and I had that mess to straighten out—about fifty horse collars, and fifty sets of harness to untangle. Then everything went fine till it began to rain; then it snowed; then we had to quit to gather beef. When things dried out we started up again, and by November we wound up with about 600 tons of well-stacked hay. We kept it for emergencies for years; it took a lot of hay to carry all our calves and yearlings over, and we never sold a head till it was three or four year old.

What we sold, we sold to drovers right here on the range. In 1924, for instance, we sold our beef to a chap named Kindlespier—real nice feller—fifty bucks a head for three-year-olds, forty bucks a head for drys and spays. This Kindlespier bought most of the beef in our area that fall; he hired cowboys, had a wagon and camp outfit, took delivery on the range, then crossed the Line at Willow Creek and trailed 'em to the railroad pens at Havre for shipment to Chicago. In those days our closest market was the States; cattle were appraised—not weighed—for duty as we crossed the Line. The duty paid was just so much a head; the only health inspection was for mange.

But then, disaster! In 1931 prices hit rock bottom. On top of that, the Americans put a protective tariff on, and duty doubled. Of course, there'd been other years when the market across the Line hadn't worked for us: As far back as 1895 my father-in-law, Tom Hargrave,

This is how range hay was put up with horsepower.

A. *Cutting wild hay with five-foot mowers on the CL Ranch on Jumping Pound Creek.* —Copithorne family

B. *Gathering it with a sweep.* —Montana State University Libraries, Wilson Collection

C. Putting it up the beaver slide with a push-pole stacker on the W.C. Gardner Ranch near Nanton, Alberta. Mr. Gardner was away at World War One; Mrs. Gardner is driving. —Glenbow Archives

D. Pulling it up on the bull pole. —Glenbow Archives

E. Stacking with an overthrow stacker. —Glenbow Archives

F. Topping the stack with manpower. —Copithorne family

had shipped fat cattle all the way to England; during World War One, again, our cattle went to Britain. So, eventually, in 1931, somebody remembered the cattle boats tied up at Halifax and got 'em out of mothballs. They saved the day!

ED McKINNON

A pioneer cattle feeder, working on his father's ranch when hard times came. He recalls how silk trains and steamships helped them beat the crunch.

My dad remembered northern Montana cattle being driven north to Calgary for shipment over the Canadian Pacific Railroad to Chicago. That was before the Great Northern reached Montana.

Dad came west on the CPR in 1886. He planned to work one summer and go home with fifty dollars—enough to save the family farm in Ontario. By the end of that summer, he used to say, he wouldn't have given fifty dollars for the whole of Ontario; he stayed and learned the ranching business when cattle could range clear from the Bow to the Missouri. He rode on many a roundup in the early days and started the LK Ranch and Farming Company.

I quit school in June of 1929, and went to work for LK with my brothers, Charlie, Angus, Don, and Arthur. They sent me down to run our little feedlot at Dalemead on the Bow River east of Calgary. Our barley-fed LK steers went east to Winnipeg, South Saint Paul, or Chicago, and the first we really noticed of the Depression was when the Hawley-Smoot Tariff took effect in 1930. Then our markets went to hell. Buyers had to be coaxed to come and look. Grass steers dropped to two dollars a hundred, and there was no market at all for cows or bulls, some of which were purchased, shot, and buried by the government.

Then somebody noticed the British pound was worth $4.85 Canadian. That would work—if we could get 'em across the pond! Somebody else remembered cattle boats, tied up at Halifax since World War One, all fitted out with stalls for pairs of cattle up to eight years old. Before long, those old boats had been refurbished and pressed into service; the stalls held, easily, three head of our younger, lighter two- and three-year-olds, which cheapened-up the freight which was based on space instead of weight.

Department of agriculture people in Ottawa helped with shipping arrangements. The Western Stock Growers' Association scheduled cattle all along the Line from B.C. to Ontario. Trains would pick up one- or two- or ten-car lots—consigned by different owners; they'd stop at Dalemead Siding for our cars, then on to Medicine Hat, and finally Montreal: a six-day trip with, normally, three feed stops en route.

The CPR outdid itself in getting cattle through—sometimes even stopped a "crack" silk train to hook us on. Those transcontinental freights, rushing Oriental silk from Pacific ports to New England textile mills, had priority over everything on the line, and they could get our cattle through with just one stop en route, which saved two feeds along the way.[2] It was quite a thrill to get word of a silk train coming. The cattle—already brand- and health-inspected, with export papers ready—were loaded onto cars bedded down with wheat straw two feet deep; the cars were hooked together. Everything was ready when that fast express arrived.

I can still hear that big old locomotive panting while it unhooked, backed into the siding, pulled the cattle cars out onto the line, backed again, and coupled with the silk cars; you could hear the clatter roll right down the train. Then, in no time, it was gone, oozing off into the night, with the cattle riding comfortably in front, and a couple of lucky cowboys behind.

At Montreal a boat was ready and the cattle went on board, loose, tie-ropes draggin' from their necks. Then the cowboys and the sailors had to tie 'em in their stalls before they hit rough water out at sea. In earlier times, I guess, those older, bigger cattle gave 'em hell; they'd have to rope 'em in the hold, then use a big long hawser rope and winch 'em with a capstan to the stalls. Our feedlot cattle weighed 1,200 pounds, but handled easy; though I suppose those "shortgrass country" Gilchrist steers were wild as hell. On the second trip Dad established a tradition: he had his cattle tied up, fed, and watered, and was sitting on the deck when the boat passed Quebec City— that's where the St. Lawrence widens out and things get rough.

The crossings took a week. The cattle went ashore at Liverpool, and were driven through the Mersey River tunnel to Birkenhead, held off feed a day, and slaughtered. Next day the carcasses were shipped to London's Smithfield Market where they sold "by the side" at auction, and were very well received. I guess the British liked the hard, white fat on our barley-finished cattle; they paid a premium for everything we sent.

My brother Charlie went across with the first shipment, and stayed all summer collecting money, making transfers, taking care of small details for everyone. He found that when the boats touched

Charlie McKinnon showing Alberta range cattle to English buyers.
—McKinnon family

shore, the sailors cut the tie-ropes with an ax—just threw 'em away—sold pails and forks and everything for junk. He gathered it all up and shipped it home to be used over and over again, the way you'd expect a good businessman to do.

While it lasted, it was worth six cents a pound to ship our beef to England. But, in 1933 the Brits went off the gold standard; the pound sterling dropped to $3.60 Canadian, and all the frosting melted off the cake. For a year or so our government pegged exchange back up at $4.60 a hundred, and the shipments continued for awhile, but then the Canada-U.S. Trade Agreement was signed in 1936, and our natural market opened up again. Trade always follows the path of least resistance; the English shipments stopped.

I never got to go on one of those exciting trips. It would have been great fun, but somebody had to stay home and do the chores. And room got to be a problem since so many people—doctors, lawyers, homesick immigrants—wanted to work their way to England on those boats. One who did go on a trip was an adventurous young Albertan named Harry Hays, who returned to make a fortune exporting cattle, and went on to become Canadian minister of agriculture; it was he, of course, who opened up the North American continent to European cattle. But that's another story. It was quite a joke on Harry that a silk train came through on his wedding day. The knot was hurriedly tied, and Harry kissed the bride, and departed, all alone, in the caboose.

MAYNARD SMITH

This Montana rancher, speaks of good times and depressions in the cycle.

I remember my grandad telling me about a real good year right after World War One—a year when cattle made good money and it rained! I was helping him drive cattle in to market, and he was telling of better times. I was about ten years old and I remember it real well: we were trailing from the ranch right to the packer, and those big old grass-fat steers brought three cents a pound! That was 1933, the depths of the Depression.

The next good year—I was grown by then—was 1950 or '51. After that, golly, we were hanging by our coattails till the sixties. Then came a little spurt—like, thirty cents or so for steer calves—not as much as 1951. The price slid off again to a low in '64, then slow improvement till the Nixon "freeze" of 1973.[3] Ka-boom! Then, 1978 was good, but '81, a crash! There's really only been a few years of good prices in several generations in the cattle business.

I'm getting old, I guess. I listened to a young fellow talk the other night: "You gotta change," he said. I'm sure we all change to some extent, but too much change can be disastrous, too. I've seen a lot of ranches go down the tube. I'm a director of a financial institution that has livestock loans out all over the state of Montana, and during the latest crisis—in the mid-1980s—I've seen a lot of people go under because they changed too fast, while older outfits that have operated more or less the same for generations are still going strong.

The big thing that has broke most people has been timing—picking the wrong time for expansion. That sounds elementary, but throughout my lifetime land values have generally increased: anything you bought twenty or thirty years ago has doubled or tripled in value until the last few years, you know, when land has gone the other way. That's been a shock to many of us. But some of the good old operators who've been taking care of their land for many years, not overstocking, never getting into too much debt—however they managed that—have survived.

JOHN CROSS

Ties down a global range problem that still exists today.

In 1931 cattle prices in Canada dropped in half—from six to three cents a pound—and to get that, we had to feed 'em barley worth eleven cents a bushel. Of course, land values dropped the same; grass land wasn't worth much money at the time. What *should* rangeland be worth?

In '31 a three-year-old steer was worth an ounce of gold; and so was the animal-unit of land required to run him—that's about twenty acres in these Porcupine Hills. Today, a 1,000-pound steer is worth two ounces of gold; the land's worth ten. That makes it tough to buy much grass for steers.

The trouble is, a lot of people think that rangeland is a whole lot more productive than it is, even at the best of times. There's lots of would-be cowboys around who have gone into the banks and bought a bunch of cows and now they're broke. And government has often backed 'em. We've seen banks competing with politicians instead of with each other. Who needs that? It puts the entire system out of kilter.

ALEX JOHNSTON

Southern Alberta historian who remembers the dust bowl and the Dirty Thirties as continental problems.

I was born on a southwestern Saskatchewan homestead farm, and have always been interested in agriculture. In fact, I knew very little else when I eventually went to university in 1940. At that time some pretty responsible people had just about given up on this whole part of the continent, and there were very, very few individuals in the mid-1930s who thought it had any future at all. The exact same conditions existed here in western Canada as in the United States, you know: the so-called dust bowl you've read so much about, if you don't remember. The same thing was going on up and down the whole interior of the North American continent. The damage here had come, primarily, from abusive farming practices. What happened was that early farmers brought techniques suited to humid climates, and simply not suited to our arid or semi-arid conditions. This all culminated, actually, on two occasions: there was a tremendous

Pulverizing the range with 16 mules in a Shenandoah hitch near Nobleford, Alberta, about 1921. —Glenbow Archives

amount of soil drifting in the early 1920s that lasted about five years; and then we had the economic depression that lasted for a decade.

One old, hard-held traditional technique is that of summer-fallowing—a very old idea, of course, perhaps as old as agriculture. In moister parts of the world it's used primarily as a weed-control measure. You shouldn't have to stop cultivation to control weeds, there are other ways of doing it, but nevertheless that's what's always been done.[4] Gradually, the farmers, summer-fallowing moist areas, plowing deep, began to take tremendous pride in having clean fields; they turned the soil completely over, burying all the stubble, making their fields look neat and tidy. But, out in this semi-arid region, the technique was disastrous.

The experience has been that it takes about seven years, let's say, for the organic matter in prairie soil to break down, and for the soil to convert into a condition that blows readily in the wind. A lot of land was broken in this area, for instance, in 1903, and extensive soil drifting started in 1911. That's about the interval one encounters.

The people in the Nobleford-Barons-Monarch triangle, north of Lethbridge, were particularly hard hit. They went through the same experience of breaking the native prairie sod, and then went through the brief period when there wasn't any problem because the soil had enough aggregation and structure to withstand the wind. Those soils, however, tend to be fine, sandy loams that blow very easily, and when the original organic matter—the root content, and so on—broke down, then the drifting started with a vengeance. The farmers in that area were faced with simple survival, it was as simple as that; either they did something about it, or they were going out of business.

Well, necessity's the mother of invention, and so a lot of people began to devise techniques. The practice of cover-cropping—seeding fallow land to oats in mid-summer, hoping for lots of growth before a killing frost—originated near Fort Macleod, Alberta. That sort of crop stays green all winter, provides valuable pasture, and holds the soil. And then a farmer up at Monarch by the name of Koole—a horticulturist and shoemaker who'd come homesteading—came up with the concept of strip-farming just out of sheer necessity. He noticed that drifting started toward the center of his fields, and that gave him the idea of cultivating summer-fallow in narrow strips, at right angles to the prevailing wind where possible. He was quite confident strips would work; in fact, they did, and carloads of farmers were soon coming up on tour from neighboring Montana to observe and study the idea.

In 1941 I was at the University of Saskatchewan, very much involved in curing land deterioration through regrassing. People at the Swift Current Research Station had developed techniques whereby they seeded rye grain into deteriorated fields; then, when they got a bit of a crop, they seeded crested wheatgrass into the stubble. This new technique just stabilized the land, and, as time went on, new ways were found to turn those fields of Russian thistle and other annual weeds back into productive pasture.

We Canadians are apt to think we originated these ideas; in fact— in many, many cases—we picked up on ideas from people down at Mandan, North Dakota, and Stillwater, Oklahoma, and a variety of other places. Responsible people up and down the continent were

Soil drifting along a fence line in the Dirty Thirties. —Glenbow Archives

Narrow strips, just a binder swath in width, helped to stop soil blowing.
—Montana State University Libraries

meeting constantly all through those years, conferring with each other, and everybody was terribly, terribly concerned about getting this whole continent stabilized and back into some sort of production.

GERALD HUGHES

grew up on a Judith Basin sheep and cattle ranch that survived the awful crunch of the Great Depression. Gerald has a twinkle in his eye as he recalls some of the challenges in his eighty-five years on The Range.

I've seen a few depressions in my time, but, as time goes by, they might be getting worse; people have a lot of debt nowadays. In the thirties, $500 was a lot of debt, though—as for us—we never went in debt back then because we always had a cash flow. We used to milk a lot of cows; that old barn up there held fifteen, sixteen cows, so we got about five gallons of cream a day. At the end of the week, we'd ship it on the bus to Lewistown or, when that creamery went belly up, to Great Falls. No matter how tight things got, we always had a cash flow from our Holstein cows.

And then, we always had a herd of pigs runnin' out on the range. One year, after an early snow, Pa says, "Maybe you and Harley better go up over west, and see if you can bring some of them sows home with their pigs."

Well, we had a hell of a time. We'd run onto a sow and, "Eeeeh!" There'd be pigs runnin' every direction. So we told Dad: "Can't get 'em yet. We'll have to wait for colder weather."

In October you'd see old sows headin' down out of the hills and brush all by themselves. Then Pa'd sort out the pigs, and he'd put 'em in and feed 'em barley and skim milk, and then in February or March we'd take 'em to Great Falls and bring home hams and bacon. So we had cream and pigs and wool and wether lambs; and we sold rams and ewes—always somebody around the country wantin' ewes—and, that way, Dad had a cash flow all the time, and he never had to mortgage anything.

After 1929, a lot of banks went under, and Pa was a director of the First National in Stanford at the time, and he took it on himself to pay off all the depositors at ninety-five cents on the dollar; that made things pretty tough around the Hughes ranch for awhile. When I came home from college I had to find an off-ranch job. The customer-owned production credit associations (PCAs) started up in the thirties, and I went to work for the PCA in Lewistown in 1934. The bank down there went broke in '29 or '30, and a few years later Ben Forbes, who'd been president, was made head of the PCA. He wanted somebody who could go out and read a brand, or tell a calf from a yearlin'—stuff like that—so Ben asked Pa, and Pa said, "Maybe Gerald...."

So, Dad and I went over, and Ben took us out to dinner at the old Fergus Hotel. And then, by gosh, he says, "Well, Gerry, you better come on over and go to work for me."

My territory covered six counties—maybe I'd be way down in the Missouri Breaks today, and tonight be at the Collins Hotel in Roundup, and tomorrow over on the Musselshell. And every night I'd have to write reports, you know, and mail 'em back to Lewistown— to the office. I had an old pickup and they paid five cents a mile. I had my saddle in the back and a tarp to throw across it, and most of 'em'd give me a horse to ride, but they wasn't always helpful; some of those old horses, they was bastards!

And then I had to carry a little book that had the name of every customer, and his brand and how many yearlings, how many cows, and how many steers. There was one rancher way down in the Breaks—my boss says, "Now, you watch that bugger, Gerry." Well, this ol' fella thought he was pretty smooth. He says, "Okay, the riders got all the cattle right down in the bottom, Hughes. They'll bring 'em right on up this coulee, see."

Well, when they come up the coulee, him and I was standin' there a-countin', and everything was workin' real nice. But pretty soon, here comes a damn ol' cow with her horn turned down a certain way, and I says, "geez, I seen that cow before! What the hell!" And, here they were, a-bringin' 'em round again; and that's the truth! The bastards! [Gerald laughs].

So I went back, and old man Forbes wrote 'em a letter—says: "You people get those cattle of yours into the goddam corral where we can count 'em and, by God, if you're gonna be foolin' around with me, you can just go get your money somewheres else." And, money was tight, tight, tight in the Dirty Thirties.

They had some other guys working for the PCA, but a lot of 'em couldn't ride a horse or read a brand, or couldn't tell the age on a horse, you know, or nothin'; they wouldn't have known a yearling steer from a three-year-old. You could've run the same cow by 'em several times; they wouldn't have known the difference.

A lot of the land Pa bought, why, the homesteaders had plowed it up and left. They plowed that country up before the First World War—1915 and '16, and like that; Hansen, down here, plowed a slug of it. He was going to raise wheat, with prices all that high. Then 1915 and 1916 were the real good years; the dry years and the dust storms came later. That's when they starved out. And 1919 was drier than hell; Pa shipped his cattle east in July that year—no grass, and they were thin.

You'll find old plows still layin' in the fields where the homesteaders walked away and left 'em—even high in the Little Belts where they tried to plow the valleys and gravel benches. Just look at old Pigeye Basin: people thought you could just stick a plow in the ground up there and grow a crop. Well, nothin' but gravel under it; just try ridin' a saddle horse over it today. Whew!

And, later, in the thirties, up here on the bench, Pa says, "Damn, we gotta do somethin' about that land. We're payin' taxes on it, and it ain't producin' nothin'." So, we got the county commissioners out, and they drove around and changed the classification from farm to grazing land. After that we bought some Crested wheatgrass seed, and Pa got an old Case tractor and a four-horse drill that held a ton of seed; we put a tongue in it for the tractor, and I went to seedin' day after day after day. Some places I got a good stand of Crested wheat; some places I got nothin', but it was the best thing we could do up on that dry, windy bench. In the end, we were able to get a lot of it back to grass.

CLAIR WILLITS

agricultural banker, got his start as a pioneer in the artificial insemination business. He went on to a thirty-year career providing credit on The Range through the PCA.

The West has been a capital-starved area right up to modern times. There was virtually no capital here at all in the thirties, and what little bit there was, was tight, tight, tight. As a banker, I'm proud of the chance I've had to help a lot of people achieve their goals.

The U.S. farm credit system followed a European model. The basic unit was the Federal Land Bank, whose objective was to accumulate eastern capital through the sale of bonds, and put that money out to producers who could then buy land and make improvements using their land as security. The Federal Land Bank bonds were the first of the so-called agency bonds—not totally guaranteed by government;[5] each district paid a fee to use the money. Units of the system were considered independent and, by 1968, we'd paid back every penny of original government capital. In other words, at that time there was sufficient capital in the system, nationwide, to handle normal needs.

By the 1930s the federal government had set up the intermediate credit banks to take care of short-term credit. They were meant to loan their money to existing banks who would then lend it to farmers, but the regular banks wouldn't touch it; so, in the tough years of the thirties, production credit associations were established. They were organized along true co-op lines in twelve districts across the country, and, while they paralleled the federal land banks, they used the federal intermediate credit banks as their discount agencies, borrowed money from them, and, on the advice of farmer boards-of-directors, loaned it out to members.

As we accumulated capital, we were restricted to certain capital levels that we could borrow. In other words, if we had $100,000 capital, we could maybe borrow a couple million dollars from the intermediate credit bank, and this was a very effective way of doing business and one of the principal driving forces behind the tremendous revolution in agriculture from the late 1950s clear into the 1980s, at which time the farm credit system almost came a cropper.

One of the problems with the system, early on, was that conventional wisdom said "Never buy land." But if you do, "never pay top dollar; everything's always too high; let your wife wear the same coat for five years; you're farm people, and you're not supposed to have it

98

good." That's the way it was in the thirties, and those people that were in banking, then, came out with that same attitude, and so did most of their clients.

Old Walt Fellows, my first employer, had gone through all the bank closures of the thirties, and I never knew him ever to say "That's a good buy," on a piece of land—and that was when good wheat land around here was selling for $35 to $40 an acre. Later, it got up to $400 to $500 an acre, but Walt was a seat-of-the-pants banker and he had really no way of judging except by judging people—their integrity, their ability, and that kind of thing. Numbers on paper were almost irrelevant to him.

And then, in the 1970s, a lot of folks began to think the time would never come again when we'd oversupply the market. I was skeptical, I remember, because of worldwide efforts to help the Third World countries improve their standard of living—preferable as that was, I thought, to giving them straight-out dollars or bushels of wheat.

On the one hand, if a substantial borrower came to me and said, "Hey! The government's tellin' me to grow every bushel I can, so I just bought ten thousand acres of grassland over in such-and-such county; I have adequate capital, big machinery, and I'm going in there early in the spring and break it up and seed it; and I can get into government programs and be insured and draw allotments," why, sure, I'd go along with him, and lend him money. Who wouldn't? I think even most farmers knew this was a fallacy, because we'd all seen surpluses many times before. But, on the other hand, as John Greytak—who probably broke a quarter million acres of Montana sod, himself, in the 1960s and 1970s—says: "If the government throws money on the floor, you might as well pick it up." That was the attitude.

In retrospect, a lot of things we did were wrong, but—taking the side of my generation in the banking business—many of the things that farmers and ranchers did that got them in hot water were done without our blessing. Our PCA never urged people to borrow money; in fact, we maintained a pretty tough stance. We would absolutely not lend to anyone unless it penciled out, and by "pencil out" I mean draw up a program with a cash flow budget, and determine if it would work or have a chance at working. At the same time, deals that worked out beautifully at six or seven percent were disasters at seventeen percent, as many people found out in the eighties. But, if a man is determined to spend his money, you can tell him no, but someone else will tell him yes. He'll find a way to do it; many did.

But, it's part of apple pie and motherhood that every farmer and rancher should be able to keep his land intact, forever and regardless. That's the American tradition. I have a cousin in Boston—just like your cousin anywhere. She listens to Dan Rather on TV, and feels sorry for the farmer who's lost everything to the bank, and his family walking off the farm with just their clothes. How tragic it is!

And it may be very tragic, too. But, wait a minute! Before you feel too bad, go back and get the facts. What did they walk onto that place with? Did they walk on with some cash of their own? Did they actually have a reasonable chance of making it when they started? Or did they take the market-value increase in land, and borrow against it, and invest it? I want to know the history before I judge each individual case, positive or negative. Today, in the late eighties—there's probably fifteen to twenty percent of the total farm population that don't borrow a dime from anyone, and if thirty percent of those who do borrow are in trouble, that still leaves seventy percent okay. It's tragic to see anybody go under. Plenty of small businesses go under here in town, all over the country, every year. That's tragic, too; you just never see them on TV.

BOB ROSS
remembers horses running wild as a major rangeland problem.

One thing that helped a lot in growing grass and getting some range improvement after the Dirty Thirties was weeding out thousands of those wild horses Zane Grey wrote about. He called 'em wild, and they were wild all right.[6] But every one descended from domestic horses that somebody had turned loose; they weren't worth catching, shipping, or stealing. And watch a bunch of horses—all day, every day, heads down, grazing, and terribly hard on rangeland. Around the time of World War One, with wheat two bucks a bushel—that's eleven bucks today—a lot of land was plowed and most of it with horsepower; you didn't farm a whole lot in a hurry, but you seeded all you could; at two bucks a bushel you kept a lot of horses busy. After the war came the dry years; prices dropped out of wheat and cattle both; folks walked off and often turned their livestock loose on the open range.

My dad was foreman for the HX, near Delphia, on the Musselshell. The outfit ran a lot of horses in the breaks, and Dad ran horses, too; he got his stake that way. One of my first recollections is a train load

Branding wild horses in the early 1900s. —Museum of the Rockies

shipped to Saint Jo, Missouri, back in '24; they brought enough to pay the freight. Dad shipped another bunch in 1928; they brought five bucks a head. "Dog horses," we called 'em. Lord knows, we might have eaten some ourselves, bought back over the counter—except we never bought anything over the counter in those days. But somebody probably did.

JIM BAILEY
veterinarian who grew up around wild horses, knows the problems, and has a tongue-in-cheek solution.

My grandpa came from Arkansas with his mother, his little brother, and his sister. He was sixteen years old; his pa had died, and they came north with a team and wagon. They spent their last two dollars in Sheridan, Wyoming, buying horse feed to get 'em to the lower Rosebud Valley in Montana, where an uncle had a homestead; that was in the 1880s. Eventually, Grandpa homesteaded there, himself, and got married, raised a family, and provided a ranch for each of his kids. There's still Baileys hangin' out down there.

But, first thing he did, Grandpa Bailey went to work as a horse wrangler for the Double Diamond Cattle Company, owned by Frank

101

Robinson, one of the old-time Texas trail drivers. After a few years with Frank, he signed on with the FUF horse outfit; his brother worked for 'em, too, but he got kicked in the belly—ruptured his spleen and he died right there in an FUF horse camp. The FUF brand was reverse F, U connected, standing F. I don't know who owned the outfit—never did—but they ran horses from the Big Horns to the Missouri—couple of hundred miles—and Miles City was their headquarters. To the best of my knowledge, when the horse business folded up they just kicked the last few horses out on the open range and left the country.

We had a lot of wild horses on the ranch where I grew up, down on the Rosebud—running free. One of my uncles thought they were nice to look at and he didn't believe in fences; it wasn't any problem to him if they tore things up, ate a hell of a lot of grass, ran the cattle out of the water holes. But, finally, that uncle died, and the rest of the family ran 'em in, shipped as many as they could, and Winchestered the rest. That was in the 1960s; matter of fact, there was thirty head left in one stud bunch that you couldn't get within three miles of on horseback. They had radar of some kind, and all you ever saw was a cloud of dust three ridges over from where you were; they were wild, all right—that last bunch—until they finally went and rifled 'em in the seventies.

But, don't misunderstand! Those were all domestic horses just gone wild, is all they were. So-called wild horses are the exact same species as domestic breeds, with the exact same genes and chromosomes as Seattle Slew, Steeldust, or Justin Morgan; the only difference is they don't run quite so fast or quite so far. Most wild horses are very poor quality—idiots, really—the progeny of cast-offs. If you had a good horse, you used him, sold him for cash, or traded him off; if he was an idiot bronc or ugly or crooked legged, or you didn't have a market and didn't want to shoot him, you just turned him out and let him run on the range. That's your wild horse: the kind Zane Grey wrote about. If Zane Grey did one bad thing, he made wild horses romantic with his *Wildfire* and the rest. You won't find Wildfire running in a wild bunch.

There wasn't any horses here at all before the Spaniards came trundlin' over and brought 'em, starting in the sixteenth century. So, wild horses are imports and, in my opinion, pretty much the culls of the importation. My personal feeling is: Okay, protect our real endangered species, but wild horses are no separate species, and they certainly aren't endangered. We've got about eight million horses in the United States, damn near every one of 'em better than the wild ones. My feeling is: Eliminate the wild bunch, and both the taxpayers and the range will be better off, and the world won't lose a thing.

Now, the federal government has charged the BLM with running a wild horse program and you don't know it, but it costs you lots of money. They maintain wild horse ranges around the country and, as numbers grow, they sift through 'em and bring old crocks and cripples into feedyards where they hold them till they die—at your expense. There's a feedyard in Nebraska where 11,000 old, unwanted horses—some of 'em seventeen, eighteen years old—are kept until they die of natural causes; no provision to send 'em to the great can in the sky. And, a colleague of mine runs a wild horse processing yard at Rock Springs, Wyoming, where the BLM brings in horses off the Red Desert, and hires my friend to examine, identify, classify, castrate, vaccinate, deworm, whatever needs to be done—expense, no object. Only the youngest ones are put up for adoption; the rest are fed forever. I asked him how much money he made, and he laughed! It was a happy laugh, too; it wasn't a sorry kind of laugh.

You can adopt a young wild horse, a yearling, two-, or three-year-old; every one from a long, long line of culls. It'll cost you $100, and after a year you'll get full title; and that first hundred bucks you spend will be the cheapest part of the deal. It's gonna cost you a hundred and fifty bucks a month to do it right; I don't care if you steal the hay, you'll spend approximately $150 a month to maintain that horse humanely. If you're around these parts, I'll love ya for it! Forty percent of my business is with horses.

Of course, people who adopt wild horses are often the kind who don't want to spend a nickel on 'em. We were called out recently to treat a terrible wire cut: adopted mustang—unbroke, never handled, not even halter-broke, and no facilities. It was a case of ropin' him like a bronc, and repairing him the best we could; then he required daily treatment by an owner with no equipment, who didn't know the first damn thing about horses or he wouldn't have paid a hundred bucks for a wild one.

And, there's a group adoption plan where a hundred people can adopt four horses apiece. They form some corporate entity and hold 'em for a year out on cheap feed somewhere, until they get free title. At that point, then, they can ship 'em out of the country for slaughter, sell 'em, do whatever they want—but they better not move 'em out of the country until they have that title.

I did a nice piece of business with that a while ago. A bunch of Red Desert horses carrying two number brands—a freeze brand on the neck, plain as day, and a hot-iron brand on the hip—had been adopted by one of these limited-partnership what-the-devil management groups, who ran 'em in South Dakota for almost a year.[7]

Well, the manager made a mistake; he gathered them up too soon, and shipped them to Great Falls, ready to cross the border for slaughter in Canada. Two weeks before title came through, that 400-head of horses was sitting here at Jacobs' stockyard, on good feed and water, just waiting for their title.

The BLM got wind of 'em. What were these wild horses doing in Montana? Which horses were they, anyway? Who authorized their removal from South Dakota? While they investigated, the yards went under twenty-four-hour armed guard, and they brought in a crew of government cowboys—wranglers, they called 'em—from California, Wyoming, a couple of 'em all the way from Washington, D.C., from all over the States, to help identify this bunch of idiot horses. Of course, they only had two number brands to identify 'em!

The good part was, they hired a veterinarian—that was me [he laughs]—to sit on the fence for two and a half days watching all this exercise go on, and charging a hell of a lot more than he was probably worth. And he did put one horse down—a horse so old he just fell down and couldn't get up; the rest of the time he was there just in case one broke a leg while the "wranglers" were putting them through the chute, reading numbers, taking pictures of each one. After all that ruckus, they shipped the horses back to South Dakota to live out the rest of their lives in a feedlot at the taxpayers' expense. The total bill for the six-week stay at Jacobs' was right on $80,000. And you wonder about government spending?

I grew up with horses—always loved 'em, and I made a pretty good hand; until I got too old and stiff, there wasn't much around a ranch I couldn't do. One of the main reasons I became a vet was that I liked to work with horses. But I haven't much use for those idiots in the wild bunch. My solution is double-pronged: We need a place to put these new wolf packs they're invitin' into the country, and Mother Nature's old way was to make the wolves love horses, too—especially young colts. So, how about giving every official wild horse range its own official wolf pack to keep the numbers down? And charging BLM with responsibility to see they get it done. I kind of have a feeling, though, that the organized horse lovers in the country might rebel. And the horse lovers are a very powerful group.

C. WAYNE COOK

range ecologist, attests to just how powerful the wild horse lovers are.

Wild horse management presents problems that can be handled well ecologically; the real trouble is political interference.

Without proper management, wild horses can be terribly destructive since nobody claims them or accepts responsibility when they leave their reserves and damage private property. Today, the Bureau of Land Management "owns" the wild horse refuges, but their management is limited by political considerations and by the very indefinite language in the wild horse act. Show me a wild horse range today, and I'll show you a range that's overused.

I'm a range ecologist, not a wild horse specialist, but I know what wild horses are; I served on the blue ribbon committee appointed by both the secretary of agriculture and the secretary of interior when the Wild Free-Roaming Horse and Burro Act was passed.[8] However, this "wild-ass" committee, as we called it, didn't have any input into the legislation; we were just supposed to tell the agencies how to manage their horses and, at the same time, maintain a viable ecosystem that included other herbivores—all under the terms of the act, of course.

I was chairman for five years, and visited most of the wild horse refuges and ranges in eleven western states during that time. I got to know the famous Velma Johnston, widely known as "Wild Horse Annie." She was a member of my committee, and she wanted to be fair and she wanted to be humane, but she didn't know what to do with excess numbers other than let them die of old age on the range or in a feedyard. After five years on that committee, studying the situation very closely, I felt the solution was to have, perhaps, six fenced wild horse ranges in the West, each with 100 to 150 head capacity. Any surplus would be culled—eliminated. But the politicians let the wild horse activists rub 'em on the shoulders—get next to 'em, so to speak—and, although they promised to consider some kind of control of numbers, the act they finally passed had no control at all.

The intention was that the surplus would go to slaughter, but the elimination had to be humane, and there's never been any definition of humane. You can go out and kill an elk or deer or moose with a .30-06 and that's humane, but you can't kill a horse that way; it's not humane. They talked of using gas; that wasn't humane. They said you could kill a horse with darts, and leave the carcass out on the range to deteriorate and go back into the ecosystem, but the spokes-

105

men for the horse lovers said that wasn't humane; you wouldn't let your sister or brother lay out there for the crows to eat. I found that a wild horse, to a horse lover, is like a sister or brother. Until we break that notion, I guess we're stuck with damage to the range environment.

Under the act, BLM is responsible for keeping numbers up to please the public, while at the same time keeping numbers down in relation to available feed, but horses reproduce very fast when they're protected. About all BLM is allowed to do is capture them, and put them up for adoption. If you really wanted to see wild horses, you should be able to go to a refuge where numbers are responsibly controlled. They have buffalo reserves where you can see wild buffalo just as they looked in days of old, but not free-ranging from Texas clear to Montana, and not in uncontrolled numbers. Horses deserve no better than the buffalo.

People find it profitable to propagate buffalo and so they take responsibility for them; therefore, buffalo are increasing. You could do the same with wild horses. There's a good market for horse meat in Europe.[9] When I was with the committee, we received bids from horse-meat packers in both Canada and Mexico, who could process surplus horses off our U.S. refuges and ship the meat to Europe. American processors—restricted by our own laws—can't do that.

Sooner or later, BLM must tell the American people about the land resource they're losing through maintaining these large wild horse populations. And somebody, someday, must tell them of the cost! It costs the taxpayer $1,000 to $2,000 for every horse that's put out for adoption. I don't think the taxpayer realizes how many millions of dollars are spent on wild horse management, or mismanagement, every year.

BILLY BIG SPRING

Indian rancher, politician, artist, and philosopher, speaks of survival in a welfare state, the Blackfeet Reservation, where times are always tough!

I'm gonna tell you a little story about horses and hard times. During World War Two, I come home on furlough and my neighbor had a that-year's colt—a sorrel colt with a big, wide blaze. Boy, what a beautiful colt!

So I asked my neighbor if he wanted to sell him; he says, "Well, he belongs to my wife; you talk to her."

106

But, "no," his wife says, "I think I'll just hang onto him." So, I forgot it.

Then, one day in Germany I got a letter from her with a bill-of-sale that says, "When you come home, you put your brand on that bald-faced colt. I give him to you."

When I got home next fall, that colt was a yearlin' and I didn't bother him, but the following spring I ran him in and, damn, he jumped that corral I don't know how many times—big, high corral. I finally ran in and "necked" him before he could jump out, and then I branded him, and let him go.

When he was three or four years old I ran him in again. Boy, was he wild! So, then, I started feedin' oats, and pretty soon he started waitin' for 'em, and got about half gentle. Damn! Just one of the best horses I ever had in my life.

But, it goes to show what happens when animals—or people— get hooked on handouts. Here's an animal as wild as anything in this world, and he starts in gettin' handouts, and gets hooked, and, next thing, gives up lookin' after himself.

I told you about my dad. He was a very impressive man, but he died poor and I swore I never would. Right now I'm tryin' to make a million bucks; I'm seventy years old and I got a million in my land, but I want some cash in my hip pocket when I die.

I only went through the sixth grade but I read a lot. I like history, and I'm an artist and collector; I collect old books and cowboy gear and Indian artifacts—some of them hundreds of years old.

When I was a kid I had horses of my own, and, of course, I rodeoed a bit in all the events. I roped in Calgary once, and I could catch anything and get off my horse real fast, but, hell, a guy could butcher a beef while I was tryin' to tie a calf. When Kathleen and I got married, we went out on my dad's old ranch with fifteen dollars in our pockets—no car, no nothing. I worked hard, worked for the neighbors and went trappin'; I used to catch 150 beaver a year, and by the time I went in the army I had some cows and horses of my own.

I was in the 35th Division, 320th, and while I was away my neighbor, Bill, that son-of-a-bitch, stole all my calves for two years. Bill and I used to run our cattle together on a lease; he ran six or seven hundred head of cattle and a band of sheep, and I would work for him sometimes. So, when I went in the Army he said, "I'll take care of your cattle fer ya, Billy." When I came home I didn't have a calf; he'd put his brand on every damn one for the past two years.

The winter I got home, 1945, wasn't too bad, and I used to ride down and help Bill feed. The next one, 1946, was hard, but I had put up thirty loads of hay for my saddle horses and that year's calf crop, which I had branded for myself. We got a hell of a snow—about four feet—in October, but I had already pushed our cattle out of the higher country, when Bill comes riding up with two cowboys. We fed 'em lunch and afterwards he says, "Billy, trail these cattle down to my winter camp. We'll feed 'em awhile, and then we'll cut yours out and you can take 'em home again."

"Hell," I says, "we'll cut 'em out right here, and you can take yours home, yourself, right now."

Well, believe it or not, two days later the wind came up and blew that four-foot snowfall clean off our winter range—cleared it off from North Two Medicine half way to Little Badger. So, here comes Bill in his car one day: "Billy, I want ya to ride down and help me move my cattle back up here. You got a hell of a lot of grass you ain't used up."

I says, "Bill, our partnership ended the day we cut your cattle out of here."

So, that's how come I started buyin' land. I had my lease, you see, but I wanted to own it; I like to own things so I can control 'em. I kept on workin' at it until I had my own land and the minerals with it. Back in 1954, I got a pretty good oil check—about $60,000—that really got me going. Sure I blew some of it and went way down, but then I came back up again.

In 1919 they issued patents to anybody that wanted them—mixed-bloods as well as full-bloods; and, as soon as the land was theirs, people mortgaged it and lost it, or just sold it outright to non-Indians. Like, where my ranch is, there was probably close to a thousand acres that was sold to non-Indians; the Great Northern Railroad bought 640 acres, which I've leased with an option to buy for many years.

A lot of Indians still don't realize they gotta pay their bills. For many years, if you had an Indian name you had a hell of a time gettin' a loan; you had to work like hell to get a loan. When a banker heard a good Indian name like Big Spring, he was afraid to trust you—he'd heard about lazy Indians. So everything I have on my ranch today, I had to work for like the devil.

In 1973 I wanted to exercise my option on the Great Northern lease and buy some other 'trust' lands that were offered. I applied for a loan from Mutual of New York, and the Mutual representative said, "Don't get your hopes up, Billy, there's two others besides you applying, you know: a farmer from off the reservation, and a mixed-blood sheepman."

"I know," I said, "I'm not." But, in the end, I got the loan, and I'll tell you why. The farmer was sloppy; when they went to see him, he had his machinery scattered all over the yard. And the sheepman had all new buildings—his home and sheep sheds and corrals—all built with taxpayers' money after the Birch Creek flood of 1964. But, when they came to Billy Big Spring's ranch, everything that was on it Billy

Big Spring had put up and taken care of and paid the bills. That's why I got the loan.

On my ranch now, I got three rivers going through it, and I control eighteen miles of the south fork of Two Medicine River. I own all the water west of the road between Little Badger and East Glacier. We don't raise cattle any more; we take cattle in for other guys, and we run them for five months, which has always worked pretty well on this reservation with its tough winters.

A lot of the native range is farmed up now. Why not? I mean, it's 'trust' land, and an Indian isn't gonna use it himself. The farmers are subsidized, so they can charge a farmer more than some cattleman or sheepman for the use of the grass. It goes right back to the subsidies. I won't let 'em farm my land at all. It's mine; I pay taxes on it, and I take care of it.[10]

The 1980s has been a dirty, dry, depressed old decade, too. I took quite a beating in the eighties, same as everybody else, but I've got so damn many things goin' right now, I don't have time to feel sorry for myself. I'm seventy years old, and I've seen plenty of ups and downs, but this is "next-year" country; it's time to make a comeback—this time BIG! I'm not hoping—I'm gonna do it! And then I'll buy a few more acres of The Range.

Billy looking over his ranch on Two Medicine River.

Here's the forecast for today: Probable northeast or south-west winds, varying to the south and west and east and points between . . . probable areas of rain, snow, hail and drought, succeeded or preceded by earthquakes with thunder and lightning.

—Mark Twain

4

Range Weather

I've watched the mercury climb from thirty-five below to thirty-five above in less than half an hour; I've battled four-foot drifts in early May; I've slept through violent wind storms that blew everything away—except the mortgage. I've seen it dry enough that even gophers packed their lunch.

There was a time when thermometers weren't allowed on many ranches: "If you wanta be a cowboy, you must play out your string," the saying went. Today we catch the weather on a Walkman, watch the tube as storms spin in across our coasts, read extended forecasts in the weekly livestock rag, but the weather's still a great unknown.

The weather can be violent on The Range. And no one—yet—knows what to do about it.[1] Any rancher can tell of record-breaking storms, destructive winds, and big losses at the hands of the Mother Nature— some true, some just a little "windy."

STAN WILSON

past president of the Canadian Cattlemen's Association, is an Alberta rancher whose word is highly respected on The Range.

The wind comes off these mountains awful strong; it's sometimes unbelievable just *how* strong. A friend of mine was ridin' from Pincher Creek to Fort Macleod one day with his hat screwed down around his ears. He was used to wind but, when his horse lifted his tail and the bit blew out of his mouth, that cowboy knew he was in fer a chinook.

GERALD HUGHES

Montana rancher/raconteur, tells how his dad was almost hit by lightning. Any closer, Gerald wouldn't have been born to tell the tale. He has an ancient photograph to prove it.

Soon after Dad come out here from Vermont in '92, he went to work for relatives freightin' wool; that's what he was doin' when the lightning hit. The Hamiltons, his cousins, had a sheep outfit on Sage Creek in the Judith Basin, and one morning Pa set out with a couple of wagon loads of wool for Great Falls, sixty miles away. Them days they run wethers for their wool—run 'em till they was three and four and five years old—and there happened to be a band of wethers travelin' with the wagons that forenoon. And Pa said there was thunder roarin' along the mountains, lightning flashing all around, and then it started rainin'. When the wind got up, they brought the sheep in between the wagons—old herder on a horse, and the sheep running along.

Well, the lightning was getting hot, and Pa, he tied the reins, you know, to a stick nailed up there like a brake handle, and he'd just jumped off his wagon and put an arm into his slicker-coat when lightning hit the bunch of 'em—sheep and horses, herder, wagons; lightning struck the whole works—killed 'em all.

Pa said the near horse on the wheel got up and squealed and squealed and kicked, and then went down for good; and his saddle horse, Little Jimmy ... [Gerald's voice breaks as he tells what happened years before his birth] ... Little Jimmy, tied behind the wagon, he was gone. Some of those horses were shod—on the wheel and the next lead team, I think Pa said—and it tore the shoes right off 'em; just tore the shoes right off 'em! And Dad, his arms were aching—couldn't hardly raise 'em. Lucky, though—Pa sure was lucky to survive. Those days, you sure took the weather as it come.

A cameraman was on hand to record this disaster back in 1892. At right, the smoke still rises from the remains of Will Hughes's saddle horse, Little Jimmy, after the lightning strike. —Hughes family

JOE GILCHRIST

Alberta rancher, has known the weather on The Range for almost ninety years. In his day, you got your forecast from the feel of wind, the look of sky, the way the livestock acted, and again—you took the weather as it come.

April of 1927 we headed west from Whitemud for Alberta with 1,700 head of Bar X Bar cows and yearlings, and a string of twenty-five horses. As usual, we were short-handed—just three of us riding, and another fellow drove the wagon with our gear: not any too much help for a seventy-five-mile cattle drive with 1,700 head. The creeks were pretty high that spring; Willow Creek would swim a cow, but not a horse.

It was a windy, cloudy evening, about forty degrees above, when we put 'em across Willow Creek, and everyone got wet; one horse and rider slipped and went clear out of sight. We tied our wagon box down so it wouldn't float away, and I was anchorman with a big, strong horse and a good rope to keep the whole outfit from taking off downstream. We set up camp that night about four miles from the crossing, and about seven o'clock the wind turned northwest with snow. I guess my brother Chay smelled trouble in the air, 'cause he turned us out to put the cattle cross't another steep-banked creek: a death trap for cows drifting from a storm. We got the cattle over to the south side just at dark, and a lucky thing we did because that night turned very bad. We turned our horses loose, except for one with lots of winter hair—we left him saddled with the blanket over his rump, tied in the lee of the wagon.

The cattle drifted south a couple miles, and piled up against a good four-wire fence; that stopped 'em till the snow built up enough so's the ones on top got over, and they drifted on another several miles.

The storm let up about four o'clock next morning and, waking up, Chay hollered at the boy who'd fallen in the creek: "Hey Art, get up and get the 'dough-gods' started."

But Art looked out from his warm bed and saw his long underwear hanging from the ridgepole frozen stiff. He says: "I'm not gettin' up first this morning, Chay! I quit!" And he cussed us all and swore he'd never work for Gilchrist Brothers again. So, I got up and, with a tin plate, shoveled the snow off all the beds and got the fire going and thawed our clothes, and Art warmed up and ate some 'dough-gods' and soon forgot his troubles. He worked for us for several years after that.

At daylight we found our horses and rode out to find the cattle, and we were lucky: we only lost about twenty head that night. We weren't so lucky in another spring storm ten or twelve years later.

In 1938 we had wintered our cowherd at the Dominion Range Experiment Station near Manyberries—they used our cattle in their grazing trials, you see—and everything was doing fine until the 28th of March, when we had the worst spring storm I ever saw: two days and nights of eighty mile an hour winds and drifting snow. The storm came in at dark; the cattle drifted before the wind into fence corners, over cutbanks, into coulees, creeks, and sloughs.

After the storm was over I rode out with my brother-in-law, Harry Hargrave, the superintendent of the station. We found dead cattle everywhere, and—days later—many others buried under drifts. The next job was to salvage what we could. I started with three men skinning—pulling the hides off carcasses with a team; we skinned out over seven hundred head, and some we missed. Losses of that kind were the exception, of course; the result of "killer" storms that track across our plains every few years with heavy losses in local areas.

The worst spell of bad, cold, winter weather I remember was in 1935 and '36; it was just as bad as 1906 and '07, although not as long. We trailed about two thousand cattle onto feed grounds in February, and, on the trail, if a yearling steer or a cow lay down, it never got up again. Our winter kill that year was five percent.

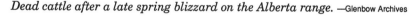

Dead cattle after a late spring blizzard on the Alberta range. —Glenbow Archives

Most of the time our older cattle did well out on the range, and we saved our hay for calves or thin cows we'd pick up from time to time. We needed hay reserves when the snow lay deep and crusted—when a thaw began but didn't last. But, most times, winter snows are light down on our range, and winds keep grassy ridges clear. And, sometimes a real chinook will come along.

I remember how I started out one winter morning to make a cleanup ride, and see what had been missed along Sage Creek. I rode through deep snow all day, and by afternoon reached Wetherelt's place—a neighbor's—where I stopped all night. Next morning it was fairly mild and clear, and the Sweet Grass Hills were a beautiful deep blue. I rode up Sage Creek as far as Wildhorse Dam, found two dead cattle, and the rest were very poor. By that time it was noon and it was twelve miles back to Wetherelt's, so I picked up a bunch of horses to break trail; I'd take the horses on ahead, then leave 'em and go back to get the cattle and, after several trips, I managed to reach a homesteader's place by dark. The homesteader agreed to feed the cattle a few oat bundles, and I rode on to Wetherelt's for the night.

That evening, after supper, the wind began to blow; the temperature rose to sixty degrees above, and next morning there was water everywhere. I rode back and got my cattle, and brought 'em home over bare ground to our winter field along the river. That was a real chinook—the kind for which our shortgrass country is famous.

LESLIE EWING KRIZ

grew up on a ranch in the Porcupine Hills. Like ranch kids everywhere, she has stories about school days and the weather.

I was about ten years old and down in the corral one day, petting the horses, when thunder started rolling around the hills; I was having fun, when—suddenly—I got a warning jolt. I saw red sparks before my eyes, I felt electricity in my hair, I got real tingly, was all, and I remember feeling foolish when nobody believed me—until they saw the blister on my finger. That's the kind of thing you're lucky to remember!

I lived twenty-five miles from town from the time I was six-months old until I finished high school. Morris Erickson, a local cowboy, or Butch McLeod, our nearest neighbor, drove the school bus, which I rode every day for about twelve years. It wasn't like the story they used to tell about Gordon Burton's dad hauling the mail in an open sleigh or buggy; we were warm. But, still, we kept one eye on the weather. I went to a one-room country school for the first three grades; we rode in style in a little yellow International four-wheel-drive school van, and the roads weren't built up in those days, so we'd take off across the fields to get around the drifts. Once, the driver even stalked a herd of elk and shot one from the school bus window. Those were the days! Freer times, without much regulation. I remember our parents' horror when they found a big old drum of stove oil rolling around the back of the bus with all the kids and guns and ammunition; if anything had happened, that drum would have rolled kids out like pie dough! Of course, us kids thought all busses came equipped that way.

But, this is an age of progress; by the time I started town-school, our road was graded up and graveled. That meant no more four-by-four "corn-binder," no more driving across the prairie; our regulation bus stayed on the road. When the snow got deep, the snow plow came or we didn't get to school. Our ranch is in the Porcupines, a thousand feet above the prairies and the town, often in warmer air; many's the time I've left a warm chinook at home, found the temperature below zero down at school, and come home after dark with the frost running off the windows. 'Course, that meant wind, and sometimes—with the snow plowed up along the road—no way could we get through when the chinook hit. And often it meant no phone: windstorm, snowstorm, rainstorm—any kind of weather at all—the phone was out. We had to plan ahead.

January of '68 was cold! The chinook stayed away; the mercury never got above minus twenty degrees for several weeks; and lots of snow! For weeks the snowplow cleared things out so we could get to school, and it piled up plow-drifts as high as the bus in many places—impassable if it started to chinook. Mom made arrangements for me to stay in town with friends; I took my suitcase on the bus, ready for anything, and, sure enough, one afternoon Mom watched the cows head up the hill to graze in warmer air on top—I wonder how they know. Then, half an hour later, the temperature shot up, the wind began to blow, and no use thinking about roads: snow from the ridges packed into all the old plow-drifts, and there it stayed. I suppose it was a week before anyone got through; the phone was out, of course, so I was out of touch with home. Even, with all our progress, still: the weather....

WARREN G. HARDING

a professional meteorologist and a rancher. He is well equipped to tell us, after fifty years of study, the how and why and, sometimes, what and where and when of the weather that has built and shaped The Range.

Montana weathermen call our range the northwest chinook zone, and the weather here can change so fast—well, you've heard what happens. Everybody talks about the weather, although, nobody ever does anything about it. I'll try to give you some factual information.

When the Japs hit Pearl Harbor in 1941, I was at Havre going to school; I went over to the weather station and signed up to learn meteorology on the job, and that was the start of a lifetime affair with the elements. They sent me to Alaska with the rawinsonde balloons, sounding the upper air, gathering information for forecasts. My wife came along as an observer; we were a husband-and-wife team on an Army Air Corps base, working for the U.S. Weather Bureau. In wartime people do strange things and learn new skills. We learned much of value for future use while in Alaska: we noticed how developments in the arctic atmosphere affect Montana a couple of days later; we visited the Gulf of Alaska Low that determines our chinook; we experienced the Arctic High at Whitehorse in the Yukon, where the cold air so often begins its southward flow. Many things came to light for us during our tour in the North that help us understand the weather on our range today.

The Range Environment

The weather has shaped this range in many ways, and it's quite consistent from Great Falls as far north as Calgary. The Lewis Range of the Montana Rockies on the west, and the Belts and Little Belts to the south, form the lip of a huge bowl that catches dense, cold arctic air when it slides in here from the north. All this is important in understanding the development of our range and its agriculture.

From November to April, our zone is a battleground between Arctic and Pacific air masses. When arctic air flows in here from the north, it moves like water. It floods over northeastern Alberta and Saskatchewan and north-central Montana, and fills our bowl and stops, dammed up by mountains, leaking through the cracks into valleys farther south, rising and falling like an ocean as pressures change above it. You have to think of the Arctic air mass as a flood: open the dike at Whitehorse and here she comes—deeper and colder over the lower land to the north, shallower as the land rises under it.

Cows can feel it coming; they sense the pressure change. When I was working in the weather office, I'd be keeping track of temperatures and I'd know an arctic front had passed through Edmonton, then Calgary, then Lethbridge. I could tell when it crossed the border, 100 miles to the north, just by watching our cows; that's about when they'd begin to get uneasy and gather up their calves and look for shelter.

When the arctic air gets deep around here, the cold can be awesome; we hold the record in this zone for the coldest temperature ever recorded in the Lower Forty-eight. In January 1954, the arctic air got so deep that the mercury hit seventy degrees below zero at Rogers Pass, northwest of Helena.

The Chinook

But something else is unique about these eastern slopes, and that's the chinook. Usually the arctic air hasn't been on us very long when here comes warmer air out of the west, and everything changes dramatically.

To the southwest there'll be a High, building out of the Great Basin; at the same time, the big, semi-permanent Low over the Gulf of Alaska will send moist air spinning towards us over the Pacific. In between the High and Low, ridges and troughs will form; the whole weather system all around the world is very delicately balanced, each system responding to the next.

The low-pressure air mass spinning towards us picks up moisture over the ocean and eventually comes ashore over the Oregon or California coast. As it moves eastward over rising ground, it has to rise, and, as it rises, it cools. If saturated, the moisture squeezes out along the coast and on the western slopes, and latent heat of condensation slows down cooling. For the best chinook, you want the Pacific air to hit the top of our mountains as warm as possible; if it's raining, it's going to be warm because of that added heat of condensation.

Of course, a lot depends on the position of the Gulf of Alaska Low. If that pulls saturated air up off the California coast, the chinook might come in here at fifty degrees Fahrenheit, and water will start running right away. Other times, cold, dry air flows in aloft from the northwest, and we'll get a chilly "Klondike" chinook. But generally, the air aloft will be thirty or thirty-five degrees when it comes over the top, and it will just run out over the arctic pool for awhile, lowering the pressure and allowing the Arctic Front to retreat.

Sometimes the warm air will run out across the surface of the arctic pool and strike high up on the side of the Sweet Grass Hills, or the Bear Paws south of Havre; you'll see them sticking up like islands from the cold. Now, watch a bunch of cows—they can sense the pressure fall that precedes a chinook, and they'll head for higher ground and warmer air.

The leading edge of that pool of arctic air can be sharp as a knife, and stretching ribbon-like from Great Falls up past Browning to Pincher Creek and Calgary in Alberta. On the west side of the ribbon, snow may be drifting and melting before a warm southwest wind; a few yards to the east—just a few *yards*, mind you—it will be still and cold. The difference can be dramatic.

On the 11th day of January 1980, the temperature at Great Falls rose from thirty-two degrees below to fifteen degrees above in seven minutes as the front oscillated. Just as quickly, with a change in pressure, the chinook can subside and the arctic air advance again.

WAITING FOR A CHINOOK: January 26, 1954, it is 32° F below zero with 20" of snow on the ground along the Milk River, north of Browning, Montana. Cattle are waiting for hay on the 3C Bar.

Four days later (January 30) the chinook has arrived. It is 44° F above zero, the snow has melted and the Milk River has flooded. It will not freeze up again for the rest of the winter.

Browning holds the record for temperature drop in Montana: in January of 1916, the mercury dropped from forty-four above to fifty-six below—100 degrees—in twenty-four hours. Tough on domestic livestock, fruit trees, and plants? You bet! Native species are better adapted.

Chinook winds of the kind that plagued skiers during the 1988 Winter Olympics at Calgary are a mixed blessing to agriculture. On open rangeland they can sweep the ridges clear of snow and make grazing possible all winter. Other places, they cause heavy drifting; and, if the overrunning air is cool to start with, the chinook can be bone chilling on the ground. It can also move anything not tied down! The strongest winds in North America come out of Crowsnest Pass near Pincher Creek, Alberta. We put out high-wind warnings for sixty and seventy mile-an-hour winds at Livingston and East Glacier in Montana, but they've howled out of the Crowsnest at better than 120 miles an hour.

What happens is this: our westerlies, blowing over the mountains at forty or fifty knots, form a trough of low pressure on the lee side, exactly as air passing over an airplane wing causes lift—Bernoulli's Principle; same thing draws smoke up your chimney. Of course, air

121

wants to rush in and fill that area of low pressure through any crack in the wall, and that makes for high winds in those mountain passes. At the same time, you'll see distinctive roll clouds of the chinook arch where the air mass undulates up and down as it comes in over the top—the warmer and moister the better. That air condenses on the lift and dries out on the fall; you can get multiple arches along the way, but the main arch stands stationary just east of the mountains. My son David flies an F-16 for the Montana Air National Guard. He can look down on the chinook arch from 50,000 feet, and see it stretched along the lee side of the Rockies, sharp as a knife, for hundreds of miles. Quite a sight!

In winter the moisture drops out of our chinook on the western slopes of the mountains, and you get good skiing at Whitefish and Lake Louise, but not much precipitation on our range—three or four inches, maybe, between October and March. If we had to depend on Pacific moisture, this area'd be a desert.

The Monsoon

Well, cold air on the surface—that's arctic air; cold air aloft is something entirely different. It's the troughs of cold upper air that bring our growing-season moisture from the south and east—an about-face in the weather flow in springtime. That cold air aloft wants to settle, and as it settles it begins to spin because of the effect of the earth turning under it. The spinning air acts as a centrifugal pump.

Closed troughs of cold upper air from the Gulf of Alaska form over our zone in the spring and pump moisture up from the Gulf of Mexico, and this upslope factor has made this area what it is. Early June is the wettest period on a 100-year "normal." Most of our big floods— 1908, 1964—have been between the first and the tenth of June. In 1953 we averaged an inch a day for fourteen days when a big closed Low stalled and stayed here for two weeks, sucking up moist air out of the Gulf of Mexico. That was what we call an "out-of-mountain" flood—the kind that soaks the range and does us so much good in June.

March is the month that brings the most severe weather, a combination of arctic and spring-type storms: below-zero temperatures, heavy snows, strong winds. April and May are generally warmer, but that's when we get those big, wet snows that kill so many new-born calves and lambs. Nineteen sixty-nine was the worst I ever heard of. It was eighty-eight degrees at Broadus, in southeastern Montana, on the 25th of April. On the 26th, an upper-level low formed over the Black Hills; first it rained, and then it snowed, and then it froze, and two days later there were twenty-six-foot drifts. When it was over, they'd lost 100,000 head of cattle and sheep in the area—the biggest loss of cattle in thirty-six hours I've ever heard of.

Our mountain valleys seldom get that kind of storm. The plains are noted for them; the air mass needs room to spin before it can suck up moist air from the gulf. Such storms are like tornadoes: pretty localized. They're violent, but they lose their energy quick.

But, occasionally, our closed lows stall farther west, over the continental divide, and they pump tropical air out of California and deluge the high country with warm rain, often just as the winter snow pack is beginning to melt. That's when we get our "in-mountain" floods—so damaging, and maybe something relatively new in recent decades.

My wife Grace's grandfather came from Wales as a blacksmith back in the steamboat days; he shod the bulls that hauled freight all around Montana and up the Whoop-up Trail to Canada. He put up shop at a place they called The Leavings near Fort Shaw, where the Mullan Road left Sun River and struck out over the hills for Helena. Grace was born and raised beside the river on her dad's homestead, and we've made it our permanent home ever since the war. This river is part of our lives, and it has changed.

Sun River starts high up in the Rockies, in the Bob Marshall Wilderness Area south of Glacier Park, and runs south for quite a ways before cutting through the Front Range to empty into the Missouri just above Great Falls. It provides irrigation water for a large farming area on these high, dry plains where rainfall averages only about fourteen inches a year. You can see the old stream bed just as the old-timers remember it—a meandering stream, by all accounts—with sod right down to water's edge. Then, in 1908, came a flood that started to erode the banks and scour the channel, another followed in 1916, and then, in 1953, the Sun cut across its banks and went straight down the valley. You can see how it scoured and straightened out all the old horseshoe curves. At the turn of the century it was hard to find gravel around here anywhere; now, all we've got is gravel.

The Glory Hole wasn't big enough—water floods over the top.
—George Roskie

The Flood of 1964

In 1929, they built Gibson Dam where Sun River comes through the mountains. They studied the records and the signs from prehistoric days and designed a sort of relief valve to take fifty thousand cubic feet of water per second: the largest flow imaginable over a 500-year period. The overflow shaft was named the Glory Hole, I suppose by the miners who drove it.

Well, in June of 1964 a weather pattern with tropical moisture and thunderstorms stalled over the divide between Rogers Pass and Waterton National Park, dropping fourteen inches of rain in twenty-four hours on the melting snow pack. We've presented those figures at weather symposiums around the world, and they're impressive even to people used to tropical moisture. Fifty-three thousand second-feet of water came down the Sun and through the Glory Hole. Incredibly, it wasn't big enough; water came over the top. Rivers all

124

up and down the mountains left their channels, flooded homes, tore out bridges, and caused great loss of property and life. Thirty lives were lost along Two Medicine and Birch Creek on the Blackfeet Reservation.[2]

Written records don't go back too far, but I think there's been a little-recognized change in climatology that's caused the devastating in-mountain floods in this century. We had spectacular floods in 1953 and '64 and '75. The 1930s were dry with tough winters, while the 1980s were dry with mild winters. Can we recognize eleven-year floods and fifty-year droughts? The thing to remember is that historic times are just the wink of an eye compared with the geologic time over which the weather has been at work, making our land what it is today.

I used to be lead forecaster in the weather office at Great Falls, and I've made a lifetime study of the way our winter storms move in—out of the Gulf of Alaska at thirty knots or so, bringing the chinook to Browning and Pincher Creek, or allowing the arctic front to slide up as far as Cut Bank. We do the best we can, and we've made great progress using all the new tools, from rawinsonde to satellites to computer models; however, science is still looking for the key to long-range forecasting.

People are always suggesting simple explanations and clues to the weather—El Niño, sun spots, the greenhouse effect, and so on—but it's not that simple. The weather is produced by an extremely complex combination of all those factors and many more around the world. To this day, forecasts are usually not reliable for more than three to five days, but it beats the times when bull trains and trail herds struck out across the prairie with no forecast at all.

DICK CASSUTT

Montana rancher and storyteller.

I can tell you about the terrible flood in June of '64, but it's not my favorite story: too much loss, too much sadness for friends and family. It was one of those freaks of nature; this is what happened:

We were living at Fort Benton where the Teton and Marias join the Missouri. Up the Marias, near the mountains, my brother-in-law and his family had a ranch where the old trail between Fort Shaw and Canada crosses Birch Creek. The century-old log buildings of a trading post were still standing at the time.

Anyway, the first nine inches of rain came in four hours in the mountains southwest of Glacier Park where the winter snow was melting. Nine inches over an area that big was a fantastic amount of gallonage; and when the water hit Swift Dam, on upper Birch Creek, they figure it went thirty feet over the top. It took the dam out; you can go up there today and see a boulder, say, fifty feet in diameter that rolled about two miles gouging bedrock as it went. The force and amount of water was unbelievable, and, of course, there was no warning of the flood except by nature. Nature often seems to warn its creatures.

And so it was that Joyce's brother Wally had a milk cow and a saddle horse that had been on the place all their lives, as peaceful as could be. He kept them in an old corral right on the river, and they had never, ever, tried to get out before. Well, just hours before that flood they kicked the corral down, got through another fence, and got away; they never did a thing like that, before or after.

Our two older kids were supposed to be there, visiting their cousins; they'd been staying with their grandparents who had planned to take them visiting to Birch Creek, but Grampa says: "Ah, I don't feel like goin' out today, what the heck." But, for all we knew, they'd gone to Birch Creek.

Well, when the flood hit, Marilyn, our sister-in-law, was standing at the door waiting for Wally to come home. The house sat in the bottom, maybe fifty feet below the coulee rim where Wally stopped his pickup and got out to open the gate. He heard a roar. He said he could see a 100-, 150-foot column of water with horses and cattle and trees and roof tops swirling. He could see things coming up over the top of this big wave, and then dropping to the bottom. He screamed to his family, and they ran back in the house, and that's the last he saw of them: his wife and two kids—who would have been about eight and eleven years old.

Well, the water hit Wally on the coulee rim, but it didn't inundate him; but his house just disappeared before his eyes. He just *knew* his family was dead, and he went plumb out of his mind—went off across country, afoot—didn't turn up till next day down by Valier, about nine miles away.

His family ran upstairs. When the wave hit, it tore the house off its foundation and broke it up and, somehow, they got on pieces of the roof. Guy, the eldest, wound up on a floating piece of roof with the propane tank; the tank had broken loose, and he was being gassed while roaring down the valley. Marilyn, the mother, lost her glasses, but she had ahold of the girl who was about eight, and they were swept off of their piece of roof and caught a log; when the log finally went aground three, four miles downstream, she thought she had the girl but she only had her scarf. She'd lost the girl! They never found her. Many bodies were never found.

Marilyn had put the children's coats on—it was pretty cold and raw—and they would have weighed a ton, full of silt and dirt and water, but—lucky to have his coat—Guy, who was about eleven and had been gassed by the propane, was thrown ashore where he stumbled into an old shed near him on the bank and went to sleep; he must have been damn near dead because he laid there for a day and a half before he came to. A neighbor found him walking down the road.

That's just one Birch Creek story; Two Medicine, Badger, the Teton, and Sun River had big losses, too. Over a hundred people were lost along the Rocky Mountain front that day, as well as thousands of cattle and horses, and millions of dollars in property. You bet, the weather can be violent on this range!

Swift Dam went out in June 1964, and the resulting flood on Birch Creek killed many people and swept away their homes and possessions. —U.S. Forest Service

Summing Up

I want to take time out here to add some finishing touches to this history of our range so far. In the beginning, buffalo and antelope used our "desert," as the first explorers called these northern plains (I guess they missed the spring monsoons). Largely because of the ferocity of the Blackfeet in defending their hunting grounds, the fur trade passed us by to the north and south. Then, in the mid-1800s, thousands of individuals—Indian, métis, and white—turned up to harvest hides; Fort Benton became a "hub" for river freight. As buffalo numbers declined, other hardy pioneers moved in to harvest the grass with sheep and cattle, or to replace the grass with grain. Representative government encouraged them by granting homestead rights; the newcomers settled the best land, and fought for the unclaimed "commons."

There may have been a very short period following the Civil War when absentee English or eastern capitalists controlled the range, and there has long been a common view—it persists today—that capitalism destroys public resources through greed. That didn't happen on The Range. Although much has been written about timber barons and beef bonanzas motivated by windfall profit, we still have trees and grass across the West. Consider this: Few cattle or sheep, if any, were on the Montana range before 1866. Just twenty years later the legendary open-range period came to a sudden end with the winter of '86; thereafter, absentee capitalists lost interest. The big trail herds didn't cross Milk River onto the Canadian range until about 1880—Matthew Cochrane got the first big lease in 1881. Two decades later, those enormous grants were past their prime; people like the Burtons, Copithornes, Gilchrists, Crosses, and Bruneaus had taken over. The point is this: Even if the so-called barons had tried to destroy the range (which is certainly open to question), they would not have had time to do so. Range is a renewable resource; buffalo hides were not.

The history of The Range is made of stories of poor men who left previous homes in search of opportunity, seeking fortune but ready to settle for a living. Alex Johnston honors the tough, resourceful homesteaders who endured. Ferry Carpenter points to hard up people closed out by the sheriff elsewhere. Such people came to stay, to build communities, to become modern, live-in capitalists, themselves—the tax base of a market-run society.

In evaluating history, we must look at the situation as it was. The buffalo were killed, the open range abused; nobody owned those buffalo; nobody owned the grass. Nobody was responsible for the future. Henry Sieben knew, even in 1875, that conservation was

128

important on The Range; he couldn't do much about it until he had control—control through ownership. The Gilchrist boys, arriving on the virgin Canadian prairie thirty years later, soon found that as their herd grew they were always short of grass. They learned. They settled down. They took control. They didn't build their empire by ruining The Range.

Today, while wild-horse lobbyists sponsor uncontrollable overgrazing, other environmental-elitists cry "desertification" caused by domestic cattle; "No Moo by '92" is their catchy battle cry. They say that federal agencies actually subsidize damage with below-market grazing fees. They say that, since only a small percentage of the national cattle herd uses the public land, the loss of grazing permits would not be felt. (Well, not by San Franciscans, New Yorkers, or Torontonians, at any rate.) To the contrary, recent studies suggest that public grazing fees are actually quite competitive.[3] And, more important, trained range ecologists understand that carefully managed grazing by domestic sheep and cattle can actually improve the range for other users.

Now, let's meet some people who have spent lifetimes studying, managing, and caring for The Range.

All flesh is grass. —Isaiah

5

A Range Camp

The horseman in Wanina's drawing on the previous page is Charles M. Russell's "Trailboss"; he sits his horse and thinks about The Range. Perhaps he's moving steers to market; if they're hungry on the trail, that will sure cut into profits. Perhaps he's hunting winter range; if the grass is gone this fall, that could mean a big winterkill. Perhaps he's planning to save some grass for spring.

One old friend and admirer of the famous cowboy artist, Charlie Russell, was a professional rangeman by the name of Frederick Renner, chief of the Range Management Division, U.S. Soil Conservation Service. Renner was on hand as a charter member when the American Society of Range Management was born in 1948, and it was he who made the "Trailboss" available as the SRM logo; it's used on everything from letterheads to bumper stickers.[1]

The Society for Range Management divides its jurisdiction into "sections"; our range includes the International Mountain and Northern Great Plains sections. Among SRM's objectives are: to develop an understanding of range ecosystems and management; to assist range workers in keeping up on the science and art of management; to help people obtain the products and values of the range resource; and to create a public appreciation of that resource. These are worthy goals, and SRM treasures its famous symbol of the management tradition in all the many uses for rangeland.

The Camp Meeting

I'm off to a section meeting of the SRM. Why don't you come along? You'll meet a lot of folks who share your interests; you'll be welcome in our camp.

The International Mountain Section holds an annual Range Tour on which members and their families study cattle, sheep, wildlife habitats, riparian areas, reclamation projects, seed plots, and historic sites. We always manage to learn a thing or two, but these are also times for visiting old friends, recharging rangeland batteries, and fun!

This year we're camped high on a shoulder of the west butte of the Sweet Grass Hills, right on the international boundary, overlooking the Blood and Blackfeet reservations toward Chief Mountain and Glacier Park to the west. What a view! On a clear day you can see a hundred miles across the plains to the Porcupines in the north, the Cypress Hills in the east, and the Highwoods in Montana to the south.

It's time for supper. Come on! Camp with us. Stake your tent down tight in case the chinook blows—we're not far from Pincher Creek or

Browning. And, when you're settled, come on over to the wagon; you'll find hundreds of things to eat (most of 'em beans). The boys are burning steaks and—you see those pretty girls? They're the ones who always win the grass-identification contest. And can they cook! You'll taste their specialty—saskatoon pie. Then, help yourself to coffee and join us at the campfire; grab that bale between Curt Hughes and Alex Johnston. There'll be good talk here tonight, once tongues get loosened up.

That's George Roskie pouring whiskey. The tall guy with the booming voice? That's Ryerson from Bozeman. The old-timer with the jolly wife? Bob Ross, the cowboy poet. There are visitors here from Idaho and Oregon—everyone rides the grub line in the International Mountain Section; the latch string's always out, and we have fun!

Hello! There's Harry Hargrave with a Colorado visitor—couple of old-timers, those—they go back a spell; don't come around much anymore. Harry's one of the chaps who got this bunch together; he got a lot of people started on range management. This ought to be an interesting evening.

Alberta ranchers host the July 1966 International Mountain Section range camp. Left to right: Ed and Don McKinnon, Jim Cartwright, (unidentified), John Cross, Joe Gilchrist, Sherm Ewing, Dave Jantzie, and Hal and Harold Sears.

133

HARRY HARGRAVE

born some 80 years ago, was once a one-man ag-extension service on the Alberta range.

I'm happy to be back with so many of my old friends; this is my home range, you know. Looking off northeast I can almost see the JH Ranch where I was raised, and I put in eleven happy years at Manyberries, just a good day's ride from here by saddle horse. They call the range experiment station "Onefour" now—that's Township One, Range Four—the location of an early farm and post office. But in my day it was "Manyberries," for the shipping point where Gilchrist Brothers had a grazing lease. Let me tell you just a little bit about it.

In the early days when range got overgrazed, you simply moved. Once the land was fenced, it had to be managed; but a lot more knowledge was needed, so in 1926 the Experimental Farm Service set out to find some answers, and they wisely went to the Gilchrist boys and made a deal: The government would assume a township of their lease and build the corrals, fences, scales, and buildings; the Gilchrists would keep grazing rights and supply the livestock, management, and winter feed. The deal went through, and the station grew to 41,000 acres.

L. B. Thomson, the first superintendent, specialized in animal behavior; he and his men spent months with notebooks and binoculars observing the Gilchrists' cattle as they slept, ate, drank, bred, and calved out on the range. "Doc" Clarke, the grass man, began a study of native grasses under various grazing practices, and—just to show how young this science is—the crew began, in 1931, to study carrying-capacity under several different systems, the first such study made in Canada. Their conclusion: In this part of the country, no matter what the management, it takes fifty or sixty acres to support an *animal-unit*—that is, a cow and calf for a year, and part of a bull to breed her.

Ruth and I moved down in 1936, the depth of the Depression, one of the most disastrous droughts on record. Joe Gilchrist had already been busy for a decade with teams and fresnos building dams and dugouts to catch available runoff, and—though most springs and waterholes went dry—we never lacked for water on the station. That was the way we operated in those days: we did our work with forage crops, reseeding, fertilization, animal breeding, and the like, in cooperation with the local stockmen and practical people in the field. That way we got a great deal done at very little expense to the general taxpayer.

134

In 1949 the service sent me off to visit land-grant colleges and research stations across the United States, where I already had dozens of friends and soon made many more; they brought me up to date on all the new developments in range and animal research across the continent—information I brought home to share with many ranchers in Alberta. On that tour I saw my first Charolais; I caught up with my friend Ray Woodward at Miles City, and got updated on his work with performance testing and line breeding of cattle.[2]

And along the way I met a man named Ferry Carpenter. He had a lot to do with organizing the American public domain, and he's visiting here tonight. I'd like you to hear his story of The Range.

FERRY CARPENTER

Colorado lawyer and purebred Hereford breeder, was once a bureaucrat in charge of divvying up the range.[3]

You can see a lot of public domain from this campsite, looking south toward the Missouri and beyond, and—as Hargrave, here, reminds me—I had a lot to do with organizing all the public range-lands in the western United States into what was called the U. S. Grazing Service.[4]

Here's the story: Harold Ickes was secretary of interior when the solicitor general sent me down to help work out the details of the Taylor Grazing Act of 1934. That act, you'll remember, was where the Congress said the government would sell small, isolated tracts of public land in the western United States, and set up grazing districts, where appropriate, on the rest. And that's about all they said; then they wrote *finis* to it, passed it, President Roosevelt signed it, and there it was.

Now, Secretary Ickes—the "Old Curmudgeon"—was an eastern man; he didn't know which end of a cow got up first, and he didn't care. And he didn't know what to do with the Taylor Grazing Act. And so, he put the crown on me, a young lawyer from the Colorado mountains. There were no appropriations for the job; they loaned me fellows from the Geological Survey and a couple of surveyors—seventeen men in all—to handle 142 million acres. That's a hell of a lot of land!

When they gave me the job, I went to the General Land Office in Washington for help. Now, the General Land Office is older than the Department of Interior; they'd been operating for 175 years, and I

135

went to the commissioner only to find they had no maps that could tell me where my lands were. Why? Well, every day people were filing homesteads, buying isolated tracts, making timber applications; states were trading land; the Forest Service was expanding; there were twenty-two land offices in the western states and every minute, every hour, every day somebody would take a piece of land. How could there be a map? So, I didn't know where my lands were. Nobody in the state of Montana knew where state lands were. Nobody in the federal government could help.

There was only one way to find out. I put up notices in all the public-land states that we were going to call some meetings. Anybody that wanted to get a bit of public grazing land had better be at a meeting because we were going to hand it out. Well, you don't have to say that twice; it's just like a free·meal at the church. Everybody showed up at those meetings.

I knew all about the jealousy between the cattlemen and the sheepmen; I also knew they didn't want things handled the way the Forest Service did it. In those days the Forest Service took the attitude that "father knows best," and papa will tell you what to do. Well, I came to the job with a prejudice against that stuff. I didn't think it was a good American principle—I *knew* it was poor public relations, and I didn't want to be the guy that said "papa knows best." But, there was a job to be done out there on 142 million acres. Where was it? And how were we gonna put it under supervision and get a fee for its use?

Now, you know, nobody likes to pay a fee or a tax. We would go out there and a stockman would ask, "What kind of fee?" He'd say, "My father came to this country in a covered wagon; he fought his way out here, and he settled a little ranch here and improved it; and we've always used the public land that lies next to our place—which is just as good as owning it; and now you tell us we've got to pay eight cents a head a month. How come?"

Well, there wasn't any explaining. I said, "Boys, the Congress has let you have this land for nothing as long as they could, but now you've got to stick your head through this collar. If you don't stick your head through it, another fellow will, and we'll please him and let him have the range." You couldn't go out to the range country and ask these fellows to be nice cooperative citizens; they had the land, and they were gonna keep it, and they didn't want to pay for it. It was going to be a rough old battle.

Everybody showed up at those meetings; we'd call 'em all to order, and say, "Boys, the good old days are over and there's no use crying about it. Congress is gonna set these grazing districts up, and you're gonna have to get a permit and pay a fee to use 'em.

"Now, the question is, how are you gonna do it? Are you going to have a smart guy like Mr. Pinchot write the rules and regulations?" Pinchot didn't know anything in the world about the livestock business. "Do you want that? Or do you boys want to help do this yourselves?" Well, of course they knew that Gifford Pinchot had set up the U.S. Forest Service. And, of course, they wanted to help—if they could help themselves a little bit.

We'd say: "...tell you what we'll do. We'll explain the set up, answer questions, and then you cowboys come over here and elect some advisors, and you sheepherders go over there and elect some advisors, and I won't let either of you get the downhill pull."

I'd unroll a big map of their corner of the state; then I'd say, "Gentlemen, the first thing to do is mark out the grazing district boundaries. You fellows know the *natural* grazing boundaries; I want you to come up here, and take a piece of chalk, and mark 'em on this map. And then, I'll leave a federal man out here to work with you advisors, and, together, you'll accept a set of rules and issue permits."

Well, the advisors did just that, and you'll be amazed to know that the grazing district boundaries are still practically the way those fellows set them. They knew their natural barriers, they knew where the public lands were, and it was from their initial work that the BLM grazing districts exist today.

But, a lot of problems had to be solved before we could make the grazing districts work. Who was to get the permits? That's what they wanted to know. We looked at the law. There wasn't much to say, but a lawyer spotted a clause that said: "preference goes to those with property *in* or *near* the public grazing land."

How near was *near*? If it wasn't *in*, how near did it have to be? One funny thing I found was that the drier and more worthless the land, the harder stockmen fight for it. Just why that is, I don't know. I've seen them fight over land where 640 acres wouldn't support a nightcrawler. And those were a bouncy bunch of boys; the ordinary stockman is a pretty tough guy to handle, but the range stockman had been pitched around so long and had fought so hard for his land that he was a little tougher.

How near was near? Our number-one lawyer gave me thirty-seven legal definitions from a textbook. I held a meeting in a federal courtroom, I invited the stockmen, and I got a bunch of federal Reclamation people and Forest Service people, et cetera, and I put them in a jury box and said, "We'll hear arguments today on 'how near is near.'" I felt like Moses. Hadn't the secretary said I was a big shot? I was planning a decision that would just hop 'em in the creek!

I said, "We're here because we're experts and extra smart and know all about everything. What's the use of holding meetings if we don't decide anything? We'll just have to go all through this again. We're going to make a decision. Now!"

Well, the Forest Service had furnished me with two great forest grazing men, and one was Ernest Winkler from Utah. Winkler was a good guy; he was there with me that day, and he said, "That's where you're a damn fool, Carpenter. In government we have just one rule: Never decide anything until you have to." I learned to agree with him very soon. The cowboys said they chased their cows a hundred miles; some sheepmen trailed their sheep a thousand miles to range they thought was "near." I didn't have to come to a decision; I began to see that *everywhere* is near.

We spent almost a year solving "how near is near," and we solved it by the use of some semantics. Sometimes, when you can't solve a thing, if you'll invent some words that nobody understands, they'll sit and take it—think it's solved. In the end, we kind of satisfied the people; we settled it this way: "In the issuance of grazing permits, the first permits go to the *nearest*, the next permits go to the *nearer*, and the last permits go to the *near*." It was a fool thing, but everybody in the room had gone out and hired a lawyer to have their property declared "near," and they still didn't have the answer. Sometimes you just have to pretend to solve these problems.

The Forest Service people used a rule of *commensurability*. It said if you have livestock, unless you're just running steers, you're stuck with them year-round, and you don't have any business asking Uncle Sam to let you have some pasture unless you have facilities to operate at home when the public range is closed. With six-months' summer range, in a country where they have to feed six months, an operator had to show that he had hay or roughage for his stock to live on when they weren't on public range. In the end, we adopted that rule of commensurabilty in the Grazing Service, and gave first crack at Taylor land to those with feed at home. And, after many, many battles we made a rule awarding prior rights to those who—in the five years immediately preceding passage of the Taylor Grazing Act—had used the range in connection with their land for either two years of continuous use, or for any three years in that period.

Well, that was simple. But whenever you write a rule, the boys get smart and find a way around it, and we had thousands of problems over commensurability and water rights and prior rights and transfer rights. But my idea was always to start in and do what *should* be done, and let the darn rules sit—kind of a new theory for some of the government boys. When we made a mistake, we admitted it, and that had an electrical effect on the American people. They'd never heard a government employee say: "I made a mistake and I was a damn fool and I am going to change it." It isn't done that way. But we were going to get along with the stockmen, and give them faith in the bureau that administered their lands, and we hoped they'd recognize a fair American deal. Our system worked.

But our system was so unpopular in Washington that in eighteen months or so I lost my job. I was in Albuquerque when I got a letter from Secretary Ickes ordering me to appear in Washington at one o'clock on Monday. He had the solicitor general and a bunch of other top men sitting around, and handed me a sheet with twelve charges against me. One was that I'd told some ranchers to haul their own salt out on a government range—a terrible thing to do! Some of the charges were phony, but I was fired then and there, which gives you a funny feeling.

But there's a happy ending: My stockmen friends created a disturbance. They liked my way of doing things a lot better than the ways of Gifford Pinchot, so they rained telegrams down on F.D.R. and, with an election coming, the president called the secretary in and told him he'd better hire me back; so back I went. But Harold didn't love me after that; he'd fore-foot me every time I went by him, if he could. But in government you learn to dodge those loops.

GEORGE ROSKIE

a past president of the International Mountain Section—began his career counting livestock onto national forest pastures. He later counted votes during three terms in the Montana Senate.

As Ferry Carpenter says, Gifford Pinchot was a very military guy, and when I joined the U.S. Forest Service as a brand new green-pea forester in 1936, it was still a semimilitary outfit. In those days we had *esprit de corps* and wore the uniform with pride; that was pretty much the case until about 1970, when the uniform became a casual jacket, off-color slacks, no military appearance at all. A district ranger comes to town today with shirt-tail out, in jeans; you can't tell him from a hired hand. That's okay when he's out working, but when he comes to town a lot of us old-timers think he ought to look like the responsible federal officer he was supposed to be when Gifford Pinchot organized the service. That was the tradition in my family.

I was born in 1912 in a log cabin in the Black Hills of South Dakota where my father was a U.S. forest ranger. At that time, Dad made $600 a year and furnished his own horse; he finally went to $1,200 a year and thought he was in clover, but he still had to furnish his own horse. My father's love for forests and mountains and rangeland rubbed off on me; it's my heritage and background, and I think it's why I followed in his footsteps. When I joined the service, I put in two years on the Coeur d'Alene, camping out and living in the woods of northern Idaho alone; then, I got married. Norma was from the Big Sky country and we both missed the openness of The Range, so when we got a chance we took a transfer back to Ashland, on the Custer National Forest in eastern Montana, and Ashland was a highlight of our lives. We had a little three-room house with a privy out in back and packed water from a well. In those days Ashland was a pretty western place: mud roads—the nearest pavement fifty miles away— and every Sunday afternoon a rodeo at Green's Bar down on Main Street, where cowboys brought in horses and challenged you to ride 'em.

—George Roskie.

For me, the fun part was a hundred days each summer in the saddle—maybe more. That was my job: riding range, checking water holes and brands, and counting livestock. It was the kind of country where you rode up to some little ranch at noon, and it was: "Get down, come in, and eat"; or, if you got there after noon: "Put your horse up in the barn and stay all night." And many, many a night I spent with some of those old cowboys. They'd have a one- or two-room shack, and share their bed and grub; you just took what they had to offer and were happy. You might be out for three, four, five days at a time.

From there, I went to Martinsdale as a ranger on the Lewis and Clark Forest in the Little Belt and Crazy mountains. In the years through World War Two it was still pretty much a one-man show. I had a part-time assistant, an old truck, and a big black team and wagon; we'd haul the horses to a work site with the wagon hitched behind, and work on springs and trails doing things you'd never think of doing now. Who could even harness a team today?

In those days, most of our time was spent with permitees—the folks who ran their livestock on the forest. Recreation was still just a minor use, and there was just one little "peckerwood" sawmill that sawed a few of what they called "two-by-tapers"; so, up to the end of World War Two, our main concern was grazing. Those grazing permits were supposed to be *"commensurate"*; that meant they were supposed to fit the forage on the rest of a ranch property. The cattle came from adjoining ranches; the sheep, up "driveways" from ranches down near Martinsdale and Two Dot on the Musselshell. One of our jobs was counting sheep across the forest boundary. It was fascinating; at one time there were forty bands of sheep—a thousand to a band—in the Little Belts. Anymore, I'll bet there's not three bands on the whole Lewis and Clark Forest. That era lasted only till the war, then it began to taper off, and when I left, the scheme of things was changing. They started cutting pulp, which changed the whole appearance of the forest; where we'd had trails and sheep driveways, you'll now find roads and clear-cut spaces, all of which—in my opinion—has been extremely beneficial to the forest, the country, and the range.

Lodgepole pine is a species ideally suited to our mountain ranges, and it requires fire to pop its seeds and start it germinating. Of course, forest fires were common back in earlier days; if lightning didn't start them, Indians would often touch 'em off, or sheepmen coming out of the mountains in the fall would "accidentally" set a blaze, which kept the range in good condition. In those days the young

141

lodgepole just burnt off; but then, as burning was prevented and controlled, it just got thicker and thicker until—in my time, in the early forties—most of those trees were classified as overaged, over-stocked and undersized: essentially, a biological desert with hardly any wildlife in those very thick pine stands. Once you open up the country, grazing improves for livestock and wildlife, both.

When Norma was a child in Stanford, just across the mountains in the Judith Basin, there were so few deer around that a hunter who could go out and shoot a buck was considered a real mountain man. No elk at all in the Little Belts or Crazies until about 1930, when a fellow by the name of Weaver trapped some elk in Yellowstone, brought 'em in, released 'em, and by the late 1940s they were coming out of the Little Belts in droves. And deer! You'd count forty or fifty at a time around the haystacks.

Then came the standard population irruption and die-off; game animals virtually ate themselves out of house and home. When I was supervisor on the Lewis and Clark, I'd take my advisory council out on the south slopes of the Snowies in the winter and show 'em dozens of dead deer—basically, starved to death. Plenty of grass, but the basic food supply for deer is browse—shrubs, low-growing junipers, and like that—and those plants were almost nonexistent; it's always a shock to come to understand the population cycle. And, one of the things that sportsmen seldom understand is the importance of private land to wintering game in mountain country.[5]

You'll find hundreds of deer and elk and mountain sheep on Chase Hibbard's ranch on Hound Creek and the Cobb Ranch near Augusta; they spend the winter eating the ranchers' grass and hay. Game ranges have been established as places to winter wildlife; they satisfy the public more than the game. To keep elk "home," they've even tried to herd 'em, but if you've ever herded elk, you know it ain't a very easy job.

As a multiple-use agency, we were always extremely conscious of keeping things in balance in my day. We recognized all the different values, such as protecting range for wildlife as well as domestic livestock, but we were free to use discretion and common sense. Up until the mid-1960s, the general consensus was, I think, that the management of most public lands was adequate. We depended on the professional abilities of the people that were hired to look after things. They took great pride in doing a good job.

In 1969 the public perception changed. The National Environmental Policy Act (NEPA) called for environmental impact statements, which made us justify and rationalize our every action; from that point on, everything we did came under scrutiny—in my opinion, highly subjective scrutiny. That may sound like a good idea to you, but, in fact, it has been very counter productive; it led to fear, for instance. From that act grew the fear of doing anything at all until everything was planned in minute detail—fear, great fear, of public criticism.

And the NEPA begat a brood of lesser acts: RARE I and II, which stood for Roadless Area Review something-or-other [and Evaluation]; up until then, such things had been an integral part of regular forest planning. Later, we got the Federal Land Policy and Management Act, and the Forest and Rangeland Resource Planning Act, and they piled one on another—clean air, clean water, and so forth—until it became difficult to tell whether you were complying with a law, or whether, in fact, there was a law to be complied with in any situation. If you slipped up just a little, some "kid ecologist"—some member of the "environmental elite," as it's been called—would challenge your decision, and not just through the normal appeals process, which is one thing, but in court. The interpretation of all those laws and the National Environmental Policy Act had an immediate and lasting impact on the management of our national forests; it ground almost to a standstill.

I put in a tour of duty in Alaska. When I returned to Montana, I sat in on a public meeting on the Rocky Mountain Front Plan for the Lewis and Clark Forest—a plan that had at least six years of dedicated work behind it, and one I considered excellent. That plan was challenged by the environmentalists, and was finally set aside by the regional forester at the time. As a result, from 1972 to 1986, when a revised plan was finally announced, there were fourteen years of hiatus—confusion, planning and replanning, examining and reexamining—at a cost of hundreds of thousands of dollars. And the final plan contributed nothing to the quality of management. In my opinion, the whole thing was a delaying tactic used by a few environmentalists to keep the forest managers from doing their jobs, while they gathered forces and demanded more attention to aesthetics: "wilderness," "recreation"—*their* kind of wilderness and recreation, whatever kind that was.

Well, about the time that all this hit the fan, I decided it was time for me to leave. We were entering an era of entirely new philosophies and attitudes, with quite a bit of politics creeping in. It seemed to me that freedom of choice in decision making, alternative choosing, opportunity taking, was going to be very, very limited and very, very restrictive. I retired.

I'm glad I did. The summer of 1988 was one of the driest in the history of our range. In June a lightning strike in the Scapegoat Wilderness Area west of Augusta started a fire; it was still just a little fire when some outfitters arrived to put it out. But the Forest Service stopped them; "Hands off!" they said. "Against the rules." "We'll extinguish fires set by careless campers; fires set by nature must burn out." No flexibility there; no room for common sense in the driest spell we've seen in a hundred years. And so, after smoldering all summer, in September the fire flared and got away; it burned across the wilderness area boundary; it burned into three different national forests; it burned a hundred cattle alive; it swept out onto private land, burned more cattle, and destroyed miles and miles of fence; it burnt up tons of drought-year hay and winter grass; it threatened houses, families, and towns. Too bad when professional resource managers are afraid to deal with emergencies in the face of disapproval from a few.[6]

Somehow the environmentalists have come to think they have a constitutional right to be involved in the management of public lands. That management is becoming management by committee-of-loud-voices, rather than by professional, trained, natural resource managers, and the "rights" invoked are always gained by some to the detriment of others.

It's that "zero-sum" again, but in this case there's a loser; it's the land.

BOB ROSS

cowboy poet and author who spent his life helping ranchers improve their private range.

Well, George, I know your service has its problems juggling all those multiple uses around. And—born and raised, as I was, out on the Mussellshell in the twenties and thirties—I well know it took a lot of ingenuity to unscramble all those claims to Taylor land. But what of private range? Seventy percent of the Montana range today is private, only about a third is public, and what private owners do with their own land affects us all.

My agency, the Soil Conservation Service (SCS) was organized in 1935 or '36 to give technical assistance, on request, to private owners. It was pretty hard to do very much at first, but, as private operators and public agencies started to fence more land, it became possible to make real range improvements.

For the first few years the SCS did actually manage land—ran some old reseeding programs and that sort of thing—but it wasn't long till they decided to get out of the land-management business and restrict themselves to offering technical assistance through the conservation districts. Maybe Congress made that decision for 'em, I don't know, but it was a good one.

I left the ranch and spent a couple of years at Bozeman—Montana State—before I joined the infantry and went to war in 1942; then, wounded and partially paralyzed for awhile, I went back and finished up with a degree in range in 1949. With that, I spent the next twenty-nine years as a range conservationist with SCS, helping ranchers solve their rangeland problems, always at their request, I'm proud to say.

Like anything else, it took a while for SCS to get their program rolling; people didn't jump on bandwagons and ask for help and go and do exactly what we said. When we got a chance, we'd go over a ranch property carefully—farm land, grazing land, rangeland, timberland, whatever, the whole works—and present the owner with a management plan. But, then, each rancher had to think things through himself, do his own thing, and very often conclude he'd thought it up himself.

I remember one old rancher down in southwest Montana whose range was in really terrible shape. He'd run sheep for years and years and years, just as his dad and grandad had before him; not that sheep are any worse than horses or cattle or elk or gophers or anything else, you understand—if they're out there long enough, one class will do as much damage as the other. In this case, the range had been terribly abused by poorly managed sheep.

Well, this rancher finally invited me to visit, and—first thing—we rode across a 15,000-acre pasture completely gone to sagebrush. And I mean *big* old sagebrush, higher than you could see across from a saddle horse, and nothin' growin' under it; there was very little of that in the early days.

The fella had asked me out there, so I felt I should be honest and tell him what his land could be producing. As we rode along, we'd come to a boundary fence or an inaccessible area where the herder hadn't tried to take the sheep, and I'd point to the good grass growing there—no sagebrush, just good grass—the kind of cover Mother Nature had intended. That 15,000 acres looked like it could be divided into about three different pastures with a couple of cross-fences and a little water development, and I suggested some kind of rest-rotation program.

I gave him quite a spiel. I said, "Each clump of grass is like a child, a colt, a calf; you have to give it care and lots of rest in early stages if you want it to grow up strong.

I said, "I know you can't just hang your livestock up on hooks—they gotta be out there eatin' all the time; but maybe, by changing season-of-use and grazing patterns, you might be able to have your cake and eat it too." And I explained how a grazing system might be devised to give each plant a chance to grow, mature, strengthen its roots, occasionally set seed—let Mother Nature do her thing. That's all.

Well, after poundin' on his ear for most of the day, I hoped I'd made my point. But as I said good-bye, the rancher turned on me and scored one of his own.

"You know," he said, "I had a sheepherder once who was forever tellin' me what I was doin' wrong: I shouldn't do this; I oughta do that. I finally had to ask him: 'How come, if you know so much,' I said, 'that I've got a ranch and you've got none?' "

That shook me up a bit, but I was goin' back for more the next day, except it snowed that night—big snowstorm—and it was weeks before we met again. Then, one morning, he came into the SCS office and says, right off the bat, before we'd even had our coffee, "You know, Bob, I been thinkin' ..."

He says: "You know that Elk Creek pasture we were on? Well, that's taken an awful beating the last few years. If I just ran a couple of fences across it and put in some stock-water developments and sprayed a little sagebrush ..."

Well, that was twenty years ago, pretty near twenty-five. That rancher didn't exactly hop right to it; it took him quite a while to adopt a plan—which is kind of the way things go, working with people. After that, it took six or seven years before we started to see results—which is kind of the way things go, working with plants. But after he got his cross-fences in and sagebrush sprayed, and after he'd given his grass a chance to rest for a season or two, he never had to do much water development; that dad-blamed creek just started running again. Kind of interesting: just replacing some of that sagebrush with a good grass cover allowed the snowmelt and the rain to go into the ground and feed the aquifers instead of running off. I haven't been on that place for about eight years now, but if the management is still the way it was, why, those creeks will still be running, and there'll be lots of grass, and that rancher should be makin' lots of money.

Yeah, there are some things I'm real proud of. I don't claim all the credit, by any means; just being part of it's enough. But, look at the range today; I honestly feel that over fifty percent of the Montana range is in "good" to "excellent" condition now, while back in the Dirty Thirties I doubt if there was fifteen percent "good" range. A lot of people did the work and share the credit: ranchers on their own land, agencies gaining knowledge and putting it into practice. Whoever gets the credit, our rangelands have improved tremendously, and modern ranchers have become true conservationists. They have to be if they want to stay in business; that is, where grazing really *is* their business.

Old Grass in the Spring
by Bob Ross

The days are gettin' longer
and the sun is shinin' stronger,
Some signs of spring are seen
and the grass is gettin' green,
But, the hay supply is low—
a terrible tale of woe!
'Cause I didn't save some old grass for the spring.

A cow needs lots of bulk
or she'll stand around and sulk,
She'll run from plant to plant
and be lookin' mighty ga'nt;
Green grass is mostly juice—
a pretty poor excuse
For a stand of old grass in the spring.

Your worries will be over,
you'll really be in clover;
Calves will hit the ground a-runnin'
and lay around a-sunnin';
Their Mas will give more likker
and get the love-bug quicker,
When you've left a lot of old grass for the spring.

A cow that's had a calf
will need more feed by half;
Thirty pounds of dry
puts that glimmer in her eye,
But she'll bawl herself to sleep
when there's not enough to eat.
This year I'll save some old grass for next spring.

DON RYERSON

the old professor—taught vo-ag and range, and drew the attention of a generation of Montanans to range management.

Dad used to tell me, "Son, remember this: every summer's the driest, every winter's the hardest. Stock accordingly, and, come hell or high water, you'll have grass," which we always did. Except, of course, during the Dirty Thirties, when we had three or four years of continuous drought, and grasshoppers, and hay laid in at Havre at sixty-five to seventy dollars a ton—old Minnesota sloughgrass. Break a bale, and you'd find chunks of ice, part of a muskrat house—everything you paid for, and then some!

I was just a kid when the Dirty Thirties hit and we went broke; we didn't have enough money left to leave [Don laughs]. The Federal Land Bank wound up with our outfit, but we stayed on until Dad finally got a job running a ranch in the Missouri Breaks near the mouth of the Judith River. That was a tough country down in there when I was a kid. We ran cattle and sheep on the public land, and so did everybody else, and, unfortunately, it was "them that got there fustest ..." got the grass. What usually got there "fustest" was the horses; talk about your so-called wild horses: we had 'em. The Taylor Grazing Act came in 1934, but it took about twenty years to get it going. Meantime, we realized what was happening well enough ourselves, and began to clean the horses out—sold 'em out as canners when we could—and started to build things back.

We had land seeded down to Crested wheatgrass in the thirties. Not much of it; we really didn't realize the full management possibilities, but Dad always kept some Crested for one specific purpose. He said, "I want a good calf crop; I want a ninety-five to a hundred percent calf crop. And the way to get it," he says, "is always, always have plenty of old grass—Crested wheat, if possible—left over from the previous year; that'll keep the calves up out of the dirt and mud, and give the native range a chance to start." And, of course, my dad was right. With that old stand of grass, you got good vigor, and Crested wheatgrass was the first to green up in the spring—three weeks earlier than the natives. By the first of June we'd move to native range. My dad was right! And that's what I've been preaching ever since.

It's nothing new, of course. I mean, some of the finest grasslands I ever saw were in Saudi Arabia, which has had a grazing history of, what, five thousand years? Surprised me when I went over there in 1975; I'd thought that everything was lost in the Middle East.

Heavens! We found the Bedouin have known about deferred grazing since back in Biblical times. They've kept a carry-over of grass right up till King Faisal broke up age-old rights to tribal grazing. But, the remnants of incredibly hardy, acclimated grazing plants were there, and the people wanted to bring them back to use. They have water that will last three thousand years; all they really need, they say, is a grazing system that fits the people and the land. Allah will help them do the rest.

A Fable

Charlie McKinnon rode out across the XL range one day—that's down the Bow, a hundred miles from Calgary. Topping a rise, he came upon some recreational vehicles parked across a hayfield, and a rowdy baseball game in progress. "Slide!" somebody shouted, as a runner flattened the hay. "You're out!" said Charlie, riding to the mound to discuss the situation with the pitcher.

As Charlie used to tell it: "The lady of the family fired up: 'You see that green stuff, Mister? That's called grass, *and that means this is* park, *so that means we camp* here!' " *What's grass ... is park ... is public: A fable of our modern range!*

MAC FORBES

assistant deputy minister for public lands in the Province of Alberta.

I've been a civil servant all my life, and I've enjoyed it; I've found it challenging. I guess my office has been the front line in conflicts between the grassroots and the public in Alberta. In the mid-1960s new kinds of people—many without a rural background—began to flood the range; they came from many parts of the world and, as oil and gas development increased and the economy strengthened, Alberta's cities grew by a thousand head a month and the grassroots began to lose political clout. Since then, there's been increased demand for land for recreation along with growing, mostly genuine, concern that public lands must be preserved for future generations, and I can tell you we in government have felt those pressures strongly. At the same time, we are constantly reminded of the negative perception in the cities that public land has been abused and monopolized by ranchers. All of which is nothing new, of course.

Let me tell you about Alberta; it's big country—just a little smaller than Texas, almost twice the size of Montana. Although a couple of million people live in Calgary and Edmonton and the corridor between them, over half the province is still officially *unsettled*—much of it forest, scrub, or muskeg. And, although we're Canada's largest cattle-producing province, only a relatively small percentage of our land is actually well suited to domestic livestock production.

"Crown land" is a good old British term for public domain, and by 1930 most crown land in western Canada had come under provincial jurisdiction.[7] Where, in Montana, the U.S. Forest Service and a *federal* Bureau of Land Management (BLM) are the primary public land agencies, here, forested areas are administered by the Alberta Forest Service, and public rangelands—outside forest boundaries— by a *provincial* Lands Division. It's easy to see advantages in close-to-home, provincial control of resources with responsible agencies accessible to users and accountable to local politicians; top brass in touch with local conditions forestalling the sort of sagebrush revolution that flared up in Montana a few years ago. And, over five million acres of the crown land in our province—roughly one million animal-unit-months—is under long-term grazing lease to the ranching industry; add to that large areas of native range and improved pasture in private hands, and Alberta would have twenty million acres in domestic livestock grazing.

My first real job in the civil service began in 1955 when I became a grazing-lease inspector. There was "Scotty" Campbell and me—just the two of us—and we worked the entire province, so we didn't get to inspect any lease too often, but, just the same, we lease inspectors were often the best link between the rancher and the bureaucrats in Edmonton. While we checked the range, we performed some two-pronged public relations: We tried to raise the lessee's interest in sound range management practices, and we helped him cut red tape as government grew.

And what about perceptions that ranchers get a free ride on public grazing land—"at the public trough"—and so on? That's a question we face all the time. An economist would say "fair" rent is the going *interest rate* times *resource market value*. But, remember, forage is just one component of the resource—often a small component—and that's where many people get off base. They know that public land has many expected products—recreation, wildlife, minerals, and water, as well as forage—yet they seem to want the livestock man to pay for all of it while most others use it free. In Alberta we haven't bought that, in my time.[8]

Over the past thirty years, I see much more interest in, and a far better understanding of, range management as users see the sense in managing for long-term, as opposed to short-term, gain. And, of course, these things have come about as groups like SRM, the "forage co-ops" in Alberta, Montana Range Days, Ag-Lenders schools, research and extension services, and the colleges have raised awareness in the livestock industry and shown ranchers what could and should be done.

Now, I think, we must educate the public, which has become aware and keenly interested in environmental matters but is still not very knowledgeable about rangeland. We're all in this together, after all.

ALEX JOHNSTON
Alberta historian, range scientist, and ecologist.

I believe that the term "shortgrass country" for the southern Alberta range around this camp is pretty much a misnomer; it's actually mixed prairie with large areas of speargrass, needle-and-thread, Western wheatgrass, and that sort of thing. Where true short grasses, such as Blue grama—sometimes known as buffalo grass—dominate, they would be the result of very heavy grazing, and I think many areas were kept in that condition by the buffalo that summered here, traditionally, for millennia.[9] My personal opinion is that much of this range is in just as good, or better, shape today, after a century of domestic grazing, as it was in buffalo days.

What concerns me is the plow-down of the range and what we do about it. The original ecosystem here on The Range was "closed" and self-perpetuating; it would have gone on literally forever, barring a major change in climate or a radical change in occupancy such as, in fact, occurred. After the terrible devastation that followed homestead days, we began to look at reclamation and turned to Asiatic grasses.

I've asked the question many times: Why do so many of the grasses we've found useful for regrassing the plains come from Asia? Nobody really knows. We've looked at native species, but none so far have compared with the "exotics," notably Crested wheatgrass and Russian wild rye. I don't know whether those species are even popular in Russia; we're always interested to note our Russian visitors' surprise at our extensive use of *their* native range plants.

151

In the Dirty Thirties, Crested turned out to be the salvation of the country because it took right ahold. I worked at regrassing the blown out plains until 1942. When I came home from the war in 1946, I continued with regrassing, but by then the weather patterns had changed and, instead of the drought I'd known since youth, we had some pretty good wet years—moisture and *normal* conditions, if one can use that term. The result was that the regrassing program slowed. For one thing, the land was revegetating naturally; for another, several million acres of Crested wheat had already been sown, and we'd begun to worry about utilization. The grass we'd learned could yield three times as much as our native prairie complex, had acquired a poor reputation for palatability—it got stemmy and dormant quickly.

In recent years there have been programs that encouraged plowing up the range for wheat production; there have been other programs under which millions of acres of marginal land from Colorado north to Alberta have been actually broken, cultivated, and cropped for a year, just so they could be seeded back to so-called *improved* exotic grasses like Crested wheat; the rationale being that exotic grasses yield so much more than the native-prairie complex.[10] But, not withstanding increased yield, many ecologists feel that the cultivation required for seeding results in a net loss to the system. Cultivation releases nitrogen and organic matter, and breaks down the prairie complex that's taken thousands of years to develop. I, personally, believe that native grass is the cover of choice, and I feel very strongly that plowing marginal lands is not a good idea. I definitely discourage it.

The ecological system that developed under the buffalo and the Indian was "closed": an animal ate grass, returned nutrients in its droppings, then died and returned to the soil itself—just cycled, year after year. Although nothing was added, there was net improvement through the build-up of organic content, and over the millennia a deep, organic soil profile developed, as early settlers found. We're losing it, today. As a matter of fact, in our southern Alberta prairie soils, we've used up almost half the nitrogen and organic matter that was here when farmers arrived about 1900. In less than a hundred years, that's frightening!

It's been pointed out that they're farming lands in India that have no organic matter; I spent several years in India, and I refuse to accept that information as any kind of argument at all! We need a means of working grasses and legumes into our rotations in order to return organic matter to the soil, and we have to stop our current disastrous practice of extraction and contamination.

The closed system is what we should be striving for. Our problem is we're taking too much out, we're making the wrong inputs, and we're leaving too many waste products all over the bloody place for future generations to deal with.

BOB ROSS speaks up:

The plow-down of our rangelands has been a real disgrace to rangemen and the country—it's unbelievable what went on! Thousands of acres of range plowed down to farm our government programs. As soon as the sod was broken, land could be reclassed for agriculture and might rise in market value from sixty to as much as four or five hundred bucks an acre—eligible now for some so-called farm program. We in the SCS saw what was happening soon enough, but—except for lip service—we were powerless to do anything about it. We were never a regulatory agency; we weren't set up to say "you can't do that!" It's a free country, and we take a lot of pride in being free to do with private property as we wish. I wouldn't want to change that. But, in this case, private property—rangeland—got away from us, that's all, before anybody realized what was happening. A lot of range is gone. So what are we gonna do to get it back?

Things change. The SCS is involved, nowadays, in trying to put that rangeland back to grass. That takes monetary remuneration—they used to call it money—but the damage has been done; it'll never be the same, not like when needle-and-thread and bluebunch, or even buffalo grass, grew there. Unfortunate? Lack of integrity, I'd say!

And FRANK JACOBS adds:

The range-extension people have had a hell of a time convincing us that range improvement pays. The trouble is we can't convince our bankers who like to honor cheques the day they're paid.

One problem is, despite the exploitation of our forebears, we really haven't run out of anything yet. We still buy socks and nails and two-by-fours and bread, and when you flick a switch, the light goes on. There's even too much land! Our government programs tell us so. So, why conserve it? Why not just farm the hell out of it, and get the dollars when we can?

You know about Alberta's "special areas"? Thousands and thousands of rangeland acres plowed in eastern Alberta, back in the homestead years. Well, by 1935 those farmers had gone broke and couldn't pay their taxes; I went out to a place called Richdale as a school teacher in 1937, and one of my jobs was to help distribute fish

153

and apples from the Maritimes: Relief! There was real devastation on the land. Then the Alberta government took over; the PFRA came in and seeded thousands of acres back to Crested wheat, strict grazing regulations were established, and the special areas were leased back to ranchers.

But memories are short. In other areas, not too far away, the plowdown has continued. Of course, this time the devastation will take longer. With modern tillage methods, fertilizers, herbicides, less summer-fallow, more strip-farming, it may take a hundred years to destroy the range, but, this time, we can expect a pretty thorough job. No civilization has survived the switch from animal agriculture to straight grain production; organic matter disappears all too soon.

Historians tell us the Romans sowed North Africa to salt after they conquered Carthage; modern scientists suspect that salinization probably appeared with cereal production and poor farming practices. We're seeing salinization today, increasingly, on old rangelands where Washington and Ottawa subsidized cereal crops. Those Carthaginians blamed it all on Rome, but whoever was at fault in ancient Carthage, Colonel Gaddafi hasn't got a whole lot left!

Milk River was carving hoodoos from the range thousands of years before these cattle arrived. —National Archives of Canada

154

RANGE U.

In 1951 I was riding for a California outfit that bought calves across the West, grew them out on grass, and fattened them for slaughter. One day in May my boss, Herb Lyttle, said, "Get ready, Sherm. We're shipping the steers to the Big Hole in Montana. You're goin' with 'em. You'll stay until they're settled for the summer." What a thrill for a kid to ride behind a hundred cars of cattle and a mighty, coal-fired, smoking, hissing Union Pacific engine. Sometimes an engineer would invite me up to "watch those drivers roll," like Casey Jones. More often it was a brakeman: "Sit down, kid, and hang on tight!" Those cabooses sure did "crack the whip."

Well, Montana looked pretty good to me; I decided I'd been born a hundred years too late for California, so next spring I drew my time, and Claire and I, with our brand new daughter, Nina, moved north to find our niche upon The Range. Then, green as grass in June, I spent the summer learning all I could about Montana while I scoured the country for an educational job.

"Opportunity," someone said, "just knocks. It don't kick in the door." A discouraging summer, but—finally—great luck! One day in late October I made a blind call at a ranch near Wolf Creek, and there I met a sheep buyer who knew an absentee land-owner who was looking for a man to run his cow ranch north of Browning. "Don't call him," the sheepman said, "he'll call you." By gosh, he did, and by freeze-up we were settled on the 3C Bar, a ranch made up of "patents" and "allotments" on the Blackfeet Reservation a dozen miles from Canada. There, Claire made a home for our family on the beautiful, cold, windy south fork of Milk River: a place that could use some trees, she thought. I thought trees would only spoil the incredible view and knew I'd found a perfect campus for continuing education.

One of my "professors" was the local SCS man who invited me to his lab—the range—where he coached me on the grasses, shrubs, and forbs that comprise the native prairie. He made a lifelong friend for SCS, and he introduced me to SRM—the Society for Range Management—through which, over the years, I've learned much about the environment I live in and met many wonderful people. I might never have known a "green-pea" forester, agrostologist, range ecologist, or learned very much about grass if it hadn't been for these camp meetings on The Range.

Ideas are born; they develop; they are transformed; but they never die. The history of ideas is the history of the race. They are the real events.

—Sir Andrew Macphail, 1925

6

Range Ideas

In as much as this is a history of the place I call The Range, there's room for some historical ideas. I want you to meet three rangemen whose ideas have had an impact on the science and art of managing our resource; I'll let them tell you how they came to their conclusions. Many books and papers have been written developing these ideas, and each has its believers and its skeptics. Darwin said that credit goes to the man who convinces the world, not to the man who did the original thinking. In the next chapter, you'll meet a few range mangers who became convinced enough to have tested these ideas in the field; that will help you evaluate their importance. Great ideas must stand the test of time; those that work well need no help at all.

AUGUST L. HORMAY

charter member of the SRM, is the acknowledged father of "rest-rotation" grazing, an idea long enough tested to deserve a place of honor here. Gus maintains a consultant practice well into his eighties.

I'm a city boy, myself, born and raised in San Francisco. When I was in high school, back in the twenties, I was rather sickly and the doctor said, "The thing for you is to get out into some fresh air." So I went up to a small ranch in Lake County where they had a few cattle, a few horses, and I worked around there all summer and found it interesting and invigorating—something new for a city boy. I regained my health and by winter I'd become so interested in farming that I stayed another season. By then I'd lost all interest in city life, and I went over to the university and inquired about studies that dealt with the out-of-doors. When I got around to the forestry department the counselor explained what forestry was, and added, "We also teach range management here."

I made him explain range management. He said it dealt with livestock grazing and with managing land, and that it involved riding. He mentioned cowboys! That struck a chord with me: going out on the range, riding a horse. I'd learned to ride pretty well out on the farm and loved it, so I said, "Okay, that's for me! I'll take forestry and some courses in range management," which I did.

After college I got a job at the U.S. Forest Service Experiment Station at Berkeley, at a starting salary of $1,800 a year. That was 1931, and eighteen hundred bucks wasn't bad for a kid just out of college; you could get along all right on that. That was also the first year that the station received any funds for range research; up until then they'd worked on forestry and fire control and watershed management problems. But the year I started, they got $20,000 specifically for range.

In those days people had just begun to realize the importance of vegetation to all the other values they were talking about: multiple values, multiple uses. If vegetation had been destroyed, the thinking was—and it's still widespread today: those greedy stockmen had put too many animals on the range. They'd *overstocked* it.

All through the thirties surveys were made and policies formulated, and you can get an idea of the thinking of the day from a message Henry Wallace sent the Senate: "An outstanding cause of range depletion has been excessive stocking."[1] He added that the most effective way to stop deterioration would be to reduce livestock numbers. That idea still prevails today: Rangelands deteriorate because they're grazed by *too many animals*. It sounds so logical. How else? Just too many animals out there! The idea became the basis for the philosophy of proper use, with proper stocking levels.

Well, I'm a renegade; that philosophy didn't square with what I was observing in the field. On the one hand, grazing stimulates the range. Clip off the tops, and you make the plants stool out. With bunchgrass, if you allow old growth to stand, it will ultimately get so thick that new growth can't come through; the plant may actually die—just suffocate under all that dead material. With good management, we take off excess growth before that happens.

On the other hand, go out on the range and observe; you'll find that livestock graze very selectively by plant species and by areas. They prefer some species, and they choose more accessible areas no matter what the stocking rate; they always overuse the grass around the water holes and the bottoms—same areas, same plants, year after year. Unfortunately, the best grazing sites and the most palatable plants are destroyed first. I thought, "How far do you have to go in adjusting the stocking rate to have *proper* use down in the bottoms?"

In 1934 I was investigating the theories of proper use on the Burgess Springs Experimental Range in northeast California. I decided against using different rates. I thought, "I'll just set up two pastures—one in timber, one in meadow—and I'll stock 'em both at the same rate; then, I'll go back to square-one and continue to observe grazing *habits*."

A local rancher lent me twenty heifers for the summer. I observed their grazing habits: what, when, where, and how they ate, day by

159

day, and I weighed them regularly throughout the grazing season. And this went on for four, five years. Nothing new; everything I learned had been known before.

In order to study the effects of the *degree* of grazing, I decided to mark some individual plants of four or five perennial species and clip 'em, just as I'd observed each species to be "clipped" by cattle on my pastures. I laid out a pilot area, marked a good many plants, clipped them right through the season just as a heifer would do. Amazing! Some of the less palatable species that received less clipping got bigger over the years. But, take Idaho fescue, for example, my "ice cream" plant, a favorite with my livestock. I selected some fescue plants and clipped the entire tops, including regrowth, just as the heifers did; that prevented those plants from making their own food, you see.

What effect did that have? Well, the next year those plants were smaller in diameter. I clipped again the following year; sure enough, again they're smaller. Well, certainly, they were smaller! If I didn't allow 'em any food, how could they grow bigger? On and on we went, year after year, and many of those favorite plants went right down to the point where there was just one spear left. Well, this was silly; I knew my plants would die if I kept on clipping 'em that way. Perhaps, in practice, destruction of the better sites and plants was just inevitable.

One of the real pioneers of the science of range management was Dr. A. W. Sampson, widely known as "Sammy." He had preceded me in all of this when, twenty-five years earlier at the University of California, he'd done the same kinds of studies and come up with what he called "deferral grazing." I'd read his work; he taught that you should give your plants a rest during the early part of the growing season. The thinking at that time was that a plant had made and stored all of its food when it was less than half grown. Sampson put it on a height basis: when a certain plant is six inches tall, he said, you can go ahead and graze it without damage. We now know that was wrong; we now know that at about one-third of its growth, a plant is at its lowest ebb in food reserves and highly vulnerable. Sammy's insight was a remarkable step forward, but when his theory—based on faulty information—was put to test, it was found to be flawed. You got reproduction and maintenance, but your plants were left in a weakened condition and you couldn't realize optimum production. I was trying to find a better way.

I stumbled onto my solution when I was kneeling down alongside one of my heavily clipped "ice cream" plants one day. I was looking at

160

one last little spear, and I said to myself, "If I clip this last spear off, this plant is gone for good.

"But, what if I don't clip it off—just leave it there? Well, it'll be just like a seedling. If I don't clip it, it'll grow. If I don't bother it ... Serendipity! Gus, you've found the answer!"

Using Sammy's theory as a base, and adding all the latest information, the solution jumped to light. We have to *rest* our plants for a longer period—right out to maturity. In other words, we have to give them full opportunity to make and store every bit of food available. Following a year of growing-season use, it's essential to allow our plants two years in succession to make and store an adequate food supply. That's important: one year is not enough; two years is what we need.

Then, given two green periods of rest, we can graze our plants right down to the ground—100 percent, 1,000 percent—it doesn't matter; they're still alive—a little smaller, but the roots are still alive. Give 'em that kind of rest, and they'll regain full size another year. That was the solution!

Don't worry about numbers! Put as many animals out there as you wish. But, as a practical matter, you'll need a number of pastures because you'll need to *rotate* use of the growing season. I called my solution "rest-rotation grazing."

And, there it is! It works! We've tested the theory hundreds of times in hundreds of places for forty years. There's no other way to maintain the grazing resource. Animals will graze preferred species right down into the ground, whatever the stocking rate, but with rest for two entire growing seasons you can stock up to the limit and still maintain plant vigor. Graze those riparian bottoms, yet keep on growing vegetation as lush and rank as it can be, up and down the stream, two years out of three. With proper rest-rotation management, both quality and quantity of forage will improve; animal production will increase; and, remarkably, no cut in livestock numbers will be necessary.

The range is so important to us all! Maintain vegetative cover! With grass we have the watershed, the soil, the wildlife habitat, almost everything under control. Good range management is the key to all those multiple values we talk about, and grazing animals are the tools of a manager's trade.

With the environment under control, there's only one big problem left: the people. Who's going to get how much of the pie? I've spent my life with plants and animals on the range. I'll let others figure out the people problem.

E. W. "BILL" ANDERSON

showed range people how to work together. His concept, Coordinated Resource Management Planning (CRMP), has been mused, abused, and successfully used across the West for years.

People problems! I tussled with 'em for years. How do you get people to work together? Back in the late forties, as a soil conservationist in Oregon, I was working with five ranchers who were permittees on a BLM allotment; I was working with them individually on winter range and pasture seeding and irrigation problems, but as soon as they "turned out" on their joint-grazing allotment there was friction. One day I suddenly woke to what was happening: "Hell, let's get these guys together."

I tried my idea out on the BLM district manager. "Sure," he said, "lets try it," so we called the bunch together, let everybody talk, and made everybody listen—even the DM; before long we'd made a grazing plan between us, and, finally, we agreed to make it work. That was the beginning of coordinated planning, though I called the thing "group action" at the time.

I was promoted to state range specialist, covering eastern Oregon, meeting with lots of people, and I talked group action everywhere I went. By the early sixties it was standard operating procedure to work with groups of ranchers with common problems to solve; that's when I began to use the term "coordinated planning"—just a way to help a lot of people carve the resource pie. I emphasize the *people*; you never get a resource program going until you get a lot of personal change in attitude. You'll often have a group that's polarized: strong-willed environmentalists who don't know sic-'em from straight-up about the range; range-raised people completely familiar with a problem, but not with the environmentalist point of view. We split 'em up in workshops where everybody contributes ideas, experiences, viewpoints, and we insist that only one person talks at a time—all the rest shut-up and listen. What a shock! Until now, they've never listened to each other, and sometimes a light comes on: "By golly that man *does* know somethin' about this." It happens time and time again.

In coordinated planning I try to get my people to agree on *something*, even if they can't agree on *everything* at first. When they reach an impasse, I get 'em to agree to disagree; that makes for agreement, see? And then, for heavens sake, get 'em out on the land doing things they agree on. Even on major problems—get 'em workin' together, once. It works like a dream.

I won't bore you with every detail of the coordinated planning process, except to say it provides for local groups made up of people who know conditions; they get together often to check on what's been done, and to prioritize the things they want to do. Ten projects, but only money and time for three? Which come first? Who's gonna do 'em? When?

You would be interested, though, in an actual situation—the most difficult I've encountered—on the Sheldon Wildlife Refuge in Nevada. I knew its problems—a perfect challenge for CP; so when I retired from my career with SCS, I hired on as regional range conservationist just itching to try a coordinated plan at Sheldon. I had to be a little sneaky at first.

The Sheldon National Wildlife Refuge is on land set aside by the U.S. Government in two stages. First, they set aside a small antelope refuge; then they added to it, until, today, it covers 576,000 acres— a big chunk of high-desert country in northwestern Nevada overlapping into Oregon. The bill that established Sheldon says: "Livestock grazing *shall be perpetuated* ...," but it doesn't say *how*. And when I got involved, the refuge had massive problems with livestock competing with wildlife for the range.

To start with, we had areas—very few interior fences, just *areas*— and grazing permits were granted in a pretty informal manner: one fella turned out here, another over there, and they all quarreled back and forth when another guy's cows would eat their area off. A mess! The Nevada Fish & Wildlife people didn't want any cattle at all, even though by law they had to accept them. Grazing was administered by the BLM who did nothing but set dates for turn-out and gather. The wildlife were the responsibility of the U.S. Fish & Wildlife Service, who couldn't manage wildlife because they couldn't manage *habitat* because they didn't control the cattle. All this was brought to the attention of the Congress, and Congress gave the management of the whole shebang to the U.S. Fish & Wildlife Service. And that's about when I came on the scene.

I proposed an inventory. First, let's find out what we've got to work with. I made an ecological site and condition survey. When the time came to develop the actual plan, we were fortunate to have a new refuge manager by the name of Marvin Kaschke: he understood.

But Fish & Wildlife had a guy with a Ph.D. in range. Hell, he didn't know what end of an antelope gets up first, but he had a Ph.D. and he was a planner; and he arranged to have a planning session on the project; and he proposed a big old, long, unending government planning process.

Finally, Marv, our resource manager, said, "Bill, let's look at one of your coordinated plans."

We were out at Badger Camp, in a little old stone cabin with a big old table that we used to eat on, and I laid the maps out and explained how my plan would work, and—just like that—Marv says: "Yep, we'll have a coordinated plan." He was a line officer, you see, and he overrode the regional office and planners. We had some hot times for a while, but we got a coordinated plan in operation—the most complex I ever worked with; it was beautiful.

A national refuge gets plenty of attention, and we had many competing groups to work with. We had the Nevada president of the Sierra Club; we had the Nevada president of WHOA—Wild Horse Organized Assistance; we had the Nevada Fish & Wildlife Service, who were mad at the U.S. Fish & Wildlife Service because they thought they ought to run the project—all kinds of professional jealousies. We had ranchers who thoroughly despised anybody in public service, including me, but who didn't get along together, either; and we had one grazing association whose members didn't even get along amongst themselves. It was a good test for CP.

We went through the plan in series. First, we made a field trip to survey problems, overall. And then, we sat down and looked at the objectives. Then we listed problems. We called three planning meetings about a month apart. We could only go so far with such a complex plan before we let the people go home and think about it. Then, back they'd come again and, where anything needed changing, we'd rehash it and move on a little further, let 'em mull it over again, till we finally got a plan.

All the fences were laid out with the help of the ranchers. We gave them some cross fences so they could actually manage, and they found out it was a hell of a lot easier to gather, for example, when they didn't have to ride clear across a half-million acres to find their cattle! Besides, the grass in those more easily managed pastures would be better. We built in rest-rotation programs tailored to the project; the needs of wintering mule deer were looked after, the antelope, the sage grouse on the meadows—they were all considered in the plan.

For five years we monitored progress. You know five years is not a very long time in that ten-inch rainfall area, but it was noticeable that we were making positive progress. We found something like forty new perennial plant species that were never there before. The litter and mulch on the ground increased, like, ten or fifteen times. Of course, before you can get plant reproduction, you gotta have habitat for the seedlings to survive, and that means litter on the ground to keep it cool and to keep the moisture in. Litter and mulch were the big things in getting the increase in new species.

We had an annual review where I reported to the hard-core environmentalists who were so interested in diverse habitat. I said, "You folks think a bunch of junipers over here, a bunch of mahogany over there, a bunch of sagebrush, and a meadow—that's diversity to you. I want to point out that this management program is creating diversity right out in the sagebrush, right *under* the junipers. All these new plants comin' in, many new forbs which interest wildlife, that's what real diversity is." The environmentalists were impressed, or, should have been.

We're all "environmentalists," or should be. I've worked with environmentalists all my life. Back in the thirties—dust-bowl days— everybody talked soil conservation. Then, a heck of a period when nobody paid attention; now we're back on a peak and everybody's talking environment again. When the National Environmental Policy Act (NEPA) was passed, it bothered me; I was just as traditional as anybody else, and old enough to have my traditions and my druthers when it come to what I wanted. Now, I've come to believe that act was

Bill Anderson explains a coordinated plan. —Soil Conservation Service

one of the best things that's happened, both to me and the ranching industry; it's made us realize that, whatever we do on the land, there's a second and third order of consequence down the line. Siltate a stream, you affect a fishery, and so forth down the line. Weed control—I've been skeptical of chemical herbicides ever since NEPA brought the consequences to mind.

A few years ago the halogeten weed made *Reader's Digest*; it was taking over the country—maybe a Russian plot. The government prepared to pour billions of dollars out to save our rangelands chemically. Now, all at once, the halogeten's gone. What happened? What happened was better management and Crested wheatgrass. There is no halogeten problem now. We let nature take over.

And there was goatweed: Oregon ranchers don't talk of goatweed anymore. How come? We've got a biological control on goatweed. Find a patch and there'll be beetles on it; come back in two or three years and it'll be gone! That's the ultimate answer for knapweed, too; until we get biological control, nothing's gonna beat it. There's not enough money available to go out and spray all the knapweed in just one county, but research is under way to find an insect that can live and reproduce in the environment. No more investment after that, just let nature take its course.

Back to coordinated planning: Over the years the message went out to a lot of people, and, by 1970, Oregon had 425 million acres under coordinated planning; the Oregon Fish & Wildlife Department has used coordinated plans on eleven wildlife management areas. There are so-called stewardship programs in Idaho and Montana firmly rooted in CP. It's met all situations—environment, fish, elk problems—we've had to keep adjusting all the time. What makes it work? It grew with real live people in the field. When I think of all the well-qualified professionals and ranchers who helped, it's no wonder it's successful. A hell of a tool for budgeting time and money! So doggone simple you don't even need a computer!

I spent almost forty years with SCS, and I still work with people in the field. I've loved the work, and I've loved the people I worked with. The only thing that ever bothered me was the bureaucracy; that damn bureaucracy used to get me! Do things by the book for no real reason; lots of times it'd have been better if I hadn't. And, I'll admit it, lots of times I didn't.

ALLAN SAVORY

was called from Africa to darkest North America as the prophet, first, of short-duration grazing and the Savory Grazing Method, later refined to Holistic Resource Management.

I first came to the United States with the very strong impression—gained through reading scientific journals—that everything was wonderful in America, that you were on top of the big environmental issues and had stopped desertification of the land. I wasn't prepared to find deterioration worse than anything I'd known in Africa.

I was born in Rhodesia [now Zimbabwe] in 1935. My father was a civil engineer with experience in agriculture and a great love for the bush; my family spent its holidays in the bush, and I was sent to boarding school on the Botswana border, a reasonably wild part of Africa, where—once you'd ridden two or three miles from the village—you found kudu, impala, leopard. They contributed to a normal, youthful passion for the bush, and I acquired an especially heavy dose.

Deterioration was everywhere in Africa, even as I was growing up. It was evident in the erosion and soil loss and dwindling wildlife populations of our national parks, reserves, and regular hunting areas. And those declining populations certainly weren't due to poaching; there were a pathetic few poachers armed with ancient, muzzle-loading weapons, spears, and that sort of thing. The problem was deeper.

The conventional wisdom was that domestic cattle were the cause of deteriorating rangelands, and nothing I learned at school or university countered that. Worldwide, environmentalists blamed the bulk of deterioration and the spread of deserts on overgrazing and overstocking, and, interested as I was in wildlife, I saw livestock as a tremendous evil; I longed for the day when every damn cow was gone.

At school I spent as much time as possible learning bush skills, such as tracking and survival. I went on to university at Natal, where I developed another passion: ecology. And ecology came naturally; I just listened and absorbed, although a lot of things I heard did not make sense. I got into heavy arguments with my professors over things like *animal* ecology because, ignorant as I was, I couldn't see how you could have an animal ecology when every animal in the world depends on plants. I found a total division in the plant and animal disciplines, which made me feel dissatisfied with my teachers.

After university I joined the Colonial Service and went up to Northern Rhodesia [now Zambia] as a game officer, and there, of course, my passion for the bush developed deeper; while others relied on Africans, I trained myself to track and read the bush and really observe the ground. I tried to put my scientific studies into practice and found that all my university training had left me totally unprepared for practical game management. My real education began *after* university: "self-directed learning," as we call it at our Center for Holistic Resource Management today.[2]

I worked for a year on tsetse fly control. The strategy was to kill the game and deny the tsetse fly a supply of blood then, once the fly was cleared, the idea was to move domestic livestock in. But, erosion and destruction were evident already! I had to conclude that you couldn't blame the cattle because no cattle had arrived, and you couldn't blame the game because they'd shot all the damn game. So, who the hell to blame?

I began to see our government policies at fault and said so. I recommended the culling of big game, which appeared to be overpopulating the parks, but that was not a popular thing for a government employee to say, and I came under considerable pressure to change my findings, which, of course, I wasn't prepared to do. And so, in 1963, I left the civil service and continued as a private consultant doing research as and when I could. That was the background.

Hoof Action: The Importance of Ungulates

As time went by, a light came on. I'd been watching game animals all my life; now I became increasingly aware of their importance to the land. You've seen pictures of those immense herds of hoofed animals—ungulates—stampeding across the African veldt pursued by lions or leopards, and, of course, those thousands of sharp hoofs shred plant material, hasten decay, break crusted ground, and sow the seeds of future crops, while dung and urine fertilize the soil. At first, I could only pick up the importance of herds and hoofs to the health of soils and grasses, as thousands of grazing animals move along. It was many years before I understood the importance of the predator—so obvious, now, in hind sight. The predator, of course, is behind the herding instinct. I tried to get the government to finance further research into this *herding-ungulate effect*; they ridiculed the idea, so I continued on my own.

168

Rhodesia, unlike Kenya and other African countries, was a completely independent nation where an untenable situation had developed: 220,000 whites were defying seven or eight million of their countrymen, who happened to be black, along with most of the outside world. I was in contact with all the central players on the political scene: Ian Smith, whom I strongly opposed; and Nkomo and Mugabe, whom I morally supported. I firmly believed in Mugabe's right to face elections, and I firmly believed that he would win a free election, which is what eventually transpired. My career as a consultant took me into five African countries during those years, but I was also in our part-time army and heavily involved in guerrilla warfare as a tracker—tracking people—and I began to train, and eventually to command, a tracker unit.

In 1967 or '68, I decided to go into politics, but Ian Smith had so usurped the powers of Parliament, and had seized such firm control of radio and television through secret censorship (it was an offense to even *indicate* that something had been censored), that straight forward opposition was impossible. Instead, I joined the ranks of Smith's Rhodesian Front and was elected, and then, one day in 1971 or '72, I "crossed the floor" of Parliament and publicly disclosed my true feelings about the prime minister's incompetence, which obviously caused a lot of anger—you have enough anger in a civil war, you know, without doing that sort of thing. I became the leader of the moderate whites—all those in opposition to Ian Smith—but, always, I declared my intent to simply bring about a just end to the war, to bring all parties to a constitutional conference, and to rely on proper democratic elections. My situation, however, was precarious. As things became more desperate for the government, it resorted more and more to terrorism and I knew I'd soon wind up in prison— perhaps just disappear, like many of my friends.

I had been a private pilot for many years, and I kept my little single-engined Comanche fueled and ready to go at a moment's notice. As an officer in the army, I had a pass giving me free access to the airfield and, fortunately, no one thought to call it in, so I was ready late one night when I was informed I would be arrested in the morning; I simply climbed into my plane and "flew the coop," as the saying goes.

After the war, President Mugabe did some incredibly courageous and pragmatic things, which probably headed off a really frightful blood bath, and which I think the western world has overlooked. For instance, he appointed Ian Smith's commander, General Walls, to

169

command his army. When was the last time you heard of a political leader winning a civil war, then putting the losing general in command? Mugabe has my admiration, in spite of his mistakes. I left behind my family in Zimbabwe, and they survived in safety. I myself have been perfectly welcome to return since Ian Smith's defeat; I do so, often. And I still fly my Comanche when in Africa.

Time: The Second Factor

Before I made the breakthrough in my professional thinking, which brought me to the true importance of hoofed animals to the veldt, my attitude was that of any "Earth First!er" anywhere: I hated cattle. I *knew* that cattle were guilty of overgrazing and destroying the land, and, yet, I had to admit in certain cases ungulates were not the guilty party; under certain kinds of management, they were even beneficial—hard to understand, that! And soon I began to realize that *time* was implicated in the problem and a key to the solution—very fuzzy, at first; I couldn't see it clearly.

And then I heard about John Acocks in South Africa, who made the profound assertion that rangeland could be "overgrazed but understocked." He was experimenting with nonselective grazing, that is, forcing domestic livestock to graze all vegetation. I was excited. Visiting his project, I saw the same effect I'd been observing under herds of free-roaming wildlife, and I said, "All right, this *managed* herd effect deserves research."

And so, it was at that time—long before coming to America—that I asked some rancher-clients to concentrate their livestock; we'd find out just what high-intensive grazing did to land. At the same time, I became aware of Andre Voisin's work, which shows that time-of-exposure of plant to animal is a key to understanding overgrazing.[3] I said, "All right, let's incorporate my insight with what Acocks is doing with what Voisin has discovered." We coined the expression *high-intensity, short-duration grazing*, with grazing periods short enough so that no plant is bitten twice before recovery. By 1965 I realized that high-intensity grazing stresses cattle and has too many side effects, so I shortened the name to "*short-duration* grazing."

The wheel-shaped "grazing cell" that has been so closely associated with my name was another thing I came up with back in Zimbabwe, where frequent dipping through a plunge-vat was required. A wheel-like format with paddocks radiating around a "hub" containing water, feed-storage facilities, and cattle-treating equipment made livestock handling easy. When we came to America, we'd been using radial—so-called Savory—cells for thirteen years or more, but they were never designed for concentrating livestock; we already knew that was dangerous.

The Call

In 1978, Dr. M. E. Ensminger invited me to lecture on short-duration grazing at his famous International Stockmen's School, to be held that year in Phoenix.[4] I accepted the invitation and arrived equipped with slides and a report on our very dramatic African research. Only a few people attended my first session, but one rancher, who got the message, went out and gathered up his friends and packed the room.

By the end of the week, they were asking me to come, immediately, to their ranches to help them. I said, "No, I won't do that; I could be the biggest charlatan you ever met, faking slides and everything. I don't want to get involved, unless you really *believe* and have faith in what I say." I knew how much criticism there would be.

I said, "Why don't you pick one very cynical member of your group, and send him over to Africa. I'll take him 'round; I'll introduce him to my critics; he'll be able to make up his own mind that way. And, if such a cynical person recommends my help, I'll come. And they did so, and that person returned impressed with what he saw. And they called me, and I came to America.

Well, once I began working in America, I found this very big gap between the literature and the land. For instance, much is said about the loss of soil from croplands, but I find very few references to "desertification." Now, the term desertification is unfortunate because it implies camels and so on; I don't know who coined it, but it's come to be accepted, and it really just means the deterioration of the ecological system—the mineral and water cycles and the flow of solar energy that drives all biological succession. It means the deterioration of agriculture in our "brittle" environments.

Brittle Environments

The concept of *brittleness* was the third discovery (following *herd effect* and *time*) that has enabled us to solve the problems of deteriorating range and spreading deserts. For many years some environments have been considered fragile—some dry, some wet, and so on— but *fragile*. We were missing the point: *all* environments are fragile, I know of none that aren't. We now identify what we call "brittle"

171

areas (as much as two-thirds of the land surface of the earth) where natural decay of plant material takes place *slowly*, through chemical oxidation and weathering. In brittle areas, the physical action of ungulates speeds thing up.

Nonbrittle rangelands, with their fast biological decay, have no need for physical action; they become complex and productive soon enough. Your Montana and Alberta rangelands, though, are brittle. In the absence of herds of ungulates under pressure, those brittle rangelands—subjected, as they've been, to concomitant *understocking* and *overgrazing*—tend to become less productive, simpler in complexity, more vulnerable to boom-and-bust as dry years become droughts, rainfalls become floods, and small populations of weeds and insects become serious infestations. I'm sorry to find vast areas of Montana invaded by leafy spurge and knapweed. Millions of dollars are spent on eradication, yet those weeds are just symptomatic of degradation in a very brittle environment.

And there are other serious problems on northern rangelands; it's quite shocking to find otherwise very nice, decent farmers who actually think their erosion rates are normal. In Zimbabwe we'd remove such ignorant managers from the land—just take 'em off, even from private land. We have that capability in Zimbabwe. Here, land abuse is all too often accepted.

Periodic disasters are expected. What with low animal-densities in overgrazed management systems lacking sufficient disturbance, plant spaces open up; lichen, club moss, and weeds take hold between the plants; productivity steadily declines. Deterioration of a brittle environment, anywhere in the world, is what we call "desertification."

Holism

With our insight into brittleness, my break through with the ungulate effect, and the discovery that time—not number of animals—governs overgrazing, I now had three keys to the desertification riddle. To those I added a concept that brought fuller understanding of the complexity and unity of nature. That concept is known as *holism*; it allows us to plan the end to desertification. The philosophy of holism was first pronounced in 1926 by the South African statesman and naturalist, Jan Smuts, and I had been using the word in planning for about fifteen years before it dawned on me that "holistic" was not the same as "integrated" or "interdisciplinary" planning. That was a revelation. Once we made that breakthrough, we were on our way toward mastering all terrestrial situations. Let me explain with a non-example first.

You may have read of holistic medicine, by which is meant the treatment of *whole people*. That's not "holistic" in our sense; we wouldn't agree that you can treat a patient in a vacuum, divorced from his environment. In true holistic medicine, a patient would bring his banker and his broker and his accountant, as well as his home and family, and perhaps his county agent, into the doctor's office; all are important to his overall health. Similarly, we can't manage land, alone, holisticly; we must consider the people of the land along with cultures, values, economics, and everything else involved in "quality of life."

The essence is that the world is made of greater and lesser "wholes," and you have to treat with wholes in the environment. The *minimum whole* involves a unit of land—be it farm or forest or park; it's people—be they clan or family, or tribe, who share a common interest; and it's financial resources available to those people. For holistic management, then, we've identified three components: the land, the people, and the financial resources.

Resource Management

Worldwide, resource management is, and always has been, reactionary, *crisis* management: the only kind of management mankind has ever known. From our Center for Holistic Resource Management, in Albuquerque, we teach *proactive* management: we set desired goals, we consider available tools, and we test before we make decisions. As we proceed, we monitor and control; we test the air, like old-time miners carrying canaries: when a bird drops off the perch, get the hell out of the mine—an early warning system.

Over many years, we've adapted a very ingenious planning method with biologic goals: we plan holisticly, test our tools, and monitor results; we stay in full control as we go along. And it's a very, very simple method—nothing a fifteen-year-old can't understand—very, very flexible, and it works! In fact, the only way we know for it to fail, once a student understands it, is to ignore it—not to practice it at all.

The problem is, we usually talk to people over twenty, or to people who have agricultural degrees or backgrounds, and it's terribly hard for them to switch to our *proactive* form of management, with three-part goals and putting off decisions until the tools are tested. That's very, very tough, and so we offer recurrent training and support. Those who attend just a single course don't make it; serious students return for regular, supplementary training and succeed. If these major resource problems could be mastered in a single week, they wouldn't have plagued mankind since the dawn of time.

On The 3C Bar

In 1952 when I went to the 3C Bar Ranch, I was twenty-six years old: too old for proactive management, just right for crisis management—which was good, because one crisis followed another.

In those days the northern part of the Blackfeet Reservation was a beautiful sea of grass: miles and miles of fescue-covered ridges cleared of snow by chinook winds, underused, decaying. The buffalo and the wolf had been gone for seventy-five years; bands of sheep came through each summer, heading for the mountains, but they didn't use much bunchgrass. It was said no range-wise Indian ever left the sheltered valleys of Two Medicine or Badger to winter horses on the wind-swept Milk. The few hardy ranchers who lived there mostly overgrazed the coulees in the summer, and fed hay on low-lying feed grounds in the winter. Yes, that upland grass was underused, like money in the bank: falling behind inflation, but better than being broke!

One neighbor with range savvy advanced my education on the principles of multi-species grazing. As I rode out across the ranch one morning, I surprised a band of woolies—two thousand head (the 3C Bar didn't own a single ewe). As I approached, they scurried under a fence—the bottom wire had been raised—while their herder calmly watched the operation from his wagon on a hill; he knew what he was doing. I rode on up the valley to visit with the neighbors, Levi and Daisy Bird, and their grandson, Dick Cassutt, the sheepman.

Dick looked at me with a twinkle in his eye and, with disarming courtliness, he said, "Deepest apologies, Good Neighbor; we sometimes eat the neighbor's beef around here, but we never steal his grass. It's our danged old sheepherder, Johnny C.," Dick laughed. "Old John's a talented thief—spent his life in jail. We try to keep him from temptation, but he just ain't happy unless he's stealing somethin'."

"Well, damn the neighbors, anyway!" I thought, but Cassutt became a lifetime friend and, in fact, stole very little grass, for, among those tough old fescue crowns, his sheep sniffed out the tender shrubs and forbs—their "ice cream" plants. And, as Dick's larcenous herder and his dogs moved the band along, I'm sure hoof action did the 3C Bar a favor.

Real desertification hit that range in the 1960s, after farmers were encouraged to plow it up. Fly over it today and you'll see miles and miles of cropland, and, when the wind blows, clouds and clouds of dirt. A plague hit the Montana range, a plague of plowshares. That's what desertification means to me.

My professor of range planning at Range U. was a wizened old lawman, A. R. "Porky" Sellars. "Since Prohibition days, along this border, I've sent two hundred men to the pen, all by myself," he said. He didn't teach group action.

Porky had ridden for the Winder Ranche near Fort Macleod, Alberta, back in 1904. He soon moved to Montana where he talked so much about the Porcupine Hills that they hung a nickname on him and it stuck. He cowboyed for several years, then had some exciting times working for the border patrol; later, when I knew him in the fifties, he was working as a stock detective for the Blackfeet tribe, the stockmen's association, and the county. Now, that took coordinate planning.

He packed a .45 revolver under his belt, where the barrel must have dug him in the groin—that was the way he looked; I never saw him laugh. He rode the grub line. He kept six horses stashed around the range, and he'd show up unexpected at a ranch, stay a day or two, then turn out Roanie, catch up Froggy, and be gone—where, no one knew. I rode a lot of miles with Porky, soaking up his stories—not believing many.

One cold January afternoon we rode into Fred Stone's yard on the middle fork of Milk River, and accepted an invitation to "pull your saddles off, and stay all night." The minute the sun went down, old Porky pulled the window shades without leave from Mrs. Stone (two hundred convicts would have relatives, you know). Then, backs to the wall, we sat, spinning yarns until we turned in on the sofa-bed. I was careful not to twitch during the night. That .45 under Porky's pillow was ready to come up firing—and to hell with Mrs. Stone's nice wallpaper and pictures!

"You won't last long," said Porky, "unless you plan ahead!" He taught proactive management and coordinated planning.

175

Give the people ideas, they'll put 'em to work.
—James Tompkins

7

Range Know-how

Around any ranch the landmarks and the pastures all have names. On our Porcupine Hills ranch, say, "Drop some salt on Shirt-tail Butte," or "Push those cows off Bee-sting Hill," or "Those bloody elk have wrecked the gate on Windy Pass," and everybody knows whose tail was out, and who got stung, and where to fix the fence. The Eatout Field? I'll tell you how the Eatout *got its name.*

Years ago the grass grew thick on Shirt-tail Butte. Beneath it, on the flats by Dead-horse Spring, grass grew so tall that Noah Sitton, the owner at the time, could put up prairie hay. That was during the war, when men were scarce, and young Butch McLeod, his neighbor, helped him. "Old Sitton gave me a team and rake," Butch said, "and had me rake in spirals, dumping curls of fresh-mowed, knee-deep prairie wool—finest thing in the world for wintering calves! The old man called it 'war hay' and left those curls out in the field all winter—just turned the weaned calves in to feed themselves and bed down on the leavings. No worry about elk eating it, them days—there was no elk in the Porcupines, them days."

Well, Noah Sitton died, and the next owner used that pasture hard. For the following twenty growing seasons, his cattle "ate it out," every May, June, and July. It never got a rest. Soon, thistles grew on top of Shirt-tail Butte, and there wasn't "wool" enough on War-hay Flat to keep a tick alive. Half-starved cows and calves came off that range in startlingly poor condition.

In 1965 the land changed hands again, and somebody gave the Eatout Field its name. We call it that today; it reminds us of the wages of poor management. But unplowed rangeland—badly overgrazed though it may be—is a renewable resource. Rest it spring and summer for a while, and—amazing! It comes back. The remnants of tough old plants survive. Now, Shirt-tail Butte grows fescue, once again, as winter feed for cows and calves, and elk. Now, it's hunters *that wreck the gate at Windy Pass.*

At *Squaw Butte* near Boise
JIM LITTLE
manages range for future generations.

To be a survivor in this day and age, you'd better take care of the land, and you'd better take care of it *first*. And you'd better improve it and harvest your grass in an economical fashion. You're the caretaker for future generations.

The Great Depression broke my grandad. He had become the world's largest sheepman; when he died, he died sheep-poor—he left his business completely riddled with debt. From the ruins, his children built an outfit called the Highland Livestock and Land Company. See what I mean? They put the livestock first. "The livestock always come first," my uncle said.

Dad didn't agree with that; he understood that properly managed land is one true source of wealth. He worked hard to get his unit out of debt, and in 1967, when I came home from college to help him run the outfit, we were among the first to adopt rest-rotation grazing; we even got the jump on the BLM.

Dad went on a field trip and heard the guy who dreamed up rest-rotation explain his theory: use one-third of your range in the spring; stay off one-third until fall; don't use one-third at all. Two-thirds, then, can produce that vital seed crop every year. It sounded like common sense to Dad; he came right home and built some fence to get our first rotations going. And—whaddaya know—it worked!

Rest-rotation really proved its worth after the huge range fire that burnt over most of our permit land in 1986 and left our wooden fence posts in ashes—we've put 'em back in steel. After that fire the environmental groups came up with something called the Squaw Butte Rehabilitation Project; they gave "informed" opinions, made strong statements, and clearly showed they didn't know what they were talking about. They said, "We'll have to keep the cattle off that burnt-out Squaw Butte range for at least two years."

They finally let me sit on a committee. That was nice! I was the permittee. I said, "No way I'm stayin' off that range."

So, they brought in a range consultant who carefully studied the situation and reported, "Look! There's seedlings coming on this burn already! Whatever the permittee's been doing, don't argue with success; don't cut him back at all. Just keep that system going."

The point is, those folks had that famous mind set: When anything goes wrong, get the cattle off the range. But they were right to call a very prominent rangeman—the consultant's name was August L. Hormay.

On *Hound Creek,* northeast of Helena
CHASE HIBBARD
uses rest-rotation grazing.

My great-grandfather, Henry Sieben, worried about the range 100 years ago and later bought the ranch his cattle found near the Hole-in-the-wall. My brothers and I still own that ranch today. One day, in the late seventies, I was invited to a demonstration of rest-rotation grazing, and I was thoroughly impressed with what I heard and saw. I scratched my head and thought, maybe this is what we're looking for; maybe this could help preserve good range and heal old scars. That was the day I first met Gus Hormay.

Henry Sieben ran sheep on this ranch for many years. He didn't really like 'em, but that's where the money was; at one point he had ten or twelve bands, roughly a thousand to a band. The ranch was almost exclusively in sheep until good lambing help got scarce in the 1960s; that's when the ranch switched over to cattle.

Now, our range has a rich variety of grasses, but it's primarily Rough fescue country, and—odd as it may seem, considering our success—sheep don't really like Rough fescue. They use it last. As a result, we had fabulous old fescue stands, *underused* and stale; range like that is not very productive. I believe cattle and sheep complement each other on this range; they prefer different plants. Sheep like short, tender grasses and forbs; cattle can use coarser stuff. And, in this mountainous country, you've got to fight cows out of the creeks to get 'em on the ridge tops, and you've got to fight the sheep to get 'em off the ridges. You can see how two species might be more than twice as good as one, as I believe they are. When I took over in 1976, I went back to sheep; in 1987 we sheared 1,300 or 1,400 head.

There's another problem caused by following continuous grazing patterns year after year. We have to get the cattle off our hay meadows early so the hay can grow; so, we take 'em to the mountains. Then we have to pull 'em out of the mountains to wean and ship the calves early in the fall, even though there's plenty of grazing left up in the high country. That's been going on for years. It leads to overgrazing certain areas and underusing others; neither is good management. That's some background: when I met Hormay, I was sensitive to range deterioration and looking for a better way to handle it.

When I saw what Gus was doing, I asked if he would visit me at Hound Creek. He wasn't interested at first, but after a while he decided he'd come. He made himself familiar with the lay of the land

and with our strengths and weaknesses, and he helped design a classic rest-rotation program that went into place on our forest allotment in 1981.

By arranging things so every pasture gets two out of three full growing seasons of rest, we've been able to increase cattle numbers; heavier stocking removes the stale old fescue. I'll admit that when we leave a pasture after a full and heavy season it looks tough—especially the lower range near the water. We know, though, that it's going to have two full growing seasons of rest; it'll be in great shape before it's used again. And we're seeing lots of new growth: little Idaho fescue shoots, new Bluebunch wheatgrass plants coming in on old bare sites.

After our first experience with rest-rotation grazing, we liked it so much we put in a second system on our deeded land; we'll be using it on all our summer-grazing areas eventually. Rest-rotation grazing is simple—almost fool-proof. Design a plan to fit your ranch; then, when the time is right, just open the gates and turn the cattle in. That's it—not much capital required. Old Henry Sieben would have liked it.

Allan Savory's Holistic Resource Management (HRM) is more sophisticated and philosophical. I attended HRM school in Great Falls a couple of years ago, and the quality of instruction was impressive; I'm sure HRM can give you maximum performance if you thoroughly understand it, but—like a highly tuned Ferrari in the hands of a twelve-year-old—it has the potential for a major wreck if anything goes wrong.

At *Shipwheel Grasslands*, 200 miles to the north of Hound Creek
BLAKE and MARY HOLTMAN
manage the range holistically.

BLAKE: Grandad used a "ship's wheel" for a brand, like the one that steered his immigrant ship from Sweden in the early 1900s.

My brother Jerry and his family are on our grandfather's original homestead now, at Taber, on the prairie between Medicine Hat and Lethbridge. A few miles north, Mary and I grow grass and cattle and run a custom feedlot, and we also own some rangeland in the foothills. Mary and I met at college down in Oregon. She was trained as a teacher, but when she came to the ranch she hired-on immediately as a rider, riding pens and working cattle.

MARY: It seems this family has always been intrigued with new ideas—Blake and Jerry always attending seminars and courses. Blake was at the International Stockmen's School at Phoenix when Savory first lectured in America. Blake came home so excited about this person from Rhodesia that he talked for months about the Savory concept for managing grassland, something he had never heard of before. The rest of us were saying, "Right! Sounds good! So what?"

But next year I was persuaded to go to San Antonio and hear Savory for myself, and after that I knew what Blake was saying. It really was interesting! We talked to Allan privately, and right away we said, "Let's go for it!"

But Savory said, "Hold on! Don't go off half-cocked! I'll be starting my own school soon, and you must come; in the meantime, you must read and prepare."

He and his partner, Stan Parsons, were promoting their handbook for planning and managing land with short-duration grazing, a term they'd coined in Africa years before.[1] It seemed to us, quite simply, that they were recommending extremely high stocking rates, although for very short periods of time. Time was controlled very carefully to let each plant recover between "bites."

In order to control the grazing properly, they described a wagon-wheel pattern of paddocks requiring lots of fence and recommended innovative fence-building techniques requiring much less capital per mile than traditional methods. They sparked a whole new industry as new materials appeared upon the scene, many imported from New Zealand: high-tensile wire, stays, posts, and solar-electric chargers.

And, right from the start, Savory and Parsons preached sophisticated planning: do all the studies, identify weak links, get everybody in your organization involved; they were talking *holism*, even then. The term was new to us, but it meant simultaneously planning every aspect of a business; it meant giving full consideration to financing, marketing, and everything in between, as well as grazing management. We didn't do all that! We just jumped in and started building fence. That's the way we are—not very conservative. At first, we did just about everything wrong: built elaborate paddocks before we'd really studied the land; never got our entire crew involved; and incurred a lot of debt in the process.

BLAKE: I was among the handful of people who listened to Allan Savory back in 1978. Mary came with me in 1979, and later that year we bought some overgrazed rangeland in the Porcupine Hills with prices near their all-time high. We had to make it work.

182

By 1981 we were practicing what I thought was SGM (Savory grazing method): building fence, double-stocking, triple-stocking—expecting miracles. I put up everything and went for it. At first, we ran it as a system. Now, looking back, I realize goals and planning must come first, but we weren't all that holistic back in 1981: we didn't plan, we didn't monitor. Then came the drought of 1983-85. Before we knew it we were digging into savings—I mean, organic soil-bank savings—to survive.

But, HRM is new: a continual learning process, continually changing year after year after year. Ten years ago, in 1980, Allan seemed quite an angry man; what he believed, he believed passionately, and it made him angry when others missed the point. Just five years ago, Allan seemed a pretty frustrated man; he knew his weak link was people, but he didn't know, yet, what to do about it. Finally, he hired a fellow named Don Green whose *expertise* was people, team building his specialty; he helped us see that team work is more important than all the fences in the world. We made all the mistakes, you see, but we didn't quit; we still go back and take more training every year.

MARY: Nowdays, we contemplate and plan holistically before we ever sink a fence post in the ground. We look at all the options, set our goals, choose our tools, and monitor results; and it's become a family, if not a community, project. As Allan says, no one person—now, or ever—manages a resource alone. Not ever, anywhere. And so, Blake and I work together and encourage our family and employees and everybody else to help define the goals and visualize the way we want the land to look as production goes ahead. HRM teaches a three-part goal: first, *quality of life*; then, *landscape*; then, *production.*

• Quality of life: That's new, I think, but usually easy to agree on. We want an outdoor life; we want to give something back to the earth after taking so much out; and we want our families to be involved, as much as they wish.

• Landscape: One thing we visualize here is a scene in which the spring of ecological succession has risen to its highest point. Our land is sandy, and we'd like succession to move toward a more complex environment, as complex as possible with bushes and shrubs and grass. We'd like to see that happen, and we'd like to help it happen, but we don't force it to happen by planting in rows or using specific crops.

We visualize clean water. We have clean water now, and want to keep it. A couple of years ago an oil company planned a waste-disposal site a quarter-mile from our main water supply, at a higher elevation, on straight sand; we went "bananas" until they reconsidered. And, every member of the family loves trees; we'd like to grow more trees. We can get as specific about the landscape as we want.

• <u>Production</u>: Basically, we harvest sunlight; the only consideration is how we're going to do it. We have to decide whether to harvest the sunlight through straight farming, or through grass and livestock, or perhaps even through processing manure for the market. But, whatever our production goal, we definitely consider profit; it's imperative to turn a profit in our business!

Well, Blake and I hammer these things out from time to time, and, as much as we can, we involve our entire staff. Some of our people have been through various HRM courses; others are allergic to school of any kind. That's just the kind of business we're in. But the toughest part—and potentially most exciting—is working with other ranchers in the area. A proposed housing development in our community? We see ourselves working with the county, the developers, and our neighbors, adopting three-part goals. It's possible; there are places where it's happened.

In addition, there are tools. There are only a few tools, in general terms, available to mankind, and [reading from an HRM checklist] they are: Rest, Fire, Grazing (animal impact), Living Organisms, Technology, Money, Labor, and Human Creativity. That's it! No others anywhere on earth. Technology is the biggest; Living Organisms is the most important to succession—it includes insects and soil micro-organisms. We pick the tools that fit the goals for our operation. Want to plant grass? We use Technology. If we do grass, nowadays, it'll probably be a "timing" thing with animals; we'll broadcast seeds and let hoof-action put them in the ground. In practice, we test each option to find the one that best suits our goals.

And it's important to monitor results. Many farmers never fully realize what's taking place. We're learning to monitor trends in species, ground cover, quantity of forage. Well, let's be honest, here at Shipwheel we still don't monitor enough. We talk about it and mean to get it done, but we often put it off until we panic. And panic comes when we remember the awful mistakes we made when we beefed up management without first beefing up our knowledge. Make mistakes holistically and you do more damage than just through old-style bumbling.

BLAKE: I hope by now we've learned to manage for the whole, with our sights on the horizon. Our foothills range, unused or underused, runs heavy to Rough fescue; our prairie land is ideal for Crested wheatgrass. But a monoculture, of any kind, is inconsistent with our three-part goal; we'd like to build a real complex ecosystem, more stable than any monoculture.

Where we find solid Crested wheat, we can find ways to diversify— perhaps move cattle from a paddock where desirable grasses have recently gone to seed; let them carry the seeds in their rumens and plant them with their feet. But, of course, that might take two, or five, or ten years to accomplish, and we aren't used to waiting that long for change.

The first change has to come within ourselves, and sometimes that's the hardest part. For example, several years ago we had a beautiful piece of irrigated pasture: alfalfa, orchard grass, and wheatgrass—beautiful catch. We didn't put enough cattle on; we overgrazed but understocked, and kochia weed took over, choking out the grass.[2] So, what to do?

In the old days, I would have ripped it up and carefully reseeded, using lots of petro-dollars in the form of fuel and heavy iron in the process; that's still my first instinct today. But, instead, we had a meeting. We decided: one, we certainly needed a profit; and, two, we'd encourage natural succession and cut the petro-dollars. With those two goals in mind, we chose animal impact, Grazing, as our primary tool.

Using some Technology, we partitioned off the kochia into ten-acre paddocks, crowded 800 yearlings in a paddock—almost like a feedyard—time-controlled their movements, moving every day during the growing season, allowing plenty of time for forage regrowth. And, look here! In places grass is coming back already and crowding out the kochia. And all of it is making seed. This is the most extreme thing we've done so far, and it's following the model like a dream.

Managing land is rarely a simple question of doing right or wrong; it's more the process of picking a destination, and moving in that direction. You can do that with Savory's method; HRM is a continual learning thing—continually changing, like the sky or sea. So we run a check on progress. Off track a bit? Just spin the wheel and bring the ship on course, as Savory—and Grandfather—would have done.

185

Not far away at *Never-Idle Farm*
IKE LANIER
repairs some damage done in earlier years.

We're farmers and proud of it. Diana and I and our son Rod
continue to farm the prairie south of Lethbridge because of economics. Dryland pasture simply can't produce a satisfactory return on the
dollar value of our land today in competition with ranchers who
have—or should have—a smaller per-unit capital base. And, in
grazing livestock, there's just no way to control per-unit input; that
makes it hard to keep a handle on production.

Legume hay is good for the soil, but it doesn't make economic sense
to me, either. In this semi-arid country, dryland alfalfa does not
usually produce enough to pay for seed, but it sure as hell does use up
all the moisture. It's true that alfalfa fixes nitrogen in the soil, but it's
very high-cost nitrogen; we now know a well-fertilized wheat plant
will return as many nutrients as alfalfa. And, I'm not a real fan of
irrigation; we've got the water to irrigate about 300 acres, but, even
with modern pivots, I think the return would be too low to justify
investment in labor and equipment. No, what we understand is
farming—dryland farming.

We grow cereal and oilseed crops, as my dad did before us, but we
do it in a way that satisfies our personal environmental standards—
we hope to go on living on this planet and this farm for many years
to come. We use a technique called *no-till*, or *zero-tillage*.[3] Unlike
conventional farming, it eliminates all plowing and maintains the
supply of nutrients from which we produce our crops; it also leaves old
root channels in place to carry water. It sounds very simple now, but
it took a long time to understand that we were living off the organic
matter built up in the native range over millions of years. For the past
sixty or seventy years we've been saving low-value trash and spend-
ing high-value residues while using more and more expensive chemicals. That's a no-win situation, and a little of the history may be
interesting.

My dad came north with a group of young Kentuckians in 1909.
He'd grown up with farming, but Kentucky had long been settled, and
its opportunities didn't seem attractive. The experiences of southern
Alberta homesteaders sounded pretty exciting. Land developers
advertised forty-bushel yields of winter wheat and twenty-five of
flax; that was enough to start a sort of gold rush. A prime consideration in selecting a place to farm was a short haul for your grain. Dad
had heard harrowing stories about hauling twenty or thirty miles

with a team and wagon in the dead of winter, so he located close to the elevators here at Wilson Siding. And he chose land that was well drained yet not too hilly—we appreciate his good judgment today. But conditions on the prairies were very different from those the newcomers were used to. My mother, who came up in 1917, found nothing higher than a fencepost between here and Medicine Hat—all the trees were in the river bottoms and invisible. Coming from a land where every growing thing has a bloom on it, that must have been a psychological shock.

When Dad arrived, it was already standard practice here to let half your land lie fallow. Summer fallowing is a very old scheme, of course; the idea is to preserve moisture—two year's moisture for one year's crop, as the saying goes—and to give the soil a rest. To make it work, it's necessary to control the annual weeds that rush in to fill the void, and, farming with horses and without chemical herbicides made that a difficult task. But, Dad and his neighbors worked hard at learning to farm in this semi-arid environment. Their greatest concern was preservation of moisture; they could see it was critical to cut evaporation on the fallow land, so they tried the famous dust-mulch technique. Dad actually took a widely popular correspondence course which taught that after a rain you went out and harrowed and packed and pulverized the topsoil, thereby sealing in the moisture.

Well, Dad was hailed out twice in his first ten years—totally hailed out with no insurance, of course—but, the freedom of life in the West was mighty appealing, and the crops, when they were good, were good enough to encourage him to stay. But the high prices and good moisture around the First World War were followed by bad years in the late teens and early twenties. Then, even though the sod had been recently broken and organic content was still quite high, when the wind blew, the pulverized prairie topsoil began to move.

I think the major topsoil losses in our area occurred in about fifteen or twenty years of misguided farming practices. The first reaction was, rather than to harrow the soil to dust, to find a way to keep the trash—the stubble and straw—on top. That wasn't easy. Rod weeders were designed to do the job—simple machines with shanks supporting a square rod that rotated at a shallow depth under loose soil. The rods cut off the weeds and left the trash on top, but you could only travel at about one mile an hour because you had to have three or four men walking behind with pitch forks to help the straw flow through, between the shanks.

Soon, C.S. Noble, of Nobleford, Alberta, brought out an improvement—a long flat blade that floated along just below the surface, severing the roots; the Noble Blade would not plug up with trash and has become popular worldwide. But—whether you left dust or trash on top—eventually, good farming practice dictated that you turn all residue under, leaving your topsoil "clean"—and unprotected.

I think we have to reconsider the whole concept of summer fallow. A lot of the damage has been done by the idea that the stubble is the valuable part of the residue, and that you have to turn it under. In fact, recent studies show that ninety-eight percent of the total residual nutrient value is in the root material—already under the ground. The stubble is just carbon, a valuable source of energy if left on top to crumble. In tilling that stubble under, you bring up valuable nutrients that oxidize and disappear into thin air.[4]

And, soil scientists have found that no matter what we do to cut evaporation our fallow land retains only about one-third of the total moisture it receives. Water drains away laterally along the first impermeable layer until it eventually surfaces, bringing up alkali with it. Much of the saline problem in this part of the world could be alleviated if the water that falls on summer fallow were used to grow a crop instead of absorbing salts and draining away. We could remove the cause rather than treating the problem.

The people at Lethbridge Research Station have started saying these things—but only relatively recently, and with a lot of caution. If they say "don't turn your stubble under," many farmers may take the easy way out and *burn*; soil scientists are very careful about saying anything that would lead to burning. Stubble does have value; it just has less relative value than the really good stuff underneath. You lose them both when you burn and cultivate.

Most of my good neighbors are not equipped for zero-tillage, and most good conventional farmers don't really believe they *can* crop continuously—the land must have a rest. That mind-set has evolved into tradition—a neatly fallowed field with all the trash turned under is the mark of a good farmer. It may also be a matter of convenience; fallowing half your acres is the easy way to farm—easier than continuous cropping. You have a whole year to prepare your land for seeding; then, in spring, one operation and you're done. The rest of the year you can cultivate your fallow land, and, for a few people— truth be told—a modern air-conditioned tractor cab is the best place on the farm to spend the summer.

The belief that you must cultivate to prepare for another crop is a fallacy. In fact, you have a perfect seedbed waiting; nothing you do will improve upon it. What you need is a furrow-opener with enough rigidity to prepare a nice firm furrow for your seed. We sold all our

A heavy hoe-drill replaces other tillage equipment on the Lanier farm.
—Ric Swihart, Lethbridge Herald

tillage equipment in 1983, and replaced it with a heavy hoe-type seed drill.

We've been zero-tilling all our land for six years now, and they have been terribly dry years—drier, really, than the thirties. With the drought, crops have been minimal, but we get seventy-five to eighty percent of what's grown on summer fallow, and that puts us way ahead of the game. The fallowers only produce on half their land, and they have many extra tillage operations. We put more money into chemicals, but we're gradually cutting back, and fertilizer requirements are decreasing. I know by the feel of the ground, and soil tests verify, that we have increased organic matter; it's like walking on a lawn—so soft and spongy. And we're under much less stress these days because the danger of soil blowing is almost nil.

We know of the limited market for so-called natural foods, grown without benefit of chemical herbicides, pesticides, or fertilizers, but we aren't attracted to it for at least two reasons: first, the premiums paid are far too low to make up for loss of production, and we want to stay in business; second, organic farming would continue to deplete our soil. "Natural" or "organic" farmers still need to plow the ground.

189

They may plow down a green manure crop, but plowing of any kind is a dirty word to me—it wastes the root material, which is critically important. It's possible to do more damage with tillage than with carefully chosen organic chemicals, which break down in the sunlight before they touch your food.

As for fertilizer, I'll never understand why people want food grown with animal manure. There's a contradiction there: much concern with purity, so pile on the manure. And you never know exactly what you're getting—too much N (nitrogen) or not enough P (phosphorus); whatever the source, all nutrients must be turned into the same chemical form before they can be utilized. Plants can't tell the difference between Cominco and cow manure. When I balance chemical fertilizer and herbicide with animal fertilizer and tillage, the benefits are all with zero-till.

The patented herbicide Roundup, which we use once a year in the fall, used to be expensive. Now, with patents running out, Roundup is our only major input that's dropping in price, and we're using lower rates than we ever thought possible.[5] And we handle our fertilizer carefully. We monitor the soil and put on just the right amount to get a twenty-five- or thirty-bushel crop with average rainfall. If we happen to get more rain, we'll mix another twenty pounds of N with our late-spring 2-4-D. That gives us a double-edged benefit—the fertilizer makes the weeds grow faster and therefore more susceptible to herbicide, so we can cut back on the herbicide. It's especially effective on winter wheat.

Winter wheat is my favorite crop; it's a wonderful management tool. It spreads machinery and labor costs over a longer period. It's harvested at a most favorable time of year. It's a great conservation crop, providing soil protection in the fall. And winter wheat is a crop that's not harvested or disturbed while ducks and geese are nesting. Ducks Unlimited has expressed an interest in funding research into new and better varieties, in order to increase the acreage seeded. There's lots of room for improvement, especially in Alberta, because Canadian varieties produce too much straw. It was bred that way with the thought that all the trash would be tilled into the soil—we can do without that today.

No-till is the only way I know to build a healthy soil and stay in business. Nowadays, we farm whole sections instead of strips—the logistics are much simpler. We grow four oil and cereal crops in rotation—it's just as easy to rotate big square fields as narrow strips. We make significant savings in fuel, equipment, and labor—at least 300 tractor-hours a year—by eliminating tillage. We have just two operations, spraying and seeding, and my son Rod and I can do them both quite easily, independent of outside help. The longer we zero-till, the more mellow our soil becomes. On the northern plains, I believe that zero-tillage is the sustainable course for agriculture.

At the *Antelope Creek Ranch*, near Brooks
SYLVESTER SMOLIAK
designs pastures for use by cattle and ducks.

I spent many years at Manyberries and the Lethbridge Research Station, and the highlight of my range career has been acceptance of my work by people—all kinds of projects, all kinds of people: ranchers and the general public. A lot of my work has been with Russian wild rye: such a successful grass, I think, because it provides early season grazing and can take the pressure off the native range. You're always pleased when people use your work. I remember, once, when Alex Johnston and I were traveling and saw a place with rows of grass going up and down, over the rolling hills. We stopped and found

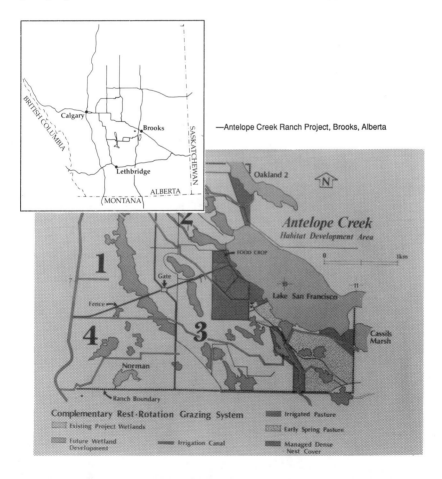

—Antelope Creek Ranch Project, Brooks, Alberta

Russian wild rye and alfalfa planted in alternate rows with three-foot spacings. Unbelievable!

We asked the rancher—never saw him before—"Where'd you get the idea to seed in alternate rows?"

"From you," he said.

"From me?"

"Yeah. I was there at the Manyberries Field Day about two years ago, and you told us how to seed grass. I came right home and tried it on this old farmland of mine, just like you said. It's doing great!"

I was very satisfied with that. A lot of times you think nobody pays attention; nobody will go to all that trouble. That fellow did!

It's tough to make a living on a ranch. It takes good management, and some studies indicate a twenty-five percent increase in production where native range is rested until the third week of June; that's a management decision. But, if you're going to stay off native range, you've got to have an alternate source of forage; you can't hang up your cows. A field of Russian wild rye makes ideal early grazing.

But grazing is just one use for rangeland. I take great pride in my work with Ducks Unlimited. In 1983, Alberta Fish & Wildlife Division and Canadian Bucks for Wildlife Foundation bought a beautiful ranch on Antelope Creek in the Eastern Irrigation District (EID), near Brooks. The EID covers 600,000 acres of farm and pasture land; it's a wildlife habitat famous the world over.

Goose nest on Antelope Creek habitat development. —Antelope Creek Ranch Project

Ducks Unlimited (DU) wanted to use some native range at Antelope Creek, but the EID was reluctant to go along, assuming a conflict of interest with grazing. The DU people knew that cattle and wildlife can often be compatible, so they came to me and asked for a grazing system that would please the farmers while enhancing habitat for ducks and other wildlife. I devised a rest-rotation system and convinced the EID that they would benefit as the DU people developed wetland sites. There'll be high-producing sedges growing on wetland sites, and cattle will graze those sedges and require less dry range; there will be more sloughs, and cattle won't have to travel so far to water.

Well, the EID went for it. By gosh, they're happy as the dickens with it now! Coupled with native range under rest-rotation is irrigated pasture and dryland Crested wheat. The irrigated land had been used for hay, but I suggested that Ducks Unlimited seed it down to pasture. That way, the cows start out on Crested wheat, the first thing to green up in the spring. The native range is split in four parts—some grazed, the rest protected—that's the rest-rotation part. Ducks and geese want cover for nesting—just sort of spotty cover—and with grazed but rested native range that's exactly what they get; rested pasture provides clumps of grass, perfect for building nests. During the nesting season the cows are moved to irrigated pasture. That's good for the cows, and it gives the ducks a chance to waddle around the prairie, undisturbed, nesting and hatching on dryland Crested wheat and the resting native range. See how it works for all the different interests?

I'm retired from the research station now, but I monitor the Ducks Unlimited program every chance I get. It's an ideal opportunity to practice what I've preached for thirty-five-plus years. Who should be so lucky?

On the old *Milk River* buffalo range
KEN MILLER
runs a modern livestock business.

Our farm is just north of the border, at the west end of the old Gilchrist Brothers' range. Before their time this was buffalo country, and we use those aboriginal animals on our farm today. Here's the story: One Saturday night, about 1977, my wife Mary and I were sitting in the bar in our little home town of Warner, Alberta, when somebody mentioned a newspaper article about Elk Island Park. It seems they wanted to get rid of some buffalo. We submitted a tender for twenty-five yearlings and won.

You always hear about sixty million buffalo on the plains when the white man came along. The last of the Canadian herd wintered right here on the north slopes of the Sweet Grass Hills and ranged farther north on the prairie in the summer. I doubt if individuals traveled more than a few hundred miles from winter to summer range, whether they were in Texas or the Midwest or here in the "shortgrass country." I suppose they split on natural barriers—rivers and that sort of thing. The young bulls would have traveled around looking for action, keeping the genetic pot stirred up; then they'd dominate a group for a year or two before they got kicked out. The old cows would have formed the local bands and become the wise old leaders, and don't forget those cows could still have calves at thirty years of age.

If I recollect properly, plains buffalo got down to less than a thousand head on the whole North American continent before the turn of the century. In 1908 the Canadian government had the foresight to acquire a few hundred survivors from a rancher in Montana and turn 'em loose on a buffalo reserve near Wainwright, a couple of hundred miles northeast of Calgary. They multiplied fruitfully until, after twenty years, they had overrun their range and were moved to Elk Island National Park, near Edmonton, or sent to join their cousins at Wood Buffalo National Park in the far northeastern corner of Alberta.

When we heard about the Elk Island buffalo sale, we were looking for something to scavenge excess roughage—the aftermath of our grass-seed harvest; we bought 'em and they've worked out fine, once we got set up for them. Our management plan is simple. In May—our early growing season—we calve out on a dry, sandy patch of native buffalo grass. The calving pasture's small; the buffalo pick it clean in just a couple of weeks, but they fertilize and trample in new seed. It's a bit severe; we sometimes call that pasture our "un-Savory" grazing cell.

For June, July, and August there's an irrigated breeding pasture of "tame" introduced varieties: Meadow brome, orchard grass, Troy bluegrass, and some legumes. That pasture has to last right through the summer while our seed crop's heading out and the native range is building up its roots. We turn-in on our seed fields after harvest in mid-August and let the buffalo graze the trash, along with unplowed native range in coulees, fence corners, and a forty-acre, mesh-fenced holding trap. Nutrition's good year-round, so we expect a ninety percent calf crop every year—occasionally, we get lucky and hit 100 percent.

Our buffalo started out as a bit of a hobby; but, by turning range and seed crop residues into high-priced specialty meat and hides, they've more than paid their way. We built herd size by keeping all our heifers and selling only excess three-year-old bulls, which provide a cash flow. We've been able to sell buffalo meat, by the side, at three dollars a pound. That means a three-year-old bull will gross between $1,800 and $2,000; in the 1980s that worked! It paid the bills.

Our buffalo are legally "domestic," but they aren't what you'd call tame; there's a real difference in their acceptance of man, and it's interesting to find two separate mentalities in our herd. We have a "socialist" variety—*Bison fabianis*—more inclined to hang around and make a nuisance of themselves until we feed 'em; and the "rugged individuals"—*B. smithii*—that'd rather go and hustle for themselves.

I think it's important to emphasize the role that private ownership has played in saving the buffalo. During the great annihilation of the 1800s the vast herds belonged to nobody; no individual or group or government took any responsibility for, or made any claim upon, a single animal. As public property, they almost vanished from the face of the earth. Then, a few private individuals like Michel Pablo and Charles Allard in Montana gathered up survivors, claimed ownership, took responsibility, and slowly built the herds we have today.

Herds are maintained in public parks on both sides of the border. Montana has its National Bison Range with a population of about 350 head; Yellowstone probably strained its carrying capacity with an estimated 2,500 in 1988; Banff and Waterton maintain demonstration herds of fifteen or twenty head, but the largest herds of plains buffalo in Canada are the 800 head, or so, at Elk Island and the few thousand up in Wood Buffalo National Park. It's been largely through private ownership—responsible management by individuals acting for enjoyment and/or profit—that buffalo have experienced such a tremendous increase in numbers over the past thirty or forty years. Far from being extinct, there are 100,000 buffalo in North America today.

Mary and I are primarily grass seed producers; the seed we grow revegetates The Range. We're rather proud of what we're doing. We didn't break the sod or exterminate the bison; rather, we're replacing what's been lost with something better and more efficient—at a profit!

Near the *Beartooth Game Range* in Montana's Big Belt Mountains
CHASE HIBBARD
copes with other native herbivores.

One of the big concerns on our ranch today is unmanaged public property, namely, elk. You go out to combine oats only to find elk camped in your field. The crop is ruined; you take the combine back to the shed after just a couple of rounds. Or, again, go out to cut a second growth of hay—looked good a week ago. Now, the alfalfa regrowth is gone, along with your brand new under-seeding of orchard grass, all grazed down to nothing by the elk. I'll admit that one of the enjoyable things about ranch life is the sound of elk bugling in the fall—so loud it's hard to sleep sometimes, but always a great thrill. I also know a certain amount of wildlife depredation goes with the turf as just part of owning land and ranching in Montana, but there's a point where all this gets mighty expensive.

In theory, a state-owned wintering ground should take the heat off private land and be a real asset to the country; we have such a place—the Beartooth Game Range—as our neighbor to the west. But, in its early stages, at least, it's been a disappointment. There are parts of it that elk rarely touch; they still descend on us for the winter.

Here's the problem: In setting up the game range, the state took over places that were irrigated and hayed years ago. They cut domestic grazing, and those native meadow grasses have become so coarse and woody they're practically unpalatable to the elk. As a result, such areas are of little use for anything anymore.

But there's hope. In 1987, and again in 1989, our cattle were used to "treat" those meadows during their "seed-ripe" season, that is, to prune the old, dense growth. Two things are apparent: first, there has been little or no damage to riparian areas—creek banks—when used that late in the year; second, there has indeed been improvement in quality and quantity of winter feed available for elk. And so we hope the program will be expanded; we'd be glad to have our cattle "treat" a larger area.

There's considerable self-interest here, of course. But not, as you might think, because we get more grass; after all, we still pay the full-shot fees for forest grazing, plus we stand a number of unusual costs not borne on private leases. Public grazing is no free lunch. Rather, the big advantage comes from making the game range more attractive to the elk so they'll leave us alone in winter. There's gotta be some give-and-take somewhere. If the public owns the wildlife, then, surely, they're responsible for habitat. So far, they haven't taken this seriously in Montana.

196

A Montana elk herd on winter feed ground. —Museum of the Rockies

On *Dry Wolf Creek* in the Little Belts
GERALD HUGHES
remembers:

There wasn't any elk around the Judith Basin when I was a kid. They brought 'em in from Yellowstone in the twenties and early thirties—didn't ask, just brought 'em in and turned 'em loose for us to feed. I remember our neighbors Reed and Flannigan—madder than hornets up there close to the forest. Them damn elk!

Like, just the other day, one of our neighbor says, "Damned elk is tryin' to eat us out, and you folks, too." And he said he counted a hundred, hundred fifty goin' through his place, and, up around our sheep camp, sixty or seventy more. He said if they was a rancher's strays he'd fight, or sue, or eat a few, at least. And now, they're tryin' to bring back wolves—the range needs predators, some say! I suppose we'll have to feed them, again, too.

I was secretary of the stockmen's association when they got the old white wolf of Stanford—last of 'em around the Judith Basin; that was back in May of 1930. That bugger, ya know, he come over to a ranch where Dad had a bunch of cows corralled at night. He got two or three; he'd only eat the hind end out of 'em and leave the rest.

197

So, one nice, clear night Dad says, "Mother, I better go up to that place and get him!" All we had was lanterns or lamps, you know, but Dad climbed up on a hay rack loaded with feed, and he got his rifle ready, and long about midnight here come the old white wolf. Well, the cows started bawlin' and millin', and Pa fired off several shots in the dark, but he couldn't see very good, Pa couldn't, so he didn't get him—just scared him good. But the bastard never come back.

Next he was killin' yearlin's over at Charlie Taylor's place. Bunch of us kids went after him—tracked him way up a mountain on the Taylor ranch; but we never seen him—makin' too much noise, I suppose. Then Dobie Neil and his brother Earl, they run onto him one afternoon while they was checkin' cattle. They had an old half-breed trapper with 'em; Al Close was his name, and he was a "Dead-eye Dick." He got him.

So they kept his teeth and hide, and they took some pictures; and they wrote a lot of stuff that wasn't true and named a motel for him on the highway. That was the last wolf seen in the Judith Basin; we didn't miss 'em, but I suppose we'll be seein' more.

In the *Porcupine Hills*, fifty miles from Calgary
JOHN CROSS
explains a quandary.

You may find the ranching fraternity split over which is more difficult to manage: the hunters or the hunted. We ranchers are full-time resource managers living on the job, and we often have a mix of public and private range. Our livestock use only part of the range resource, and we don't get paid—in fact, we aren't allowed—to manage the rest. It's not always clear who's *supposed* to manage it.

I jokingly told some pheasant hunters once, "If we managed the C7 properly, we'd get rid of you fellows, too." That was years ago, before we had alfalfa. We grew a lot of oats; you'd throw a bundle on the ground, and—bang!—there'd be oats to feed the pheasants. I remember counting 200 birds just riding across a field one morning, but now, in place of "stooks" of oat bundles from our binders, we have stacks of good alfalfa hay. The pheasants are gone—we miss 'em—but alfalfa's certainly better for the land than oats, and the modern system saves an awful lot of work, both in feeding cows and closing gates behind the hunters. When you're only fifty miles from a city as large as Calgary, that can be a big, big problem.

Nowadays, of course, it's elk! They make hunters seem the lesser of two evils. The first herd of elk I ever saw was right after World War Two. Maybe transplants out of Yellowstone worked their way up through Glacier Park; anyway, since the forties, they've increased until, in 1984, we had an elk for every two cows on the ranch.

It's quite funny—looking back! We had been very successful in seeding a field to grass and didn't want to use it at all that season. A government pamphlet warned: "Don't graze that grass for at least a year, after it's seeded down." Then, here came 400 government elk to pick it clean.

And I was at a wildlife meeting once; I said, "Those elk read brands! As soon as they see an C7 on a critter, they stay right with 'em; they graze along behind, getting salt and mineral and cubes—they know they're gonna get fed when the weather gets tough."[6] Of course, they didn't all believe me about the brands.

But, certainly, we worry about the cost of wintering all those elk. Wouldn't you? They use a lot of range—and eat our hay and oats and freshly seeded grass and mineral and salt—and tear down fences. And the government people raise lease-rental fees and cut the amount of lease a ranch can have; no mention, ever, of taking off some elk. We've had our thinking about that!

There aren't so many elk here during hunting season in the fall; they stay back in the mountains where it's safe until the snow gets deep. Mid-winter is when we wish we had more hunters; that's when the elk are thick, and the fire hazard's down. But we can't just open season, so, what to do? We invite the Peigans and Stoneys in. Here in Alberta, Indians have the right to shoot elk any time, though not free right of access to ranch lands. They're good friends to have. Even though they don't kill many elk, they sure scare the hell out of 'em! [John laughs]. It's a very successful conservation program.

On *Two Medicine River*, adjoining Glacier Park
BILLY BIG SPRING
manages with a sense of humor.

I can get along with anybody, Indian or white—even green environmentalists, although I don't believe we need more wilderness or wolves or grizzly bears. But hunters don't bother me much; I post my land "No Trespassing. Survivors Will Be Prosecuted!" and even the bears understand those signs.

199

You know, city people will believe almost anything you tell 'em. One time I was at a convention in Detroit, and a fellow asked me what were these [deer horn tips] hanging from my homemade necktie. I said, "They're grizzly teeth."

"Grizzly *bear?*"

"Yeah."

"Why, how'd you get 'em?"

"Well," I says, "I'll tell ya. Us cowboys all wear spurs, you know, and they're not only to ride horses with. We also use 'em to get grizzlies."

"How do you do that?" he asks, and his eyes get big!

I says, "Like I got these. First I had to find a bear up on a mountain. Then I set somebody to makin' lots of noise down in the valley to get the bear's attention; while he's looking down, he don't notice me up here.

"Grizzly teeth" hang from Billy's necktie. —Big Spring family

"So, I puts on my spurs and sneaks up behind him, quiet like. I got a knife, but I don't wanna kill that bear 'cause he's an endangered species, so I just jump on his back, and sink my spurs into his belly. Then, while he's tryin' to bite, I reach around with one arm and get busy collectin' teeth.

When I'm finished, I give that bear a kick in the ass with my spurs, and he rolls down off the hill with a terrible roar. I'm always careful to let 'em get away, because they grow more teeth, ya know."

By damn, I think that fellow really believed me [Billy chuckles].

At *Riske Creek* across the Rockies in British Columbia's Chilcotin
NEIL HARVIE
provides free lunch for bighorn sheep.

The whole Chilcotin area has been studied to death; there are deer, sheep, moose, elk habitat studies—make-work projects, mostly—that the public doesn't fully understand. But just let urban people believe the game is doing well, and the game biologists look good—a symbiotic relationship, if there ever was one, but a terrible waste of money!

A few miles south of Williams Lake, 500 miles west of Calgary, Lynn Bonner and Grant Huffman and I run 2,000 commercial, crossbred cows with bulls drawn from across the *Beefbooster* system.[7] Much of the range is provincial lease, and it's shared with other user-groups; for those who live on the land in British Columbia, control is a big, big problem. Real conflicts build between ranchers and game biologists and those who want to manage the game to suit themselves. Nobody has a claim on all environmental issues; we are all environmentalists. As a rancher, I have as much at stake as anybody else.

Well, a few years ago, we did a land trade with the B.C. government: We got ownership of a former grazing lease; they got full control of land along the Fraser and Chilcotin rivers as an exclusive home for a herd of California bighorn sheep. Now, the young fellow that promoted the trade was a highly trained biologist, but he didn't savvy "sheep speak"; if he'd asked the sheep, they'd have said they didn't like the deal. But, have you ever tried to tell a game biologist anything? In my opinion, that young man was blinkered; he wanted his own little game preserve or kingdom, and then the bureaucrats got into it.

What happened? Well, as soon as the bighorns were on their own, they looked around for all that nice, green, tender regrowth they'd been used to. In a few years time, their winter range got old and stale and tough, and they followed us home to graze behind our cattle. There's obvious compatibility between range cattle and bighorn sheep—sheep of any kind, for all I know.

The ostensible reason for the trade was to save a very unique and valuable resource. Now, I don't know that the California bighorn was ever in need of saving; it sure as hell isn't endangered in that valley. Those sheep have become so used to alfalfa hay and all the other good stuff we grow for cows, that they've proliferated far beyond the biologists' wildest dreams—not so much from anything the biologists have done, as from all the feed they've "borrowed." I don't think us ranchers get much credit for our help.

As the bighorns proliferated on our ranch at Riske Creek, the game people decided to trap some for transplanting. So, they hung big radio-controlled nets from poles over our hay stacks and baited them with apple pulp—a delicacy for sheep. Expense: no object. Permission: not required when bighorns are involved. Imagine going out and finding a crew of eager young civil servants training wild sheep to make a mess of your winter feed supply—on private land, no less. We couldn't believe it! We still boil over when we think about it.

On the up-beat side, Ducks Unlimited is a private organization that has been in partnership with ranchers throughout the west in developing resources, a great example to resource managers everywhere. A private organization can make things happen fast. When Ducks Unlimited wants shoreline for more birds, it simply helps the local land owners and managers store more water; that's exactly what the ranchers want, as well. At Riske Creek we've done some interesting joint ventures with Ducks Unlimited. They have helped our ranch tremendously, while improving habitat.

On our range at Riske Creek we have—besides DU and game biologists and bighorns—the timber industry and a military reserve where they carry on extensive training programs; the summer maneuvers harass our cattle most. This is the sort of situation where coordinated resource planning is effective, and it's been used a lot of times, a lot of places in British Columbia since Bill Anderson introduced it. It brings the players together: graziers, foresters, game biologists, military, and what-have-you. I think it helps each understand the other, although it doesn't necessarily stop the conflicts. With the army exploding shells while we're moving cows about, I guess there'll always be potential conflict.

Waiting for a handout. —Harvie family

At *Bridge Creek* in Oregon's Blue Mountains
BILL ANDERSON
pioneered a big idea.

In the 1950s elk were drifting down out of the Blue Mountains to winter on the steep breaks of the north fork of the John Day River near Monument, Oregon. The Monument country is a tough place to make a living, and the ranchers were unhappy with the elk for wintering on their turn-out range. The hunters loved it! It was easy hunting, so, by 1960, friction between the ranchers and the state game commission had heated up the atmosphere.

When it got too hot, the commission took action. They thought they'd buy a ranch near Monument for the elk to winter on, and they found a rancher who was ready to sell out. It was a hell of a place, you know: so darn steep and rocky you could hardly ride a saddle horse across it. But that's the kind of country elk prefer, so the State of Oregon bought the place and kept the cattle off, and, a few years later the elk moved on to another ranch on Bridge Creek.

The game commission said, "We must have misjudged where the elk were gonna winter; that Monument country must have been too tough," and—not knowing why the elk had moved—the commission bought six small ranches in that high, dry, marginal-farming country, and put together the Bridge Creek Wildlife Area.

They kept all domestic livestock off, again. And three years later the elk moved on, again. Bridge Creek had taken on what I call a "wolf-plant" aspect, that is, lots of rank, leached residue that elk don't like. At that point, the game commission came to me (I was SCS State Range Specialist at the time). "What's goin' on?" they asked.

The Soil Conservation Service had a big advantage; it wasn't hampered by a lot of old tradition—the ranger vs. cowboy thing, for instance. We just worked with private land owners and tried to pass on what we knew about grass and how it grew. So, when the game commission came to me and asked me what to do about their elk, I went right down and studied the problem on-site for a while, and finally, I could say, "I know what's happening. You've got to put the cattle back."

We made a range survey; we had a fifteen-year record of use to go on, and an estimated winter herd of 120 elk. We estimated there was 350 AUMs (animal-unit-months) available for cattle in the summer; that wasn't much, but the range was pretty well beat up. We planned a good rotation system, and the commission looked around for a rancher who could make our program work and found the Colvins— typical old-time ranchers—who understood their cattle and the country. After we'd explained what we wanted to do, they came up with the idea of running yearling steers and heifers, which fit in nicely with their operation. Well, that was the best we could get! Yearlings cover country a whole lot better than cows and calves and can be shipped to market earlier, leaving more feed for elk.

So, we laid out six accessible pastures, three on each side of a road, which kept the sexes separate, and we took down more old fences than we built—just a dream to lay the darn thing out. The game boys developed lots of water holes, and we figured out a rest-rotation program: One pasture got complete rest from domestic livestock every year; one was topped off first thing in the spring, and then allowed to grow; and one could be used heavy during the growing season. The cattle loved it; those yearlings grew like weeds.

What happened? We started with 350 animal-unit-months of forage available for cattle and stocked accordingly. Immediately, the herd of wintering elk began to grow; in about three years, as I recall, elk numbers were over 500. Within ten years (and this is hard to believe) there were 1,200 head of elk and counting, maybe 1,800 wintering—at least a ten-fold increase in a decade. Seeing what was happening, the commission soon doubled the domestic stocking rate to 700 cattle AUMs; three years later it went to 900; it was up to 1,400, the last I heard.

There've been other spin-offs, and not all good ones. Elk, like cows and people, develop social problems when they're crowded; when Bridge Creek numbers approached a couple of thousand head, some split off and went looking for other wintering areas, which made the local ranchers mad. When that happens you need a cow-elk hunt to cut the numbers down; that's what they've had to do at Bridge Creek.

Well, Bridge Creek got the attention of wildlife people in the neighboring states. For a long time, ranchers had been saying their cattle could *improve* the wildlife habitat; they had research to back 'em up. Not till Bridge Creek, however, had anybody gone right out and done it; that's where we started listening to each other.

On the *Big Hole River* in southwestern Montana
MAYNARD SMITH
and family talk with many interest groups.

We listen to a lot of different groups here on our range. There are thousands of sportsmen and fishermen in our area who want to use the range for recreation, and I appreciate how they feel. When I was a kid in California my folks leased out our ranch, and I couldn't hunt at home because we didn't want to infringe on our lessee. On our Montana ranch, today, we aren't required to allow access to our state or private lands, but we do. And we don't charge; if we're gonna cry about the numbers of deer and elk, we've gotta let the hunters harvest them. But we do make 'em hunt on foot or horseback; no motor vehicles allowed. That's because of knapweed; we don't need people driving around scattering noxious weeds.

As early as 1961 the elk were getting to be a problem on all the private ranches in our area, so the government went out and purchased a ranch adjacent to our own just for wintering elk. That sounded like a good idea at first, but the elk range went practically unused for many years while the elk were happily grazing private pastures. The Fish & Wildlife managers have learned a lot over the past twenty-five years and now understand that elk aren't interested in range that hasn't been grazed by something else. Cattle keep the grass from getting rank.

Holley and I have four grown kids; Meg and Randy are on the ranch full time—fifth generation in the ranching business. We run on 50,000 acres of federal, state, and private land with two or three thousand animal-unit-months of "permit" grazing. You can talk about environment all you want, but nobody—I mean, nobody!—has more concern for the local range environment, public or private, than we do. Everything we have is tied in to it.

You may ask, "Why should any one family have tenure on all that public land? Isn't that a give-away?" That's a real important question; here's the answer. With genuine tenure on intermingled public and private lands, our interest becomes *long-term;* we treat the public's land exactly like our own. We try hard to improve it. It's human nature! Long-term private interest is very much in the public's interest, too.

Of course, when you use public land there's politics involved, and a lot of people are opposed to grazing domestic livestock of any kind—especially those who don't understand animal behavior. Nowadays, the Forest Service, BLM, and Soil Conservation Service are really pushing coordinated resource management, and one plan in particular has the official blessing of the federal government. This is what developed: Sometime in the 1970s, an environmental group brought suit against the BLM for overgrazing public lands in Idaho; that's when PRIA, the Public Rangeland Improvement Act, was born. Under Section 12 of PRIA, Challis, Idaho, became the center for an experimental "stewardship" program, based on Bill Anderson's coordinated approach. In 1979, the PRIA people called a meeting in Butte, which I happened to attend with other ranchers, BLM, and Forest Service people. After much discussion, we agreed to work together on the so-called East Pioneer Stewardship area.

Under PRIA guidelines, we set up a steering committee. In addition to the national forest supervisor and the district manager of the BLM, we chose eleven members: four ranchers, representatives from the governor's office, the university system, and Fish, Wildlife & Parks, two local sportsmen/environmentalists, the SCS man, and the county agent. The first job of the steering committee was to nominate and prioritize some range-improvement projects.

Next, we chose a technical action group, or TAG, composed of a rancher-permittee, a Fish & Wildlife person, the area biologist, a sportsman, and a BLM or Forest Service range-conservationist. Our TAG surveys each project and reports to the steering committee.

Originally, there was mention of federal money for range improvement, but the money never came. Of course, we get lots of help with planning, and materials for water projects and fencing, but permittees contribute most of the time, machinery, and capital. That's good; it gives 'em a real interest while it saves the tax payers money—a big "plus" for CRMP and the stewardship program.

The biggest success, I think, has been improved interagency cooperation. BLM and the Forest Service both have rangeland in our area, and there's been lots of friction between them. Now, through group action, we move fences so that BLM and forest land can be enclosed in the same pasture—an unheard of thing, before. Now it's possible to make decisions based on know-how instead of politics, although the steering committee chairman may have to go and knock some bureaucratic heads together: "Hey, boys, you're getting 'that way' again." That's happened several times, and the working relationship has improved.

A most important spin-off has been raising the trust level. At first, our groups were wary and suspicious; since we've started listening, we've learned to say our pieces and respect other opinions. Still, some folks refuse to get involved with government agents. You still hear, "That s.o.b. couldn't make it on the ranch, so now he's working for the guv'ment," but we have to cut that out. Good people—many of our own kids—are out there working for the agencies. They're working hard at worthwhile jobs, and they sure won't fade away.

At *Wall Creek* on the Madison River
FRED KING
is learning to live with cattle.

We still get quizzical looks from sportsmen, including me, when somebody says, "It's springtime in the Rockies and time to get some cattle on the game range." I think, "Golly, what in the world will happen next!"

I'm no cattleman! My interest has always been in wildlife. I'm from Pennsylvania, where I wanted to be a game protector, but those fellows can wind up in Pittsburgh as easy as Bucks County, so I came to Montana where I majored in wildlife management at MSU and went to work for Fish, Wildlife & Parks, shocking fish, checking hunters, and catching grizzly bears for research. I've been with the department ever since.

I'm a wildlife area manager. That means I'm responsible for maintenance on a game range—specifically, the Wall Creek range in southwestern Montana. I don't make policy, I just carry out programs for the biologist and the regional wildlife manager, but they let me have some input. I love the kind of work I've chosen, and I've come to see elk habitat as a prime indicator of quality of life here in Montana.

Elk once ranged from Pennsylvania, right across the country. When Lewis and Clark came west there were elk along the Missouri, elk on the plains, elk in the foothills, and most of them made seasonal migrations—to high country in summer, back to lower country in winter—just as they do today. Elk aren't, basically, a mountain animal, but those that stayed on the plains just basically got eaten. By the early 1900s the only elk left were in Yellowstone National Park; they were gone from their old ranges—the victims of market hunting, like the buffalo.

In 1910 they started reintroducing elk onto Montana ranges. The first transplant of twenty-five head came out of Yellowstone to Fleecer Peak, near Butte; they made continuous plants thereafter until they had elk herds around the state—soon, more than they knew what to do with.

There's a famous herd that winters in Jackson Hole, Wyoming. Long ago, the Wyoming people decided to feed them hay all winter; they're quite a tourist attraction. When elk began coming out of the high country to winter on Montana ranches in the forties and early fifties, our Fish & Wildlife people decided to try something different. If the state would buy some natural winter range, eliminate competition, and allow the vegetation to rest, recuperat, and grow year after year, they figured they could greatly increase the number of elk for hunters.

West of the continental divide elk will browse on woody shrubs and forbs, but they prefer grass when they can get it. On our winter range that means, mostly, native bunch grasses like Bluebunch wheatgrass and Idaho and Rough fescue. That's what elk like best—their bread and butter—and it puts them in direct competition with domestic cattle. Back about 1951 they were already having problems with an elk herd migrating to an already overgrazed range around Big Sky. There never seemed to be enough vegetation, so the state bought 7,000 acres from the Great Northern Railroad and a private rancher.

You can bet here was lots of criticism when the state began acquiring private land for wildlife, and one big fear was interference with the tax base of the counties. That criticism was addressed right from the start: our department pays money *in lieu* of taxes, and every cent comes out of hunters' pockets; no general tax funds at all. That's what makes our Montana game ranges such a feather in the sportsmen's bonnet! Hunters want more animals to shoot; they put their bucks behind the project. And we get additional support from Pittman-Robertson, a fund collected nationwide with a federal excise tax on ammunition.

In southwest Montana, the Blacktail, Fleecer, and Wall Creek are classic examples of the potential of game ranges. When the Blacktail was purchased in 1972, 400 to 600 head of elk wintered on that privately owned ranch. The cows went off; the vegetation grew. Twelve years later 1,700 elk were wintering there—herd growth stimulated by the increased food supply.

But ranchers in elk country have always had problems protecting their winter feed, and quadrupling elk numbers can only increase those problems. One of our good neighbors went to chopping his alfalfa and blowing it into hundred-yard-long plastic bags that lay out on the ground. Nobody thought the elk would get into those bags, but last year when the range locked up with ice and snow the elk came down and punctured them and loaded up and waddled away back up the hill, so full they could hardly walk. In spite of best intentions, under the best of management, with adequate winter range, elk may still attack private hay supplies. We're sorry when it happens, but our business is maintaining healthy, vigorous elk for our primary constituents: the sportsmen of Montana.

Elk winter range at Wall Creek. —Fred J. King

Still, there are exciting new developments that sometimes work to everyone's advantage. For instance, the Fleecer wildlife area, like the Blacktail, was hard-core winter range when it was purchased. About 200 elk summered in the high country and came back to lower ground in winter. We kicked the cows off Fleecer, let the vegetation grow, protected the antlerless segment, and watched that herd increase to 1,000 head by the early eighties. But those elk wouldn't stay "home"; they crossed over onto private land and pestered Maynard Smith. Ownership doesn't mean much to an elk. Now, Maynard is the most tolerant of neighbors, but finally he came to us and said, "Look, guys, on top of wintering elk, I've got more hunters on my place than ever. This may be good for the state, but it's pretty tough on me. There must be another way."

We had, at that time, been in close contact with Gus Hormay and had already had a go at rest-rotation grazing. So, our biologist, Mike Frisina, worked out a program whereby Maynard's cows would prune the lower elevations of the game range to make way for springtime growth. Maynard would rest portions of his winter range which were useful to the elk. That solved some common problems. Maynard had been wintering elk already, but now he was getting something in return; now he could be more tolerant of all those wintering elk and all those hunters. It's a good deal for our elk. And—come spring, when hay supplies are low—it's a good deal for Smith's cows to have that early grazing on our low-elevation pastures. It's not a one-way street; it's symbiotic. And, that's how come we tolerate cows on the Wall Creek range.

Wall Creek is my immediate responsibility. The adjacent land is owned by the Forest Service, with over 800 animal-units of grazing under permit to a group of local ranchers. With help from Gus Hormay, we've designed a nine-pasture, three-year, rest-rotation program, modified to make best use of pasture type, lay of the land, and elevational changes. Here's how it works: About May 1st we put cows on a low-elevation pasture on the Madison—a field that's had a couple of years' rest; they stay there till June 1st, pruning the decadent growth; then, on to a mid-elevation pasture where they graze for a month and a half. About July 15th, they go to high forest pasture where they perform a "seed-ripe" treatment; that's the seed-stomping, threshing, planting action of hundreds of sharp hoofs—a process more important than any of us realized.

September 1st, the cattle come down to mid-elevation pasture and do another seed-ripe treatment for the next couple of weeks. Then, on to lower pasture for the last seed treatment of the year. By September

30th the cattle are gone, it's early fall, and the range is in great shape for elk as they move down out of high country for the winter.

Everybody benefits: The Forest Service has more pasture without hammering the environment; ranchers get more production with less risk from the weather. But to me, what's most important is the benefit to our elk. Sure, we tolerate cattle, but we don't open up our land to help the ranchers. We use livestock simply as tools to improve elk habitat, and we've seen the Wall Creek wintering herd grow from 200 to 1,400 head. With that result, we can deal with neighbors as partners rather than as adversaries. We're improving a basic resource to the benefit of sportsmen, ranchers, farmers, and everybody else.

As a wildlife manager, I like to point to a special meaning elk have for Montanans. Elk are a tolerant species, very adaptable to many of man's activities. They survive clear-cuts, roads, agriculture, housing, everything, up to a point, but they need their seasonal range. They need a quality wintering place with plenty of feed and security from storms and hunting pressure, and they need safe calving grounds—exactly the kind of landscape many Montanans visualize and value. As long as we maintain habitat acceptable to elk, we're looking after quality of life for humans. I say, disrupt things for elk, and you disrupt the life we treasure here in the Treasure State.

From a range state university
C. WAYNE COOK
speaks his mind.

The Range: A natural, biologic complex with plants, bacteria, insects, birds, and animals interspersed, feeding on one another, dependent on the soil and water resources.

It's important to think of *ecosystems*: the flow of energy, water, and nutrients between sun and cloud and soil and plant and animal. A range ecologist thinks of *primary producers* (plants) and *secondary producers* (animals), and a good range manager knows he cannot manage one without the other—manage one and you are only half a rangeman.

Range management is a difficult science. It's young, as sciences go, and it has identity problems because of all the disciplines involved. There's range-animal nutrition, for example, which is different from general animal nutrition, you see, because a range animal selects its own food, rather than receiving it in a box. A range scientist, therefore, has to know how much, which plants, what nutrients they contain, as well as the nutrients required for physiological functions at various stages of different animals' lives. It's not a simple science!

I know I can improve one range for deer by putting on sheep at a different season and at a different intensity. I can graze another range with cattle at a different season still, and improve it, again, for deer. Or I can improve it for sheep, or I can improve it for elk. If I want elk-deer range, I handle it one way; if I want cattle summer range, I handle it another. But managing range for multispecies grazing introduces a lot more features into the system, and makes it a lot more complicated, and you have to be astute to make it work.

I say you're almost always better off if you can rotate animals and pastures, and I say you'll usually get more production through grazing several species than through any one alone, with any grazing system. But you have to be astute; unless you know a great deal about your plants and soils and everything associated with them, it's too easy to rotate *wrong*, and do a lot of damage. You must know what you're doing.

I recently wrote a management plan for an agency that wanted to divide a forage resource among deer, elk, antelope, wild horses, sheep, and cattle, all on the same range. The plan is fine, but it will take qualified, practical rangemen to carry it out. None of the agencies think they need trained range managers anymore. And I think they're in trouble! We're at a dangerously low point in training young range managers. In 1988 only five seniors graduated in range at Colorado State, perhaps ten at Utah State; Montana and Alberta, much the same. Properly trained range managers, it seems—the life blood of our western resource agencies—are fast becoming another endangered species![8]

A band of sheep can be a useful management tool in the care of a well-trained herder. —L.A. Huffman photo, Montana Historical Society

The greatest service that can be rendered to any country is to add a useful plant to its culture.

—Thomas Jefferson

8

Range Grasses

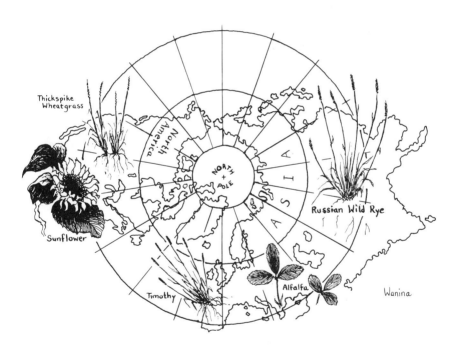

Thus far, we have encountered users *of rangeland—ranchers, farmers, and other managers—and* secondary producers, *such as buffalo and elk. But it wouldn't be right to leave The Range without more about its* primary producers: *the grasses.*

Doug Dewey, a plant breeder and explorer, calls our continent a "have-not land" to dramatize the fact that most of the species we use for food, including all of the grains, all of our main food animals except the turkey, and most of the forage crops we feed them, had to be imported before civilization could proceed.[1]

In 1720 colonist Timothy Hanson broadcast his trove of hay seed along the Maryland shore; today feral "timothy" is found across the continent. In 1854 farmer Grimm, a German immigrant, sowed old-world seed on the California gold fields; Grimm alfalfa still makes hay and pasture on The Range. This year, Marshall Copithorne planted spuds on Jumping Pound from "eyes" his grandad brought from Ireland. Your own immigrant ancestors most likely included seed stock in their baggage.

That our continent has become a land of plenty, where its inhabitants now eat better than any people in history, is due to many things: farmers free to profit from their produce; farmland blessed with excellent soils and climate; a haphazard collection of heirloom seed stock multiplied a thousand-fold. And don't forget that group of unsung heroes, the plant explorers, botanists, and geneticists who discovered, preserved, improved—and more recently, engineered—the germplasm of American good-eating.

GUS HORMAY

a student of grass at twenty-four, range consultant at eighty, reminds us how grass builds topsoil and holds water.

Soil erosion, deterioration, desertification—whatever you want to call it—has been going on, quite literally, forever. We won't stop it; what we have to do is control it where we can.

The development of organic matter in the top layer of the soil is so important in watershed control: It makes the soil more receptive to water; it lets the water sink in and percolate slowly rather than running off the surface. Reservoirs of ground water make modern, manmade lakes seem puny by comparison. The deeper the relatively spongy topsoil horizon, the more water can be stored in the soil and available to support life.

Many topsoils are only a few inches thick; the deepest in the world are the *chernozem* soils of Russia, where the organic horizon is four or five feet deep. And all that organic matter came from plant residue, mostly from the decaying roots of range plants. Grass, with its fibrous, hair-like roots, is the best topsoil builder known to man. The goal of any range management plan or conservation project should be to maintain the most effective ground cover, using the best available vegetation. Vegetation, you see, controls fertility, erosion, and almost everything else to do with land. No doubt about it: Grass is *the* superior vegetation!

TOM LAWRENCE
plant breeder, spent a lifetime learning to grow grass.

Many people think grass is sort of a static thing—leave it alone, it's there forever. We know that's not the case. Native range is actually dynamic—always changing; it must be treated in a way that will allow seed production before the plants die out—that's nature's way. They talk of establishing a native grassland park near where the Gilchrist brothers got their start; they think they're going to save the grass by not using it at all. That won't work. Our range developed under grazing; quit grazing it entirely, and you'll get all kinds of changes in the stand. You can't just preserve grassland; you've got to handle it in a *natural* way.

When early explorers like Palliser saw this semiarid corner of the world, they thought it would be limited to stock raising.[2] Fifty years later, though, it was opened up for homesteading, and by 1920 thousands of farmers—my father among them—had turned the short-grass prairie upside down and were trying to grow wheat. I was raised on the northern edge of the so-called Palliser's Triangle, where my father and his fellow homesteaders found they had a lot to learn about unusual soils and climates; some of their kids, like me, remember the devastation of the thirties, and have spent a lifetime learning to grow grass.

Swift Current Research Station was opened in 1920 to specialize in dryland farming studies. Along with studying tillage methods, developing erosion control, reseeding abandoned farmland, and learning to grow wheat, we've spent a lot of time with grass; I've been a grass breeder here for thirty-five years—that's long enough!

In the early years the station studied our native plants and found them too short-lived and unable to tolerate much domestic grazing. We get better production out of species introduced from Siberia and neighboring parts of Asia. I don't know why those introductions do better here than on their native ranges; they don't look impressive when you see them on the steppes, nor have the Asians tried to improve them much—not until very recently, at least. They are just the tough, resilient survivors of thousands of years of use by nomadic tribes.

Traveling in Inner Mongolia in 1982, I saw communes where the modern Mongols live in mud houses surrounded by their camels, donkeys, sheep, and cattle running all over the place. Of course, they used to be nomadic, lived in portable *yurts,* and had a traditional, very effective, grazing pattern that kept the range in shape. But, when the Communists took over in 1949, they said, "Comrades! You cannot travel around; you gotta stay in place!" So the Mongols settled down. They cut down all the trees to make their mud house rafters; they held every animal they owned on communal pastures, and pretty soon they had a desert. Now, they're sowing North American cultivars of their native grasses—some developed here at Swift Current— to help reclaim the dunes.

SYLVESTER SMOLIAK

Manyberries agrostologist, found himself "retreaded" as a grass breeder.

At Manyberries we have one stand of the Siberian native, Crested wheatgrass, that was seeded in 1928 and is still productive sixty years later! Sixty years isn't bad, and it's an easy grass to establish; I tell people, "just broadcast it on pavement, it'll grow!" But it declines considerably in value from spring to fall.

Russian wild rye greens up in early spring and stays green late in fall—big advantage—but it's tough to get established, and it doesn't adapt to "favorable" conditions. We had an experimental plot on the Q7 Ranche in the Porcupine Hills: Russian wild rye just eight inches high beside a three-foot stand of brome—same field, black soil, and plenty of moisture. Russian wild rye is more competitive in heavier alkaline soils and tougher conditions.

Cicer milkvetch, another introduction from the Urals, is a legume—a *non-bloating* legume! Tested at Manyberries in the early

1930s, it looked promising, very promising; it should have been a natural for cattle, and Alex Johnston and I released a cultivar called Oxley that we hoped would suit the industry, but, again, it was too hard to get established. I've been working on improved seedling vigor ever since.

When we wanted a better grass for foothills pastures, we thought of orchard grass, which is great in early spring. With an orchard grass for spring and a wild rye for fall, foothills ranchers could have almost year-round grazing, but we needed a hardier line for the black-soil zones. So, when Lethbridge got the job of improving orchard grass, I was told to go and learn plant breeding. Range management had been my love, and I didn't want to switch, but Lethbridge could afford just one range manager. It was Alex or me, and I was junior, so, after years of wear and tear, I got retreaded.

There are at least two ways of breeding more productive grasses. The modern, high-tech way is with interspecific crossing; once you solve the technical problems, you can make a lot of progress in a hurry. Doug Dewey is doing a lot of this at Logan, Utah. The old way is through selection—performance testing, to use a rancher's term— which can be a long-term project; we're doing this with Cicer milkvetch, germinating it in two-and-a-half inch trays of vermiculite. Anything that survives in that environment is transplanted into the field for

Alex Johnston and Sylver Smoliak inspecting a Cicer milkvetch sample.
—Lethbridge Research Station Archives

propagation. The same with orchard grass. We're testing it in growth-cabinets where seedlings are subjected to freezing temperatures. Survivors go through the cycle over and over again—it takes a very long time.

Alex and I got involved in the search for useful "natives" for use on seismic lines, pipelines, roadways, and so forth. It was just too easy to say "seed Crested wheat." We figured we needed natives, so we developed Walsh, a cultivar of native Western wheatgrass, and Elbee Northern (Thickspike) wheatgrass—two of the three cultivars of Canadian natives released to date.

In Canada, you have to prove your new plant is equal to, or better than, an existing Canadian variety. With our Northern and Western wheatgrasses, we had a problem: ours were "firsts"—there were no existing varieties. We finally cut through miles of bureaucratic jungle by proposing them for revegetation, rather than for agriculture, and they let us go ahead. But what red tape! When you finally prove the value of your work, it must be tested on two or three locations over a three-year period with a lot of other disciplines involved: the insect men, for instance. The final product is a joint effort, and royalties in Canada, if any, go back into the forage-breeding program; it's a labor of love—certainly no get-rich-quick scheme for the breeder.

I've been working on a cultivar of native Basin, or Giant, wild rye, a beautiful collection that grows five or six feet tall! I call it Coulee, and I'll follow it along. But, this is another "first"—not comparable with anything else and strictly agricultural; that means it'll be hard to license by-the-book. Gosh, I hope they change that book while I'm alive to see it, but sometimes that takes a terrible long time!

DON RYERSON

MSU professor and range scientist, thinks we've overlooked some valuable natives.

Most of the stuff we're using, unfortunately, came from across the pond: from off the Mediterranean coast and from off the Russian steppes. I've seen grasses in Saudi Arabia that would work; but why go there when we have good stuff at home? Of course, some introductions have certainly proved their value; they do fit into management programs with special seasonal grazing, but we should get a better handle on our natives.

Botanists and plant explorers have combed the United States for useful natives, but they haven't paid enough attention to eco-type in making their selections. I've paid a lot of attention to it in my work; I've released a Thickspike wheatgrass (the Canadians call it Northern), and was working on a Spike fescue when I retired. Some of my Spike is even earlier than Crested wheatgrass, and absolutely unbelievable as forage. It's usually found above 6,000 feet in a high-rainfall environment; I found mine at a low elevation out of Big Timber, which gets ten, twelve inches a year. There it was: big, beautiful stuff! That was 1958. I took it to the university's Red Bluff ranch on the Madison, but it was very slow coming; we wrote it off— gave up on it. Thank heavens we didn't destroy the plots; ten years later I dropped by, one day, just to see how that old Spike was doing. Holy smokes! There it was on the 10th of May, already twelve inches high, shooting seed, and grazing-ready—just an example of the stuff that's floating around right here at home.

Thickspike (Northern) wheatgrass is found throughout the plains from Alberta, across Montana, into the Dakotas, down into Wyoming, Idaho, and Utah. I found good Thickspike down in Canyon Lands in Utah, and if I'd been reseeding in that area I most certainly would have collected it, but my practice is to select within a given area, for a given site, to meet a specific need. I looked all over Montana before settling on a rhizomatous, high-producing Thickspike on a southwest-facing, eroded site near Havre.

Find something that meets your grazing needs? Go ahead and collect it, but be sure to maintain genetic diversity. When breeders play around with plants, they "select" under simulated grazing conditions for ten, fifteen, or even thirty years before making a "release" and often lose *genetic diversity* in the process. We need to look for outstanding individuals adapted to given soil, site, and climate situations. When we find them, we should capitalize on them; the genes have been here since the last ice age and have survived under eons of heavy grazing. I think that's what we need.

KEN MILLER

our buffalo man, also propagates grass seed on The Range.

Happened to be, I hooked up with a seed dealer while still at university. So, as soon as we graduated, Mary and I borrowed a couple of thousand dollars, spent half of it on "foundation" Russian wild rye and Pubescent wheatgrass seed, and rented enough clean land for our first seed crop. We've never looked back.

We accumulated a couple or three thousand acres of rented land in those first years we farmed; that was back in the early seventies, when times were tough and wheat was a dollar a bushel. Nobody wanted that damn dry land, so we stuck out our necks—we're more optimistic than most—and we've been in the grass-seed business ever since. We now have over 5,000 acres in grass seed.

At first we produced raw seed and turned it over to our dealer friend who cleaned and marketed it for us; when he retired, we were forced to learn marketing for ourselves. By then we had a few years under our belts, so we custom cleaned our seed and built our business through six or eight Canadian wholesalers and six or eight dealers in Idaho and Montana.

The most recent step has been a seed plant of our own, right here on the farm; that's encouraged a dozen neighbors to go into the grass-seed business, too—Tom Gilchrist among 'em. Now we're coaching them on where and how to acquire seed, and establish, harvest, and process it. Then, we clean, sack, and market it for them on percentage.

We grow most of the wheatgrasses here—the *Agropyrons:* Crested, Intermediate, Pubescent, Slender, Northern, Streambank, and Tall wheatgrass. Also Russian and Altai wild rye, plus a thousand acres of Smooth brome. These grasses are always popular with stockmen to balance out the legumes in their hay fields, but many varieties have been bred and selected for specific purposes. Intermediate wheatgrass, for instance, works better for hay production than for grazing. It likes wet areas and tolerates salinity—adapts well to areas too tough for other grasses. Some varieties are best used for pasture and are no good at all for hay. Some grasses are used for turf production, others for erosion control, still others for reseeding roadsides, railways, and pipelines.

In the last fifteen or twenty years there's been a growing demand for improved varieties of natives, the main reason being that some U.S. Government agencies require them on revegetation projects. I think it's a bit of a luxury, myself. The imports were selected for a purpose; they've been evolving over a longer period of time, and they'll probably be stronger, produce more forage, and have a lower cost of production, but they may not be as pretty as the natives. We're trying a couple of natives now: Bluebunch wheatgrass and Basin wild rye. We seeded one field three years in a row with three consecutive failures. But, we'll see....

"Crested wheat" is the common name for at least two species of the genus *Agropyron*. There is *Agropyron cristatum* which includes the old Fairway variety, and *A. desertorum*—a taller, pasture-type. Crested lasts a long time on sandy land, particularly the varieties called tetraploids, which have a double chromosome number. They are tough and vigorous, popular for seed production; ranchers in the Medicine Hat area have maintained stands of Summit for twenty or thirty years, simply spiking it every year or so. We grow a diploid, Nordan, here even though we get only three or four years out of a stand. Our American customers like it, and our customers are always right!

There's kind of a worldwide system in all this. By the time a new variety is released, the plant breeders on the experiment stations will have already put their seed through a tough selection process. They look for individual plants that do better than the general population, then they propagate it with a ratchet effect—jacking up productivity with each new generation.

Then a nursery producer will take the newly released seed stock, grow it very carefully on one- or two-acre plots, and come up with maybe 100 or 200 pounds of "breeder" seed. The breeder seed is multiplied very carefully by selected growers into "foundation" seed, then—here in Canada—commercial growers like me take over and produce "certified" seed for sale to farmers and ranchers. In the States there's an additional "registered" generation.

Some crossbreeding is being done with grasses: widely related species, crossed as much for complementarity as for hybrid vigor. For instance, Ephraim, a hybrid developed in Utah, is a very strong, creeping plant produced by crossing two *Agropyrons:* quack grass and Crested wheat. When it comes into production, it should be a very interesting grass to work with.

The actual breeding of new varieties is very subjective and is associated with certain individuals as much as it is with geography or institutions. Back in the forties and fifties, a fellow named George Rogler made Mandan, North Dakota, famous as a source of Crested wheatgrass because of its importance in revegetating blown-out farmland after the thirties. A Canadian from Saskatoon, Bob Knowles, was one of the most outstanding plant breeders of the sixties and seventies. He developed eight or ten varieties of pasture grasses in use all over North America. These days, you often hear the name of Doug Dewey—plant explorer, research geneticist, and breeder; "curator" of the *Agropyron* and *Elymus* collections at the USDA research station at Logan, Utah.

DOUGLAS R. DEWEY

research geneticist, has explored Asia as part of a
career in plant breeding.

My primary interest has always been in breeding grass and forage for western rangelands, and, in the 1960s, I became intrigued by the idea of collecting seeds from forage plants in Russia. A chance to collect seed in areas so long used for grazing seemed worth the long years of groundwork and red tape.

The grasses of the steppes and deserts of central Asia have developed and flourished under heavy grazing by cattle, horses, sheep, camels, and what-have-you for thousands of years; that's the best reason why those species are more suited to our western livestock industry than North American range plants. It's true our own grasses developed under sometimes heavy grazing by wild animals, but I'm sure the pressure of domestic—even nomadic—livestock is much heavier. Domestic animals under any system of management are much less mobile than wild game. A cow just looks at our good old native Bluebunch wheatgrass, and it about wilts on the vine, so to speak—can't really stand much grazing. On the other hand, you can grub the Asiatic Crested wheatgrass right into the ground and it will bounce right back.

The U.S. plant exploration program goes back a long, long way. As early as 1819, our foreign-service people were directed to search for useful plants and, ever since it was organized, the USDA has been sending botanists to explore the back country of Russia, China, and the Middle East with no assurance against being killed by some nomadic bandit.

Take Frank Meyer, for instance, boy, was he tough! The USDA's old Office of Foreign Seed and Plant Introduction hired him as an agricultural explorer back in Teddy Roosevelt's day, in the early 1900s, and sent him off collecting through China and Korea and Manchuria and Russia for years at a time. He traveled by foot and by mule, through blizzards and dust storms, fighting off bandits and warlords until he met his end on the Yangtse River during the revolutionary uprisings of 1918. Meyer collected tons of seeds, pits, tubers, bulbs, cuttings, and shoots—the stuff we call germplasm today—from parent stock that had survived unfavorable environments for hundreds of years. He shipped them all back home to be tested, grafted, bred, crossbred, and multiplied for the improvement of life here in the States. That kind of exploration still goes on today.[3]

I made my first exploring trip in 1972. I traveled to Iran, and had the greatest freedom of movement I've enjoyed anywhere—we'd just jump into a Landrover and take off. In the Soviet Union in the seventies, they'd map our every move; we couldn't deviate at all. We'd fly from center to center and travel with interpreters and guides. But, on our trip in 1977 we collected seed from 1,100 grasses, legumes, forbs, and shrubs in forty-five days—not bad at all. The Russians have really been very helpful in this business of plant exploring; we've exchanged more germplasm with them than with any other country. We're engaged in an on-going program: our people over there collecting grass seed, the Russians over here looking for sunflowers—that's about the only thing they're interested in. The fact is, they've got more useful plant material than we do; even the germplasm they take from us is usually from *their* natives, worked-over and improved by us.

In 1906 a plant explorer, Neils H. Hansen, exploring in Siberia for the USDA, made the first collection of Crested wheatgrass and sent it home for propagation at Mandan. Frank Meyer collected more in 1911. Now, here's a problem: The seed used to revegetate millions of arid and semiarid acres of the United States and Canada over the last fifty years was grown from no more than a dozen collections of the *Agropyron* and *Elymus* complex—Crested, Tall, and Intermediate wheatgrass, and Russian wild rye. Such a very narrow genetic base for some of our most valuable vegetation is a matter of considerable concern, and we're trying to do something about it.

Another serious problem is the loss of many old, original collections of plant material. The germplasm of many valuable forage-grass varieties, including brome, timothy, orchard grass, meadow foxtail, sainfoin, the alfalfas, clovers, and others, has been lost, destroyed, or damaged. They didn't know how to store it years ago, but we hope that situation's been corrected.

Plant material enters the United States through quarantine at Beltsville, Maryland, where all new germplasm is observed for pests and pathogens—viruses, bacteria, nematodes, insects, and so forth. Care is justified; there have been some devastating outbreaks of plant disease in various parts of the world back through history. For instance, at least two million people starved to death and millions more emigrated when a disease called late blight wiped out the Irish potato crop in the 1840s.

Different types of materials have different quarantine requirements. Cereals from parts of the world where disease is prevalent are carefully regulated. Forage plants are thought to be less critical; they usually pass through the quarantine center after a simple screening, and are then released to researchers, like me, at research stations scattered around the country. Thereafter, we are held responsible. Once a collection comes home, it's thoroughly identified, cataloged, and given its own "PI" [plant identification] number in the national plant germplasm system.

There are risks in introducing the germplasm we need into this country. Not only have some undesirable weeds like knapweed, spurge, and halogeten been brought in inadvertently and "escaped," others were introduced deliberately—with the best of intentions; cheatgrass is an example. We have a thing called "goat's rue" around Cache Valley [Utah]—goats are supposed to like the look of it, until they get a taste; it's sometimes called "professor-weed." I don't know how true it is, but some university professor is thought to have brought it in as a forage legume and let it get away. So, there are risks. But if people will only use a little judgment, they can be managed.

When you're collecting potential germplasm abroad, you're looking for genetic characteristics, not phenotypical appearance, in the native habitat. For instance, Crested wheatgrass—good as it is—has problems: first off, there's that narrow genetic base; second, it rapidly declines in forage value as the growing season progresses. Well, we've found and introduced a sub species that maintains quality late into the summer, and a major goal of future expeditions will be to expand that inventory. Some of the wild ryes have shown great promise as late fall and winter forage, but, again, their genetic base is extremely limited. We need to get out and find new collections that will add genetic diversity to these valuable grasses, too.

And then there are the possibilities for crossbreeding. Ordinarily, in plant breeding, as with cattle, when you bring distantly related genetic materials together you get the phenomena known as hybrid vigor; of course, that's what hybrid corn is all about. The more diverse the genetic material, the greater the opportunity for genetic increase; that diversity is partly what we're looking for in Asia.

Doug Dewey in a field of Crested wheatgrass. To control breeding, parchment paper sleeves are placed over female seedheads before pollination. Later, selected male pollen-bearing seedheads are shaken into the top of the sleeve. Sleeves are left in place until harvest.
—D.R. Dewey

We're heavily involved in interspecific hybridization at Logan. In fact, we're just on the verge of releasing a derivative of a Eurasian quack grass [*Agropyron repens*], and a native Bluebunch wheatgrass [*Agropyron spicatum*]; it has the productive qualities of quack without those troublesome creeping rhizomes. Of course, hybrids are usually sterile, but we manipulate around that, nowadays, by doubling the chromosomes with the chemical colchicine, and once we get fertility back, we've made an entirely new species.

Collecting plant material from the far corners of the earth is still important to our food supply. It's not as dangerous as it used to be, but it's become politicized, and, often, it's difficult to gain access—especially to developing countries. We sometimes find professional trouble-makers telling native peoples that they're being exploited; in fact, nothing could be farther from the truth. The fact is, the plant material we find in developing countries is traded for, or, at least,

227

borrowed at interest, so to speak. In other words, we take our findings home and work with them and prove their worth; later, we return them to their homelands much improved.[4]

CELESTINE LACEY
Weed management consultant—specializes in control of knapweed.

One of those "weeds that got away," referred to by Doug Dewey, would be knapweed: a problem in our western valleys. Anyone who has visited the Missoula area when the "beautiful purple wildflowers" are in bloom has seen what can happen; in many places grass production is down by ninety-five percent. And, many people have the idea that it just recently invaded Montana from Idaho or California; the fact is, knapweed has been right here and spreading for over sixty years.

Spotted knapweed (we also have Diffuse and Russian knapweed) probably came from Asia with alfalfa seed about 1893. It was first reported in Montana in 1920, and has spread at the rate of twenty-seven percent per year. As twenty-five cents invested at twenty-seven percent will grow to $4,615,305.73 in seventy years (you could look it up), so that first small infestation in Ravalli County has grown to 4,700,000 acres, according to a 1987 department of agriculture survey. Today, knapweed is in all fifty-six Montana counties.

Good range management pays. It makes it harder for knapweed to infest. I've seen it start, however, in dirt around a gopher hole and spread into "excellent"-condition range. Knapweed contains the allelopathic compound cnicin, which apparently suppresses growth in surrounding grass. It doesn't kill the grass completely. Once the knapweed is under control, the grass will come back fast. We've seen a 700 percent increase in grass on sites controlled with chemicals.

We've found knapweed growing as far east as Washington, D.C., but the immediate threat is right here in Montana to about thirty-four million acres of highly susceptible eastern rangeland sites—that's half of Montana's rangeland. And, our state spends about $500,000 a year on weed control. Part of that goes to fund preventive projects; they've drawn a sort of fire line along the eastern slope of the Rockies and committed themselves to halting the spread of knapweed. Another part goes for direct eradication; they get the best results with picloram at one-quarter pound per acre. That's expensive, but it controls weeds for a couple of years while grass makes a comeback.

About twenty-five percent of the weed trust fund finances nonchemical research, including biological control. There are insects that attack knapweed on its home range and keep it under control. Once these are found and tested and selected for reproduction in our environment, they'll get the job done with little further investment. That's the theory and, perhaps, the best hope where knapweed's taken hold. At the moment it looks promising.

A very small infestation of Diffuse and Spotted knapweed was reported in the Province of Alberta in 1974—officially, on about 300 acres. Knowing what had happened in Montana and in neighboring British Columbia, Alberta got right after it with legislation and a full eradication program with buffer zones and quarantine and hay inspection at their borders. We cooperate with them in every way, and they have profited from our experience in Montana, where knapweed got a fifty-year head start before anyone took notice.

TOM LAWRENCE

plant explorer, specializes in Siberian and Mongolian wild rye grasses.

There's always that risk of bringing in insects or disease or noxious weeds, and with millions of acres already seeded down to Crested wheat, Russian wild rye, and other "exotics," you might think we could play it safe and quarantine the North American continent to all imported food plants. That's what they did with livestock—cut off access to the vast European gene pool for sixty or seventy years. We're very aware of the risk with plants, and we keep our imports under tight security in greenhouses until we know they're clean, but some plants have a very narrow genetic base, and we need diverse types that may provide some useful characteristics. So, where do we look for diversity? Consider the work of Dr. N. I. Vavilov.

N. I. Vavilov was a famous Russian botanist before World War Two; he traveled widely studying plant populations—even visited the Lethbridge Research Station—and he proposed that the greatest diversity will be found near the center of origin of a species. The theory makes sense. Obviously, in the area of origin there will have been more time for mutation and crossfertilization, which results in more diversity, and most geneticists agree with him today. It wasn't always so, for Vavilov challenged the ideas of Stalin-era geneticist T. Lysenko, and for that he was arrested and thrown in the gulag where he died about 1942. Eventually, they realized the value of his work, and modern plant explorers use the Vavilov Institute in Leningrad in searching areas of origin for useful and diverse plant material.

Heredity and environment interact; that means some varieties do better in one place than another, and we consider that very carefully when we decide to go exploring. The area that interests me most, because it's so much like our own, is Kazakhstan, around Tselinograd, the area where Russian wild rye originated. The Russians are plowing up the steppes—as we did our native rangelands long ago—and planting wheat. On my trips in 1982 and 1986 they suspected me of spying on their wheat crop, and refused to let me visit. There's plenty of useful material in nearby China, however, and I've been there several times. When I find something I'm looking for, I bring it directly home to Swift Current, where it's kept in isolation for a couple of years to make sure it's not contaminated. Then we put it in the field and go to work.

It takes from ten to fifteen years to develop and test a new Canadian variety before we even apply for registration with the Plant Variety Registration Office in Ottawa. Once they approve and issue a certificate, we're free to turn our breeder's seed over to selected growers who produce foundation seed, which is propagated into certified seed for sale to farmers.

It takes four or five years after registration before commercial seed is readily available. For instance, Russian wild rye was a recent introduction when I arrived at Swift Current in 1954; I started working on seed-production and pasture tests and began to breed it, and we soon found out that Russian wild rye had fertility problems. My first job was to correct them. We came up with *Sawki* (a Cree word), which produced more seed than the ordinary variety of the day. I improved on that with *Mayak* (a Blackfoot term meaning "very pro-lific")—and with that we overcame the seed-production problem. Then I started selecting for establishment vigor. By keeping track of plants that came up best, I was able to improve establishment and, eventually, released a cultivar called Swift.

But, Russian wild rye has other problems; it curls up under the snow and—while it may be easy to establish, and green and nutri-tious in February—domestic cattle have trouble getting at it. An-other wild rye corrects that problem. "Altai" was brought in from the Altai Mountains by our science service people who studied it and classified it before they turned it over to us in 1950. We didn't do anything with it for a number of years—we thought it was too coarse for useful grazing. Eventually, we did some chemical and digestibility studies and built up a supply of seed. For three deep-snow years in a row we grazed it from November to the first of February, and cattle were always able to get at it because of its erectness and upright shape. Altai has another big advantage. Its root system goes down fifteen or sixteen feet, twice as far as most grasses; and Altai is a saline-tolerant grass. We think it has the capability to send down roots and actually pump out damp, poorly drained soils.

There must be dozens of other useful grasses growing around the world that haven't been studied yet. As recently as 1972 a delegation of bureaucrats went to China and was given seed of a new variety: Dahurian wild rye. We studied it at Swift Current and soon saw its potential as a "starter grass." In this dry area, we recommend seeding slower grasses, like Altai and Russian, in rows three feet apart; rapid-fire Dahurian can be seeded between those rows and provide valuable pasture during the first few years.

It was not until after Russian wild rye became commercially successful in Canada that Soviet delegations began to visit and ask questions. It was only then that we began to see reports of Russian wild rye in Soviet literature. Previously, they had not recognized its value or worked with it at all. Ironically, they still (in 1988) withhold

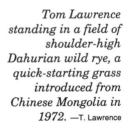

Tom Lawrence standing in a field of shoulder-high Dahurian wild rye, a quick-starting grass introduced from Chinese Mongolia in 1972. —T. Lawrence

permits to explore Soviet Mongolia where they are plowing mountain valleys said to be full of diverse grass and legume populations. My Russian scientist-friends hope to make more collections, themselves, before many species disappear from their area of origin; we should be trying to do the same before it's too late.

This is a global problem: More and more we are taking over the surface of the earth, leaving less and less for Mother Nature to play with. I've done my part to help. I've developed one variety of Intermediate wheatgrass, four of Russian, one of Altai (with two more in the works), and two varieties of Dahurian wild rye. I have the only Canadian cultivar of Tall wheatgrass; I've also been involved in the testing and registration of two of our alfalfas. I guess I'm doing all right because several of my varieties are used as far north as the Peace River country, and my Altais are in use in Utah and Wyoming. We get a good many phone calls from Montanans who are interested in their "pumping" capability.

It's very important to collect and carefully store genetic samples. When a plant disease new to this part of the world comes along, we'll be glad to find resistant characteristics in a variety in storage. We have a problem right now with the Russian wheat aphid, which attacks wheat, or, if wheat is not available, the wheatgrasses. If that aphid overwinters it could become a real problem and destroy many of our pastures and wheat crops. The aphid injects some sort of toxic substance into the plant and kills it; somewhere in storage we hope to find varieties with resistance. Another example, the wheat-stem sawfly, was once a real problem here on the prairies. In the 1940s, scientists working at Swift Current found a solid-stemmed Chinese spring wheat that the sawfly couldn't destroy.[5] They transferred the solid-stem characteristic to the bread wheats, screened them for production, and developed a useful wheat that solved the sawfly problem. That saved our farmers millions of dollars.

I first went to Asia in 1974. We were selling seed and looking for fresh plant material; we didn't have much luck. I led a four-man delegation on a visit to different research stations in 1982, and we did better. I went back by myself in '86 when *glasnost* was just starting, and they let me visit Kazakhstan and Tashkent and took me across the Caucasuses. My interpreter—supplied by the Vavilov Institute—was a very competent English-speaking scientist, and we got along very well.

The United Nations Food and Agriculture Organization sent me to their demonstration ranch in Inner Mongolia to help increase seed production. An interesting problem presented itself: a seed farm run, of course, entirely with human labor, required most of its space for growing food. As a result, not much room was left for seed.

And travel in China was interesting. My guide would deposit me in a train compartment and leave me there alone for fourteen hours at a stretch with nobody to talk to. At meal times she'd escort me to the meal car, clear everybody out, and leave me with the cooks. At my hotel in Inner Mongolia I found a screen around my table in the dining room so that I couldn't see the other diners, and couldn't be seen by them—kind of a solitary confinement.

One thing was very obvious in China in the seventies—ten years of "cultural revolution," ten years when nobody went to school, a decade when nobody went to university or was trained in scientific procedure had left the country drained. But things had changed when I went back in 1986, and the Chinese gave me the very best they had. In 1990 I can only hope it will be that way again because I'm eager to go back. I especially want to look for cultivars of wild ryes and creeping-rooted alfalfas, developed here at Swift Current, renovated in their areas of origin.

DORRIS CLARK

USDA botanist at Fort Collins, Colorado, compares his seed bank with Fort Knox.

It's startling to learn how very few of our major food crops were present when the first European settlers arrived in North America. I had thought corn was native to the United States—turns out it's from the tropics. It seems the sunflower, a few berries, and the tepary bean—a desert type—are about the only economically important foodstuffs we can claim as "natives." Generations of immigrants brought seed to help eke out a living on the land, and for 150 years, at least, plant-finding expeditions have explored far corners of the earth and sent home useful fruits and vegetables, shade trees, ornamentals, forage plants, and what-have-you, to improve our quality of life.

It's been estimated, though, that ninety-five percent of that genetic material has been lost. Prior to the turn of the century, there was no real systematic means of keeping track of what we had; specimens were kept in barn lofts, file drawers, musty offices, warm and humid warehouses—usually unprotected from rodents—and they deteriorated fast. Then, about 1900, the Bureau of Plant Industry installed an inventory system which brought to light this serious situation, and began to put it right.

I came to the National Seed Storage Lab in 1959. It was brand new, fully equipped, but not a seed in sight. We received our first seed samples soon thereafter: one alfalfa and two rye cultivars. Then, slowly, our collection grew as plant introduction stations and breeders in the United States and Canada began to back up their own inventories with samples sent to us for long-term preservation. It's just routine procedure now; we still don't get it all, but we're working at it, and every year we get a little more.[6]

Dorris Clark prepares plant germplasm for storage. —USDA-ARS archives

In the United States, regional plant introduction stations evaluate off-shore plant material; state experiment stations screen it during breeding trials; commercial seed companies contribute samples of every new variety they breed, and—in some cases—we store old, *heirloom* varieties that have been handed down for generations in families. They're important to plant breeders who get excited about primitive types that may have characteristics missing in our modern, highly selected varieties.

Genes, once lost, are no longer available to add genetic diversity, and, of course, we don't know what our genetic needs will be. Seventy-five years ago wheat breeders wanted higher yields and tolerance to drought; they weren't so much concerned with the nutritional or baking qualities in demand today. And, we can be certain of a continuing threat from plant diseases, perhaps developed by mutation; they can often be contained by crossing with resistant strains, so there's obviously a need to have such strains at hand to work with. To be ready, we search the world for specimens while learning to produce more useful varieties here at home. And we carefully store everything we find.

The importance of temperature and humidity in seed preservation has long been known, but at first there were no freezing facilities adequate for handling the volume, and we didn't fully realize the importance of *frozen* over *cool*. The advantages of cool, dry storage were probably first noticed by physiologists who found that lower temperatures lowered respiration, thus prolonging life. Samples stored in cool, controlled, dry conditions here at Fort Collins for almost thirty years before we started freezing show no loss in viability whatsoever. With cryopreservation at temperatures of minus 196 degrees Centigrade, we're confident we'll keep seeds safe for a century and more.[7]

We have in storage 250,000 samples (in 1989) from 12,000 to 15,000 species, and we're adding 12,000 to 15,000 samples every year. We expect, eventually, 500,000 samples—that's about the number of unique germplasm types we're dealing with. Most of our inventory is agronomic crops: range and forage grasses, legumes, plus a number of unique specimens used in medical research. If a scientist or plant breeder feels a plant has some potential value, he sends it and we store it; we don't go out in search of plants, the material comes to us.

And, we are charged with responsibility for every single sample—for knowing its location and maintaining its condition. At the present time, each sample is tested at five- to ten-year intervals to make sure no viability is lost. With any hint of loss of germination, arrangements are made for growing and replenishment. There's risk, however, in the testing process: Each time a seed is taken out of cold storage, genetic make-up could change; genes could be lost during harvesting or handling procedures. The less need for handling the better. And, regeneration is expensive; it can cost as much as $300 per sample if hand-pollination or isolation is required. The hope is, then, that we'll find deep-freezing so effective that we won't need to test seed quite so often. That would reduce the risk. But we still have much to learn; it just takes time to know.

We get lots of requests, like: "Grandfather had such-and-such a vegetable in his garden, and we thought it was delicious. We can't find his variety in any seed catalog now. Can you help?" We'd like to help, but our samples are very small; we're not set up to sell or give our seed, indiscriminately, to the general public. Our purpose is to distribute genes for breeding purposes—*genes*, not the vegetable itself.

In 1970, a corn blight hit the Corn Belt—near disaster; new high-producing hybrids weren't resistant. But, correction was a fairly simple matter of introducing genes from older, blight-resistant, open-pollinated corns. The National Seed Storage Lab should be able to supply that kind of plant material as required. For example, a wheat "collection" was brought in from Russia a number of years ago, and—from all appearances—it was a very inferior wheat. But, a graduate student working with a sample found resistance to sixteen wheat diseases—tremendous value for breeding new, resistant varieties, the kind of sample we hope to have available as needed.

No one would dare estimate the value of the genetic material in storage at Fort Collins. Granted, much will doubtless go unused, but no one is able to sort that out ahead, and just one sample may be worth the entire project. Sitting here in storage, carefully preserved, our seed bank backs the "genetic currency" of our continental food supply. That's why we say this collection is as good as gold, this building more important than Fort Knox.

A cold room at the USDA National Seed Storage Laboratory, Fort Collins, where almost half a million samples are stored for possible use by plant breeders. —USDA-ARS archives

THE GENE POOL

Whatever else the reader may have scavenged along the trail and added to his baggage, I hope he or she has acquired some understanding of the people and plants who live on and by The Range.

What I think I picked up, as I listened and took notes, was the importance of diversity in genetics. Not being a geneticist, I must blindly accept—as something I either noticed or was told—that nature has ways of introducing diversity into gene pools. We humans then take over, and usually select away from that diversity—unavoidably (as when we propagate a billion seeds of Crested wheat from three or four collections), or purposefully (as when we reduce domestic plants or animals to cultivars or breeds). More about that later, in another book I'll call The Ranch. *Meanwhile, experience encourages me to accept the vital importance of Dorris Clark's "Fort Knox" of plant genetics, with its steaming, freezing vats of liquid nitrogen, in which repose the "specie" of our nations' food supply. More on that later, too.*

As a matter of interest, Alex Johnston (who died in 1989) has written that there are about 350,000 flowering plants (including grasses) in the world.[8] About 17,000 occur in North America. He tells us there are 1,775 flowering species in Alberta, about 800 in the part I've called The Range. Further, of the 350,000 flowering plants, worldwide, about 20,000 are edible, but only about 250 are cultivated for food; just twenty food plants stand between mankind and famine. Just seven cereal grains provide sixty percent of the calories and fifty percent of the protein consumed on earth. Furthermore, Alex tells us, of 250 cultivated species, two may have been used for 10,000 years; 180 for over 2,000 years; only seventy have been introduced to cultivation since the time of Christ; one species (triticale) *has been introduced in the last half century.*

The point I want to make with these statistics is that freedom from famine on our continent—and, especially, on The Range—depends on a surprisingly small number of species. Our marvelous economic and transportation systems allow us to take stocks of food for granted where—just four generations ago—the people of our range depended on a single beast and forty edible plants.

Cattle roundup on Ɑ7 Ranche in the Porcupine Hills of Alberta.
—Carling O'Keefe Breweries

In my professional opinion based on lifelong study, much of our native range is in better shape after a hundred years of ranching than it was in buffalo days.

—Alex Johnston, 1986

Range Rotation

Rangeland—that vast area of earth's surface that is, or could be, covered with grass—is important to us all. As John J. Ingalls wrote a century ago in his "Tribute to Grass" essay, "Next to the divine profusion of water, light, and air—those three physical facts which render existence possible—may be reckoned the universal beneficence of grass."

Because grass stores valuable nutrients in its roots, topsoil containing the decayed roots of generations past becomes a storehouse of resources for the future. And root-rich soil holds water and releases it on demand. Unlike jungle, where nutrients are stored in treetop foliage, organic-rich rangeland is, in effect, a reservoir for water and nutrients thousands of times larger and many times more efficient than any manmade wonder.

But the range ecology includes other forms of life as well. Animals and insects eat and digest, mix and stir, live and die on vegetation. They are vital to the whole; it is utter nonsense to believe in healthy rangeland devoid of grazing animals.

And there are other mammals whose welfare is woven into the whole range ecosystem. These are the managers—the men and women who see that things get done. The story of The Range is the story of people and plants and animals. It is the story of a way of life.

TWO GILCHRIST FAMIILIES

the current generation on The Range, are still in business after three-quarters of a century.

TOM and LOIS

on Deer Creek north of the Sweet Grass Hills.

In the spring of 1914 the five young Gilchrist boys—my dad, Joe, was the youngest—formed a partnership and bought the Whitemud Ranch south of Maple Creek, Saskatchewan. The Whitemud was a great hay base, and Uncle Sandy stayed behind and put up hay and wintered calves while his brothers expanded operations to the west. By the end of the thirties, they owned strategically located ranches that controlled thousands of acres of public grazing land in the southeast corner of Alberta. They branded their cattle Bar X Bar, stacked, straight-up, right hip.

Rube—the oldest—and Mildred were on the Q Ranch, near the border port of Wild Horse, where they put up hay, kept sheep, wintered bulls, and managed the whole shebang. Chay and Mable summered yearlings and two- and three-year-olds at the Cross Z and Lost River ranches. Dad and Mother put up more hay and wintered all the yearlings here on Deer Creek. It was a 125-mile ride or cattle drive from the Deer Creek Ranch to the Whitemud. I'm sure you don't know, or care, where all those places are, but you can imagine what it was like to manage such an outfit before the days of telephones, radios, airplanes, and highways. The boys would be out on the range for weeks at a time, out of touch with each other and their families.

But, manage they did until 1945, just after the war, when they decided to wind things up. The handwriting was on the wall: large chunks of grazing lease would be lost to "community pastures." And prices were high; it was a good time to regroup. With everything sorted and tallied, there were 10,000 Bar X Bar cattle for sale, plus 6,000 sheep, and hundreds of work and saddle horses. Not bad for a family of homesteader-kids fresh out of Nova Scotia.

Dad bought the Deer Creek back after the company sold. The cattle were gone, but he bought more cows at once. I remember one bunch in particular: mostly Shorthorn-crosses with lots of color to 'em; Mom and us kids trailed them home from Manyberries—chuck-wagon and all. I remember some Hereford bulls we bought in 1946—great huge

Gilchrist Brothers' two-year-olds being trailed from Deer Creek to the Cross Z Ranch in April 1945. —National Archives of Canada

things, they were. Beef cattle have changed a lot since then, but the old-time cowmen needed the Hereford breed. Those white-faced cows could tough it through the winter and come up with a calf—some kind of calf, any kind of a calf—almost every spring.

Our Deer Creek Ranch still has thousands of acres of low-producing, dry *crown* grazing lease, but, as competition grows from hunting and recreation, we'll concentrate production on our deeded land. That means irrigated pasture for more AUMs of summer grazing. It means improved varieties of orchard grass, alfalfa, Meadow brome, and triticale for higher yields over a longer growing season. It means crossbred cattle for more efficient secondary production. And it means—as always—good management of our native range.

BILL and HELEN

on the Whitemud Ranch south of the Cypress Hills.

Old-timers still call this the Whitemud place. My dad, Rube, bought it back himself after Gilchrist Brothers dissolved. It's Cypress Cattle Company now, but we still put up native hay along Whitemud, or Frenchman's, Creek, and we still run cows on native range for ten months of the year. And we calve on green grass in May and June. You don't see deer or antelope or elk dropping fawns and calves in the snow, like so many range cows; Mother Nature still has a lot to teach us.

I broke some rangeland, once, to seed some Crested wheat for early grazing. An Indian friend stopped by and saw all the rocks we'd raised; "Billy," he said, "I think she's wrong side up." He was right! We were always gonna break some more, but we couldn't buy machinery fast enough.

Well, the flats along Whitemud and Deer Creek still grow hay, and my cousin Tom and I still stack it loose—though with Hestons instead of horses, nowadays. And native grass still carries most of our cows for much of the year on ranches a hundred miles apart, at opposite ends of the range our fathers used. We both have sons or daughters who'll be taking over someday. And one thing we never forget: Take care of the range; it's been taking care of us for generations.

ON THE EWING RANCH

in the Porcupine Hills, 150 miles northwest of Gilchrist country.

The door slams shut; the dark ranch house is empty for the first time in almost thirty years. In predawn blackness, coyotes yelp and yammer on the hill, teasing the dogs. Half a dozen cats skulk in yard-light shadows knowing that, when times are tough, the lady of the house comes through this door with milk and meat at dawn. Well, times are tough this morning—the milk cow's out to pasture with two big orphan calves to suck her dry; there'll be no warm milk for barnyard cats this day.

The dogs, Midge and Robbie, wait and wonder, too worried to bother with coyotes now. For a week they've trailed the pickup to the garbage pit each evening and watched decades worth of junk go up in smoke. Yesterday their house was gutted: furniture, barrels, boxes packed in a sivler-orange U-Haul van; the ranch stock trailer loaded with heavy appliances; the faded green Chevrolet pickup piled with leftovers. And now, this morning, suitcases—always objects of sadness for Midge and Robbie. They watch and worry until, with hugs and pats and tears, engines start and old friends drive away into the first pink light of dawn. In a few hours a new generation will take over. No strangers here, our son Charlie and his wife Sherry will run the milk cow in and feed the cats and comfort the dogs, and ranch life will go on.

Claire and I had come to the SN Ranch in the southern Alberta hills in 1955 with a brand new family of our own. We'd been "landed immigrants" then, in search of opportunity like thousands of farmers and ranchers before us. Now, as we drove away down the long valley of Cripple Creek, the fruits of many labors lined the road: forage crops of alfalfa and brome baled up for winter feed; corrals and sheds built to keep the summer rain and winter elk out of stacks of hay; round wooden troughs, strategically placed, bubbling with fresh spring water; brown native rangeland resting, to provide fresh grass next spring.

Of course, there would be no end of things for Charlie and his family to accomplish as time and cash allowed: hayfields to reseed, shed roofs to repair, more springs to develop, fences to build, pastures to rotate, the never-ending job of breeding better cattle. Ranches are living things, and even management needs reseeding and new growth. We could take some pride in a host of jobs well done; there would be plenty left to do in years to come.

On that fall morning in 1982, Claire and I left the SN Ranch, and we didn't look back. When we reached the place where the Porcupines drop off a thousand feet to the prairie stretching north and east and south, we stopped to gaze; the range and ranch and farm land of Alberta rolled away into Saskatchewan and Montana. The three buttes of the Sweet Grass Hills were a shade on the horizon.

The Leavings

There are a number of historic landmarks on the range that, in earlier days, were called "The Leavings"—places where a trail or wagon road left the water and shelter of a valley. There was The Leavings of Sun River, where the Benton Road took off across the hills for Helena; there was The Leavings of Willow Creek, beneath the Porcupine Hills, where the Macleod Trail struck out on what could be a forty-mile dry march to the Highwood River and Calgary. "The leavings," as a place name, may ring strange on modern ears: we are never far from water at sixty miles an hour.

You, the reader, have now traveled across unsettled lands, through hard times, in every kind of weather and arrived here at The Leavings of The Range refreshed, I hope, and well-supplied with history and background. From here, a trail leads to The Ranch where many breeds and crosses of exotic cattle graze. If you take that trail, you'll likely meet some characters you know traveling in the company of a colorful crew of cattle breeders, auctioneers, veterinarians, scientists, businessmen, and politicians—plus some ordinary ranchers. If there are such things as ordinary ranchers.

REGISTER of CHARACTERS

WESLEY A. ALM (1925-)

Rancher of Claresholm, Alberta, and the son of a pioneer homesteader, farmer, and cattleman. He owned and operated the Bar 15 Ranch in the Porcupine Hills for over 35 years with his wife Dixie and, lately, with their son Glen and his family. Wes is past president of the Alberta Simmental Association and a pioneer Simmental breeder.

E. WILLIAM ANDERSON (1914-)

Rangeman of Lake Oswego, Oregon, and state range management specialist with the Soil Conservation Service from 1949 to 1974. After retirement he was certified by the Society for Range Management as an accredited range consultant. He is the originator of the human-action technique, coordinated resource management planning.

JAMES H. BAILEY (1933-)

Veterinarian of Great Falls, Montana, raised on an eastern Montana ranch. He graduated from Colorado State University with a DVM degree in 1957 and returned to general practice in the Billings area. Since 1980 he has been a partner in Associated Veterinary Services. Horses have always been important in Bailey's life and practice.

WILLIAM F. BIG SPRING (1919-1991)

Rancher of East Glacier Park, Montana, and an accomplished artist. Politically astute, Billy has served on the Blackfeet Tribal Council, the Glacier County Board of Commissioners, and the Republican National Committee. He is listed in *Who's Who in American Indians,* and *National Biographies of the World.*

GORDON L. BURTON (1916-1990)

Rancher of Claresholm, Alberta, affection-ately known to his neighbors as "the perfessor" because of his Ph.D. in agricultural economics from Iowa State University. In the early 1950s Gordon returned to the Porcupine Hills to as-sume responsibilities for his family's Burke Creek Ranch, which he operated with his wife Jean and sons Jay and Rick. He was president of the Western Stock Growers' Association in 1970-72.

FARRINGTON R. CARPENTER (1886-1980)

Rancher and lawyer of Hayden, Colorado, came west from Illinois at age 14. After college at Princeton and Harvard he came home to prac-tice law and engage in county politics. On the range, Carpenter will be remembered as first director of the U.S. Grazing Service, a Hereford breeder, and an early proponent of performance testing. In 1967 he was named Stockman of the Year by Colorado State University.

RICHARD CASSUTT (1930-)

Rancher of Fort Benton, Montana, grew up on his adoptive grandparents' Blackfeet Indian Reservation ranch, which he managed and has owned since 1978. He graduated from Montana State University in 1950 with a degree in animal science and later built a successful real estate and appraisal business.

DORRIS C. CLARK (1932-)

Botanist at Fort Collins, Colorado. He spent thirty years testing and storing seed stock at the U.S. Department of Agriculture's National Seed Storage Laboratory.

C. WAYNE COOK (1914-)

Range ecologist of Fort Collins, Colorado, born on a western Kansas farm. He served Utah State University's College of Natural Resources from 1941 to 1968 as research professor and assistant dean. For 12 years before retirement he ran the Range Science Department at Colorado State University, and continues still as a range consultant. He was president of the Society for Range Management in 1968-69. (SRM photo)

MARSHALL COPITHORNE (1937-)

Rancher of Jumping Pound, Alberta, is third-generation on the CL Ranch, a cattle and grass operation west of Calgary, which he now runs with his wife Teresa and six children. Marshall has been vice president of the Calgary Exhibition and Stampede and is one of the founders of the *Beefbooster* cattle gene pool.

JOHN M. CROSS (1916-)

Rancher of Nanton, Alberta, and a leader in the Canadian cattle industry as international director of the Society for Range Management and chairman of its International Mountain Section. He is a past president of both the Western Stock Growers' Association and the Canadian Cattlemen's Association. He and his wife Eleanor still make their home on the Q7 Ranche, now owned and operated by several of their children.

249

DOUGLAS R. DEWEY (1929-)

U.S. Department of Agriculture research geneticist at Logan, Utah, since 1956, and professor of plant science at Utah State University. He studied at the Royal Botanical Gardens in Kew, England, and the Komarov Botanical Institute in Leningrad. Dewey's research has led to strategies for the successful uses of wide hybridization that apply to all crops.

VIVIAN BRUNEAU ELLIS (1900-)

Retired rancher of Great Falls, Montana, born in South Dakota to French-Canadian parents. She lived with her parents on the Whitemud Ranch in southwestern Saskatchewan from 1905 until 1910, when they returned to the Smith River country south of Great Falls. Mrs. Ellis and her husband Richard owned and operated a sheep and cattle ranch west of Choteau, Montana, for many years.

L. MACKENZIE FORBES (1932-)

Rangeman of Edmonton, Alberta, and a well-known member of the Alberta range community since the 1950s, when he went to work for the government as a grazing lease inspector. He was assistant deputy minister for public lands in the Alberta Department of Forestry, Lands and Wildlife from 1981 to 1987.

JONATHAN FOX III (1920-)

Livestock breeder of Kamloops, British Columbia, known worldwide for his champion Morgan and Percheron horses, and Polled Hereford and Chianina cattle. Reputed as the first man ever to have judged a major livestock show from horseback (in Regina), he has judged every class of animal from poultry to llamas at the world's greatest shows. He's a member of both the Saskatchewan and Canadian Agricultural halls of fame. (Ball Studios photo)

BILL GILCHRIST (1928-)

Rancher of Maple Creek, Saskatchewan, runs the Cypress Cattle Company just a few miles from his father's 1902 homestead. Home base for Bill, his wife Helen, and their son Joe is the Whitemud Ranch, purchased by Bill's father and uncles in 1913.

JOSEPH D. GILCHRIST (1900-)

Retired rancher of Medicine Hat, Alberta, born on the second day of the twentieth century. At age 14 he became a full-fledged working partner in the Gilchrist Brothers' company and helped build it into a large-scale range cattle and sheep operation before the Second World War. His wife Murial is HARRY HARGRAVE's sister.

TOM GILCHRIST (1934-)

Rancher of Milk River, Alberta, and one of the founders of the *Beefbooster* cattle gene pool. Tom was raised on the Deer Creek Ranch and, since the late 1950s, operates it with his wife Lois.

WARREN G. HARDING (1922-)

Career weatherman and rancher of Simms, Montana, lives on the Sun River where he and his wife Grace raise Simmental cattle. Retired from the U.S. Weather Bureau after 38 years of service in Alaska and Montana, he continues as a meteorologist and partner in Northwest Weather Associates, Inc. of Great Falls. The Department of Commerce awarded him a bronze medal for his research on the movement of arctic air masses and winter storms across Alberta and Montana.

HARRY J. HARGRAVE (1909-1984)

Rangeman and superintendent of Alberta's Manyberries Range Experiment Station from 1935 to 1947; he spent 10 more years at Lethbridge Research Station. From 1959 until retirement in 1970, Harry was deputy director of Prarie Farm Rehabilitation Administration (PFRA) at Regina. He was widely known in the range and livestock communities.

NEIL S. HARVIE (1929-)

Rancher of Cochrane, Alberta, operates the Glenbow Ranch in the Bow Valley west of Calgary with his wife Robin, their daughter Katie Norman, and son Tim. He also runs a large commercial cattle ranch at Riske Creek in the interior of British Columbia. Neil is a co-founder of the *Beefbooster* cattle gene pool, and has been a director of the Calgary Exhibition and Stampede, president of Western Stock Growers' Association, vice chairman of the Alberta Cattle Commission, and director of the Canadian Cattlemen's Association.

CHASE T. HIBBARD (1948-)

Fourth-generation rancher of Helena, Montana, and a ranch management consultant who has been president and general manager of the family owned Sieben Live Stock Company in Montana's Big Belt Mountains since 1976. He has been on the board of the Montana Woolgrowers Association and president of the U.S. Targhee Sheep Association.

(George Lane photo, Helena Independent Record)

BLAKE and MARY HOLTMAN
(1942- & 1943-)

Ranchers of Taber, Alberta, long ago seeded their farmland down to grass on which they raise steers. They also run a commercial cowherd in the foothills, and operate a custom feedlot. After meeting at the University of Oregon, they transferred to the University of British Columbia at Vancouver, where Blake graduated in business and Mary as a teacher. They have been students of ALLAN SAVORY's management methods since his arrival in America.

AUGUST L. HORMAY (1907-)

Rangeman of San Francisco, California, has been in public service with the U.S. Forest Service and the Bureau of Land Management for over 50 years. He developed rest-rotation grazing and has seen its acceptance on wide stretches of public and private range. The U.S. Department of Agriculture issued him a Superior Service Award in 1957 and a Distinguished Service Award in 1971; in 1972 he received an Outstanding Achievement and Service Award from the Society for Range Management. Well into his eighties, he continues to monitor range research projects. (SRM photo)

GERALD HUGHES (1903-)

Rancher of Stanford, Montana, has lived on the same ranch in the Judith Basin all his life. Until 1971 he operated the Hughes Livestock Company started by his father and brothers Harley and Curt. Gerald graduated from Oregon State College in 1934 with a major in animal husbandry. He served 16 years in the Montana Legislature, was president of the Montana Woolgrowers' Association, and has always been active in the Montana Stockgrowers' Association.

FRANK JACOBS (1917-)

Best known as an agricultural journalist of Calgary, Alberta, Frank is a member of the Alberta Agricultural Hall of Fame and a fellow of the Agricultural Institute of Canada. Following two decades as editor of *Cattlemen* magazine, he served as consultant with Deloitte, Haskins and Sells on projects in Mexico, Ecuador, and El Salvador, as well as in western Canada. His far-reaching experience includes rancher, school-teacher, bureaucrat, and founding secretary-manager of the Stockmen's Memorial Foundation, a privately organized museum and library complex in Calgary.

ALEX JOHNSTON (1920-1989)

Rangeman of Lethbridge, Alberta, retired in 1980 from a lifetime career as range scientist at the Lethbridge Research Station. As a consultant on range improvement, he traveled in Kenya and Pakistan. Alex lectured widely on the history of southern Alberta and produced hundreds of papers, pamphlets, and books dealing with range management and the ecol-

ogy and history of the region. As SOI-TAINA (Rainy Chief), Alex was a champion of the native range people around Lethbridge and a tireless working member of the Kainai Chieftainship in the Blood Tribe of the Blackfoot Confederacy.

FRED KING (1946-)

Wildlife area manager of Bozeman, Montana, is responsible for the Wall Creek Game Range near Ennis. A native of Pennsylvania, Fred finished his college training at Montana State University and has since been employed by the state Department of Fish, Wildlife & Parks, managing winter range for elk.

LESLIE EWING KRIZ (1955-)

Mother of three boys in Rimbey, Alberta, she grew up on the SN Ranch in the Porcupine Hills. She was Alberta High School rodeo queen in 1973 and later attended Montana State University at Bozeman. (H. T. Morrison photo)

CELESTINE A. LACEY (1953-)

Agronomist of Helena, Montana, holds a master's degree and specializes in weed science. She served as state weed coordinator for the Montana Department of Agriculture, and later became a private consultant specializing in the study and control of knapweed.

IKE LANIER (1930-)

A second-generation dryland farmer of Lethbridge, Alberta, Ike has owned and operated Never-Idle Farm for over 30 years with his wife, Diana, and, since 1989, with his son, Rod. Deep concern for the land and the future of farming has led the Lanier family to be active in conservation groups and business organizations. Ike has been a member of the advisory committee of Lethbridge Research Station. He has served as president of the Lethbridge (grain) Terminal and Alberta Terminals, Ltd.; director of the Canola Growers Commission; director of the Western Wheat Growers Association; and president of the Alberta Winter Wheat Commission.

THOMAS LAWRENCE (1927-)

Geneticist, of Swift Current, Saskatchewan, bred grasses at the research station there for 35 years. After receiving his Ph.D. from the University of Alberta, Lawrence developed a dozen varieties of grasses and introduced three wild ryes to Canadian agriculture. He has received many honors, including the Distinguished Agrologist Award of the Saskatchewan Institute of Agrologists and the Outstanding Research Award from the Canadian Society of Agronomy.

JAMES A. LITTLE (1943-)

Rancher of Emmett, Idaho, where he grazes both public and private land, as his father and grandfather had before him. He was president of the Idaho Cattle Association in 1986, and in 1987 served on the board of directors of Cattlefax, the National Cattlemen's Association market research arm.

EDWIN A. McKINNON (1911-)

Rancher of Calgary, Alberta, has been raising and feeding cattle all his life. After starting with his father and brothers on the LK Ranch near Calgary, he ran his own outfit, the Running M, for many years. He has been a director of the Calgary Exhibition and Stampede and president of the Society for Range Management.

KEN F. MILLER (1944-)

Rancher and seed grower of Milk River, Alberta, mastered in agricultural economics and specialized in publicly owned pasture lands. He and his wife Mary went farming in the early 1970s; they raise grass seed and bison on their southern Alberta farm.

GEORGE F. ROSKIE (1912-)

Forester and rangeman of Great Falls, Montana, was superintendent of the Lewis & Clark National Forest in the 1960s. After a 30-year career, he retired from the U.S. Forest Service and served three terms in the Montana State Senate.

ROBERT L. ROSS (1921-)

Rangeman of Bozeman, Montana, born and raised on a ranch in the Bull Mountains of central Montana. After receiving a degree in range management from Montana State College he spent 30 years as a range conservationist with the Soil Conservation Service. Bob and his wife Nancy are well known throughout the ranching communities of Montana and Alberta. Recently Bob has gained renown as a cowboy poet and humorist. (SRM photo)

DON RYERSON (1923-)

Rangeman of Bozeman, Montana, spent a lifetime in teaching, extension, and research after receiving his bachelor's and master's degrees from Montana State College and his Ph.D. in range ecology from Texas A&M. He returned to MSU in 1957 to teach until his retirement as professor emeritus of range science in 1980. He is well remembered by a generation of students.

ALLAN SAVORY (1935-)

Teacher and consultant of Albuquerque, New Mexico, immigrated to the United States from Zimbabwe in the late 1970s, and has since developed his land-use theories into the widely acclaimed Holistic Resource Management discipline, which emphasizes human interaction with plants, animals, soils, and water in a whole environment. He has a large number of followers in both the U.S. and Canada.

E. MAYNARD SMITH (1924-)

Rancher of Glen, Montana, and a fourth-generation cattleman with a degree in animal science from University of California, Davis. He has been director of the California Cattlemen's Association, president of the Southwest Stockgrowers' Association, director of the Montana Stockgrowers' Association, director of Montana Livestock Ag-Credit, Inc. (formerly the Montana Livestock Production Credit Association), 4H leader, and supervisor of the Beaverhead Conservation District. He is on the grazing advisory board for the Butte District, and on the steering committee for the East Pioneer Experimental Stewardship Program.

SYLVESTER SMOLIAK (1926-)

Plant breeder of Lethbridge, Alberta, has been a range scientist at the Manyberries and Lethbridge research stations for 40 years. He published more than 240 scientific papers and received the Special Achievement and Fellow Awards of the Society for Range Management.

SOI-TAINA (Rainy Chief): see **ALEX JOHNSTON.**

CLAIR A. WILLITS JR. (1922-)

Agricultural banker of Great Falls, Montana, ran the Great Falls Production Credit Association from 1963 until his retirement in 1985.

STAN WILSON (1927-)

Rancher of Nanton, Alberta, is past chairman of the Alberta Cattle Commission and past president of the Canadian Cattlemen's Association.

258

Range Plants

Native Range Plants

Basin (or Giant) wild rye	*Elymus cinereus*
Bluebunch wheatgrass	*Agropyron spicatum*
Blue grama (buffalo grass)	*Bouteloua gracilis*
Buffalograss	*Buchloe dactyloides*
Green needlegrass	*Stipa viridula*
Idaho fescue	*Festuca Idahoensis*
Needle-and-thread (Speargrass)	*Stipa comata*
Northern wheatgrass (Canada)	*Agropyron dasystachyum*
Porcupine grass	*Stipa spartea*
Rough fescue	*Festuca scabrella*
Saskatoon (serviceberry)	*Amelanchier alnifolia*
Slender wheatgrass	*Agropyron trachycaulum*
Spike fescue	*Festuca spicata*
Thickspike wheatgrass (U.S.)	*Agropyron dasystachyum*
Western wheatgrass	*Agropyron smithii*

Exotic Species

Altai wild rye	*Elymus augustus*
Cheat grass	*Bromus tectorum*
Cicer milkvetch	*Astragalus cicer*
Crested wheatgrass	*Agropyron cristatum*
Dahurian wild rye	*Elymus dahuricu*
Intermediate wheatgrass	*Thinopyrum intermedium*
Kentucky bluegrass	*Poa pratensis*
Orchard grass	*Dactylis glomerata*
Russian wild rye	*Psathyrostachys juncea*
Smooth brome	*Bromus inermis*
Tall wheatgrass	*Thinopyrum elongatum*
Timothy	*Phleum pratense*

Noxious Weeds

Diffuse knapweed	*Centaurea diffusa*
Leafy spurge	*Euphorbia esula*
Russian knapweed	*Centaurea repens*
Spotted knapweed	*Centaurea maculosa*

Glossary

ADA: Alberta Department of Agriculture.

ADM: Assistant Deputy Minister, a Canadian title.

Agrologist: Agricultural soils specialist.

Agronomist: Agricultural crop production specialist.

Agrostologist: Old term for a professional grass person.

Annual: A plant that matures, produces seed, and dies in one year. Kochia and stinkweed are good examples that appear on freshly disturbed rangeland as pioneers in the natural succession.

ARS: Agricultural Research Service of USDA.

ASCS: Agricultural Stabilization Conservation Service of the USDA, provides financial assistance. Sometimes confused with Soil Conservation Service (SCS), also of the USDA, which provides technical assistance.

Awn: A slender bristle attached to the glume or lemma of some plants, such as barley, foxtail, and needlegrass, that sometimes causes irritation in grazing animals.

BIA: Bureau of Indian Affairs of the U.S. Department of Interior.

Biennial: A plant that lasts two years. Burdock, a common range nuisance, is an example; rhubarb-like leaves appear the first year, a crop of burrs the second, and then the plant dies.

BLM: Bureau of Land Management of the U.S. Department of Interior.

Border: The international boundary between the United States and Canada. The portion between the prairie provinces and Montana was established by treaty in 1818, but not surveyed until 1874.

Brittle environment: The predominant land surface on earth, where the natural decay of plant material takes place slowly through chemical oxidation and weathering.

Bunchgrass: Any grass species growing from a common base to form a tuft of culms.

260

CDA: Canada Department of Agriculture, now called Agriculture Canada.

Chernozem: Rich, black topsoil found primarily in Russia, but also in areas of the United States and Canada. (From Russian *chernyi*, black; *zemlya*, earth.)

Commensurability: The philosophy of limiting grazing permits in relation to the carrying capacity of the permittees home base.

Coordinated planning: See CRMP.

County agent: Local representative of state agricultural extension service, an adjunct of the land-grant college system by which information is extended throughout the state. In Montana, County Agents are members of the MSU faculty.

CRMP: Coordinated Resource Management Planning, a system for getting diverse user-groups to work together.

Crown land: The Canadian "public domain," which, in the West since 1930, falls under provincial rather than federal jurisdiction.

Culm: Grass stem, usually with nodes or joints.

Cultivar: A cultivated variety of plant.

DA: District Agriculturist of the ADA, equivalent to agricultural extension agent.

Ducks Unlimited: (DU) A privately organized conservation group with a record of working well with land owners, agricultural producers, and hunters on both sides of the border.

Ecosystem: A community of living organisms and their environment functioning as an ecological unit in nature.

Feral: Wild animals descended from tame stock.

Forbs: Herbs that are not grasses; wild flowers, for instance.

Glacial drift or till: A mix of soil, sand, gravel, and boulders left behind after a glacier melts.

HRM: Holistic Resource Management, a concept that considers the land and those who use it in an all-encompasing manner, including their culture, values, and economics, at minimum.

NEPA: National Environmental Protection Act of the U.S. Congress, 1969.

NWMP: North West Mounted Police, established in 1873; given the prefix "Royal" in 1904, in 1920 it became the Royal Canadian Mounted Police (RCMP).

PCA: Production Credit Association, established in the 1930s to help U.S. farmers secure loans.

Perennial: A plant that lives more than two years; most grasses are perennials.

PFRA: Prairie Farm Rehabilitation Administration, a hold-over from the 1930s, headquartered in Regina, Saskatchewan.

PRIA: Public Rangeland Improvement Act of the U.S. Congress, 1978.

Rest-rotation grazing: A management method calling for two years of uninterupted growth after a plant is grazed.

Rhizome: Underground reproductive stem, or rootstock, of certain spreading plants, such as quack grass.

Riparian: The vegetation zone along the banks of creeks and rivers.

Savory Grazing Method (SGM): A short-duration grazing plan employing the use of a radical, or wheel-shaped, "grazing cell"; this method preceded Holistic Resource Management (HRM).

SCS: Soil Conservation Service of the U.S. Department of Agriculture.

SRM: Society for Range Management headquartered in Denver.

Saline soils: Those containing soluble salts (in this area principally sulfates and chlorides of calcium, magnesium and sodium) which will not react to form new soil minerals and which may weaken or destroy plant life.

Shrub: Any woody plant smaller than a tree.

Spike (or Spikelet): The basic flowering part of a grass plant.

Taylor land: Public lands of the U.S. placed under the jurisdiction of the U.S. Grazing Service (later BLM) by the Taylor Grazing Act of 1934.

Triticale: A hybrid cross between rye and durum wheat with high yield and rich protein.

USDA: U.S. Department of Agriculture.

USFS: Forest Service of the U.S. Department of Agriculture.

Ungulates: Hoofed animals that graze.

Wether: A castrated sheep.

Notes

1
The Buffalo Range

1. John E. Parsons, *West on the 49th Parallel*, (New York: William Morrow & Co., 1963), p. 161. Greene's journal, including other letters written from Montana in 1874, is preserved in the Western Americana Collection at Yale University.

2. This "alkaline country," and subsequent mentions throughout *The Range* of soil salinity or saline seep, is a result of glaciers that advanced and retreated across this area several times, the last of which melted about 10,000 years ago, leaving behind glacial till. As the till erodes and weathers, its minerals break down and release salts into the soil. Some of these (iron and aluminum) become part of the soil; others (calcium, magnesium, and sodium) stay soluble in the soil as gypsum (calcium sulfate), Epsom salts (magnesium sulfate), and even common table salt (sodium chloride).

As water percolates into the soil it dissolves the salts and sometimes becomes so polluted that it cannot be used for irrigation and may injure or even kill animals that drink it. Water tends to flow toward higher salt concentrations, and plant roots normally contain more salt and mineral molecules than the surrounding soil, so they attract water. In a "saline seep" the amount of water in roots and soil is almost equal; therefore little or no water flows to plant roots and they die.

3. William T. Hornaday (1854-1937), an early leader in wildlife conservation, brought the plight of the buffalo to public attention in *Extermination of the American Bison, With a Sketch of its Discovery and Life History* (Washington, D.C.: Government Printing Office, 1889). He was chief taxidermist at the National Museum in Washington, D.C., and the first director (1896-1926) of the New York Zoological Park.

4. Paul F. Sharp, *Whoop-up Country* (Minneapolis: University of Minnesota, 1955), p. 41f; Sharp says that John J. Healy and Alfred B. Hamilton from Sun River "... spearheaded the invasion when they moved their trade across the boundary in 1869 ... netting $50,000 in their season's traffic." In the early 1870s renegade traders out of Fort Benton operated trading posts in what is now southern Alberta with sensational names like Whiskey Gap, Standoff, Robbers' Roost, and the notorious Fort Whoop-up. Buffalo robes were worth about $12 in trade goods, and Sharp says that as late as 1875 "over 100,000 robes and pelts were shipped annually to eastern markets by [Fort] Benton brokers. Sir Cecil Denny recalled seeing 20,000 robes ready for shipment the following spring." See also, John C. Ewers, *The Blackfeet: Raiders on the Northwestern Plains* (Norman: University of Oklahoma Press, 1958), p. 278.

5. John C. Ewers, who was for many years curator of the Museum of the Plains Indians at Browning, Montana, and who interviewed Indians born in the 1850s and 1860s, discusses this starvation period in *The Blackfeet*, p. 278ff.

6. The métis were the half-breeds who spread out from the Red River settlements. Alexander Ross, an early settler and fur-trader, left a wonderful contemporary account of the métis buffalo hunt and pemmican trade in *The Red River Settlement: Its Rise, Progress, and Present State* (London: Smith, Elder, 1856).

7. Jon Cates, *The Story of the National Bison Range* (Helena, Mont.: Falcon Press, 1986), offers the popular legend of orphan buffalo calves "trailing" Walking Coyote across the continental divide. Considering the time and place, few other explanations are possible.

8. Since most Indian languages, including those of the Blackfoot Confederacy, were not written until modern times, it is hardly surprising that many spellings are in use. I have witnessed Piegans (or Peigans, as the case may be) argue the proper spelling of their own names.

9. See Alex Johnston, *Plants and the Blackfoot* (Lethbridge, Alta.: Lethbridge Historical Society, 1987) for much interesting information and good illustrations on the uses of native plants.

10. Ewers, *The Blackfeet*, cites an 1854 report to the U.S. Indian Office in which Assistant to the Superintendent of Indian Affairs James Doty estimated the Blackfoot population at 2,550 warriors and 7,630 souls, based on a formula developed during the fur trade that allowed three warriors and nine persons per lodge. Doty counted 850 lodges.

Alex Johnston supports the population figures calculated by Sir George Simpson, governor-in-chief of the Hudson's Bay Company in the mid-1800s. He put the three tribes of the Blackfoot—including their allies, the Sarcees (Sarcis) and Gros Ventres—at 2,500 warriors and 8,800 souls; see Hugh A. Dempsey, ed., "Simpson's Essay on the Blackfoot, 1841," *Alberta History* 38 (Winter 1990), 1-14.

11. Dick Cassutt believes the Bloods are simply an offshoot of the South Piegans or Montana Blackfeet. Much evidence disputes this, but Dick does not remember Julia mentioning how the Piegans got their name; to her, they were simply The People.

12. To Hibbard's account of his pioneer great-grandfather, I have added a few details gleaned from Dick Pace, "Henry Sieben: Pioneer Montana Stockman," *Montana, The Magazine of Western History* 29 (January 1979).

13. The 1851 Treaty of Fort Laramie described the portion of Blackfoot country lying between the Missouri and the Yellowstone, but no Blackfoot leaders were in attendance to sign it.

On October 17, 1855, Lame Bull's treaty, officially the Treaty with the Blackfoot Nation, was signed in a cottonwood grove on the north bank of the Missouri just below the mouth of the Judith by 59 leaders of the Blackfoot Confederacy, plus representatives of the Gros Ventres, Flathead, Pend d'Oreille, and Nez Perce tribes. It granted the Blackfoot Nation *exclusive rights* (with some rights excluded) to a vast area in what is now Montana, Alberta, and Saskatchewan. Ratified by the U.S. Senate and signed by the president in April 1856, it is now stored in the National Archives. In 1865 and 1868 that exclusive Blackfoot territory was eroded by treaties which were never ratified.

In 1871, the U.S. Government stopped treating with Indian tribes as foreign nations, and henceforth made "agreements" instead. On February 11, 1887, an agreement was signed confirming arrangements decreed by orders in council in 1865 and 1868, ceding an additional vast area east, which included the Sweet Grass Hills. This agreement was approved by Congress in May 1888.

14. The Assiniboia district of the Canadian North West Territories became part of Saskatchewan when the prairie provinces were organized in 1905.

15. On September 22, 1887, Canada negotiated Treaty No. 7, its only treaty with the Blackfoot Indians, at a place called Blackfoot Crossing on the south bank of the Bow River, 60 miles east of Calgary. On that occasion the tribes surrendered 50,000 square miles north of the international boundary between the Cypress Hills and the Rockies.

In addition to hunting rights and reserves, each man, woman, and child received $12 cash and was promised a $5 annuity, $2,000 worth of ammunition annually, a Winchester rifle "as soon as convenient," plus stipulated cattle and agricultural supplies.

16. Sherrill MacLaren, *Braehead* (Toronto: McLelland & Stewart, 1986), offers interesting Canadiana focusing on Colonel Macleod and the Cross family.

17. As explained above (n. 13), Lame Bull's treaty is the only official "treaty" between the United States and the Blackfoot Nation. Lame Bull died in a buffalo hunting accident near the Sweet Grass Hills the following year (1856); he was about 60 years old.

18. One afternoon in 1990 I spent a fascinating hour with the Big Spring family while Billy explained the spelling of his father's name. Sounding out each syllable, the family agreed that *So-ko-yu-kris-cum*, was preferable to the traditional *Su-que-o-sis-con*, which can be found in various sources. Billy believes his spelling is phonetically correct, and he pointed out that the modern Blackfoot alphabet does not include the letter *q*. He also prefers the spelling *pe-ku-ni* for his people, as I have used it in this work.

19. Harold McCracken, *The Charles M. Russell Book* (Garden City: Doubleday & Co., 1957), p. 13, quotes "Kid Amby" Cheney regarding the artist's cowboying abilities on a roundup in which Cheney wrangled horses during the day while Russell served as "nighthawk."

20. The Pacific Scandal of 1873, a major event in Canadian history, found Sir John A. Macdonald's Conservative Administration accused of accepting campaign funds in return for favoritism on a Canadian Pacific construction contract. The government was badly defeated and Macdonald was turned out of office for five years.

21. See David H. Breen, *The Canadian Prairie West and the Ranching Frontier, 1874-1924* (Toronto: University of Toronto Press, 1983), for the authoritative history of the western Canadian cattle industry.

22. Captain John Palliser surveyed the territory between 1857 and 1860 and published his report as *Further Papers Relative to the Expedition Under Captain Palliser* (London: George Edward Eyre and William Spottiswoode, 1860); see also, Irene M. Spry, ed., *The Papers of the Palliser Expedition* (Toronto: The Champlain Society, 1968).

23. General James Brisbin, *The Beef Bonanza, or, How to Get Rich on the Plains* (Philadelphia: Lippencott, 1881); this classic promotional material is rare. A more easily obtainable contemporary report of the western Canadian range, recently reprinted and beautifully illus-

trated, is L.V. Kelly, *The Range Men* (1913; reprint, High River, Alta.: Willow Creek Publishing, 1988).

24. George Ewing's story is taken from written "recollections," a copy of which are in my possession. The inflationary horse business is reported in Christopher Ward, *The War of the Revolution* (New York: The Macmillan Co., 1952).

25. David Lavender, *History of The Great West* (New York: American Heritage Publishing Co., Inc., 1965); this work is an excellent source of general information on western land tenure and, like Lavender's other writings, is very readable.

2
Range Settlement

1. Attributed to well-known western author Marie Sandoz.

2. "Short horses" were sprinters—mostly Thoroughbred—that ran their best in 440 yards, or, a quarter-mile; thus, the name "quarter horse" evolved for them.

3. For more on the Winder Ranche, see Breen, *The Canadian Prairie West* (pp. 9-11), and Kelly, *The Range Men*.

4. Breen, *The Canadian Prairie West* (pp. 44-45), shows the boundaries of the northern Cochrane Ranche, or British-American lease, relative to the mouth of Jumping Pound Creek.

5. Heel flies, or warble flies, are *Hypodermia bovis*. In summer the females lay eggs on the heels of cattle, causing them to stampede and lose weight. The fly larvae burrow through the hide and eventually travel through the internal organs to appear in winter as warble grubs in boils along the backs of cattle. The escape holes made by the warbles permanently damage the hide for future leather production.

6. Gerald refers to a complete prolapse of the uterus following calving and a common "cure."

7. Joseph Kinsey Howard, *Montana: High, Wide, and Handsome* (New Haven: Yale University Press, 1943), pp. 295-300, gives a good account of the Mizpah-Pumpkin Creek Grazing Association, established in 1928.

8. *Report on the Western Range, Great But Neglected Natural Resource* (1936), 74th Cong., 2d sess., S. Doc. 199.

3
Hard Times and Range Horses

1. Bangs disease (named for a Danish veterinarian), or brucellosis, is a bacterial disease common in many species, including elk and bison as well as domestic cattle; abortion often results. Because humans can contract the disease (as undulant fever), control of brucellosis is bureaucratic, political, and expensive.

2. See Donald MacKay, *The Asian Dream* (Vancouver, B.C.: Douglas & McIntyre, 1986) for the story of the Canadian Pacific Railroad silk trains. In prewar, pre-nylon days, silk was big business in both Canada and the U.S. Since it originated in the Orient, there was great competition in transporting silk from Pacific Coast ports to mills on the St. Lawrence and the eastern seaboard. The so-called transcontinental railroads across the United States went only as far as Chicago; there—whether the freight was human, bovine, porcine, or silken—time-consuming switching was required between railway lines and yards. Both the Great Northern, running across the northern states, and the truly transcontinental Canadian railroads ran "crack" silk trains, which put most others onto sidings while they passed. It is a measure of the crisis of the times that such trains would stop to take on cattle cars.

3. In 1973 President Nixon froze beef prices to placate consumer groups. The resulting surplus of beef in coolers and feedlots all over the country promptly lowered prices for beef cattle, which took several years to correct.

4. See Paul De Kruif, *The Hunger Fighters* (New York: Harcourt Brace & Co., 1928), for an interesting account of summer-fallow at Indian Head, Assiniboia (Saskatchewan), during the second Riel Rebellion of 1885; Howard, *Montana*, gives a fuller and very interesting account of the invention of strip farming in the Monarch-Nobleford area; see also, Donald Worster, *Dust Bowl: The Southern Plains in the 1930s* (New York: Oxford University Press, 1979).

5. "Fannie Maes" (National Marketing Association bonds) are a good example.

6. All so-called wild horses in the Americas are actually feral, that is, descended from tame stock.

7. A freeze brand is put on with an "iron" (often copper) chilled in liquid nitrogen. It usually makes the hair turn white and the brand easy to read. The process is seemingly painless to the animal and, when successful, is easier to read without clipping than a hot-iron brand. But, in my experience, it's not always successful. Freeze

brands do less damage to the hide than a hot-iron brand, but they're still discriminated against by tanners.

8. The Wild Horse and Burro Committee was established by Congress under the 1971 Senate bill S. 1116—an *Act to Require the Protection, Management, and Control of Wild Free-Roaming Horses and Burros on Public Lands*, commonly known as the Wild Horse and Burro Act—to the great chagrin of many good civil servants in the Bureau of Land Management who have to administer it.

9. It may already be too late. See "The Flicka Factor," *The Wall Street Journal*, 26 September 1989; although the European Common Market was in 1989 the world's largest horse meat consumer (with 65 percent of the horses imported), consumption is down to one pound per person—half of what it was a decade earlier.

10. A study by Terry Anderson and Dean Lueck in *PERC Reports* 6, 3 (Bozeman, Mont.: Political Economy Research Center, November 1988), explains that 80 percent of Indian land on reservations is owned collectively by tribes; 19 percent by individuals (subject to BIA trust restrictions); and 1 percent by BIA. This oversimplifies actual land tenure because many reservations contain large acreages of fee-simple lands controlled by neither the BIA nor the tribe. In addition, 82 percent of Indian land is farmed or grazed by non-Indians.

4
Range Weather

1. Carolyn Cunningham, comp., *Montana Weather* (Helena: Montana Magazine, Inc., 1982) offers a variety of authoritative and interesting accounts and statistics.

2. See Helen B. West, *Flood: The Story of the 1964 Blackfeet Disaster* (Browning, Mont.: Blackfeet Tribal Council, 1970).

3. Montana's share of grazing fees on BLM and Forest Service land in 1988 was $125 million—a significant return to the state treasury.

John R. Lacey and James B Johnson, "Livestock Grazing on Federal Lands: A Boon to Montana's Economy," *Western Wildlands* 16, 2 (Summer 1990), point out that "income generated by [grazing] of public lands, and its progress through local economies, makes a substantial contribution to the economic well-being of Western states" (p. 24). Furthermore, grazing permits have market value which must be capitalized when comparisons with private leases are made. Federal grazing fee formulas are badly outdated and, when revised, must address items like landlord services (which are minimal), and current forage value.

5

A Range Camp

1. Ginger Renner, "Looking Backward and Forward From the Mountains: Renner and Russell Revisited," *Rangelands* 10, 5 (October 1988), 213-14.

2. Dr. Ray Woodward, an assistant animal husbandman at the North Montana Experiment Station at Havre (just across the Line from Manyberries) from 1939 to 1941, later went on to direct beef cattle research at the Miles City USDA research station, and played a major role in importing European cattle.

3. F. R. Carpenter, "Establishing Management Under the Taylor Grazing Act," *Rangelands* 3, 3 (June 1981), 105-15; this article is a verbatim and complete transcript of Carpenter's address given January 8, 1962, at Montana State College in Bozeman. With permission from the *Rangelands* editor, I have edited and shortened it without, I hope, any loss of fact or flavor. I consider the original a classic.

4. The Taylor Grazing Act of 1934 placed roughly 8 million acres of Montana's public rangelands under the jurisdiction of the U. S. Grazing Service, which joined other government agencies in studying and managing the range. In 1946 the Grazing Service and the General Land Office combined to form the Bureau of Land Management, converting grazing district graziers into BLM district managers. Over the years, BLM has bought, sold, and traded various parcels of land; in 1988 it managed 8.2 million acres in Montana.

5. Turn-of-the-century attempts at preserving big game led to hunting bans and predator control in many places. The resulting excess of deer on the million-acre Kaibab Plateau in southern Utah quickly out-stripped their food supply and the population "crashed" in 1923-24, with losses estimated at 60 percent. This experience led conservationist Aldo Leopold to define an "irruptive sequence" with four stages: 1) limited hunting and predation allow prey to multiply; 2) "deer lines" become evident on palatable browse (identifying the limits of their reach); 3) as herds peak, they begin eating unpalatable browse and the young die of starvation; 4) many adults die of disease, palatable plants decrease, and less palatable plants increase. Prey populations eventually plateau far below the pre-irruptive levels. By 1927 Leopold began to preach that there was no longer any such thing as a balance of nature; it had been upset long ago.

Alston Chase, *Playing God in Yellowstone: The Destruction of America's First National Park* (New York: Harcourt Brace Jovanovich, Publishers, 1987), pp. 24-27, describes the chain of events that led to a similar crash in the Yellowstone elk population in 1919-20, and subsequent range deterioration. In 1934 the National Park Service began a program of trapping and transplanting elk to other wild areas. Within a few years, ranchers from Montana's Judith Basin to Alberta's Porcupine Hills began seeing elk for the first time in several generations.

6. This was the Canyon Creek fire, which burned nearly 250,000 acres of Montana's national forest. It was controlled only after leaving the forest and burning across 40,000 acres of ranchland. Government lawyers at first maintained that the federal "let-burn" policy had not been negligent. But nearly two years later, under pressure from Montana's congressional delegation, they agreed to negotiate 92 claims—good news to many of the local forest service personnel charged with carrying out the unfortunate policy.

7. Prior to 1930 British Columbia and parts of Manitoba already controlled their own natural resources. The Depression made Prime Minister William Lyon Mackenzie King's Liberal government in Ottawa vulnerable to Conservative "farmers' governments" on the prairies (such as the Farmers' Union in Alberta), so he bought support in Alberta and Saskatchewan by trading off federal lands and resources to them. Since then, control of most public lands in western Canada has been provincial, and "provincial" civil services have flourished.

8. In Alberta oil, gas, and other mineral companies pay royalties and surface charges for their use of crown land. Hunters and fishermen pay a nominal fee through licenses. See Jeffrey C. Mosley, et al., *Seven Popular MYTHS About Grazing Livestock on Public Lands* (Moscow, Idaho and Tucson, Arizona: University of Idaho Forest Wildlife and Range Experiment Station, and University of Arizona Agricultural Experiment Station, March 1990), and Lacey and Johnson, "Livestock Grazing," for an interesting discussion of the "fairness" of rent paid by the livestock industry for public grazing land (applicable on both sides of the international boundary).

9. Many areas have plants that go by the common name of "buffalo grass." On the southern Alberta or north-central Montana range under discussion here, Alex Johnston would be referring to Blue grama, *Bouteloua gracilis*. In eastern Montana he would be talking about *Buchloe dactyloides*. See *Guide to Common Montana Range Plants*, (Range Management Club, Bozeman: Montana State University, 1974).

10. Johnston's co-worker from Manyberries, Sylver Smoliak, found that Crested wheatgrass and Russian wild rye produced 800 and 650 pounds (respectively) of forage per acre on sites where native range

produced only 380 pounds per acre. Johnston liked to caution, however, that native range—including the ages-old sod—has advantages that may be more important than yield alone.

6
Range Ideas

1. *Report on the Western Range*, 74th Cong., 2d sess., S. Doc. 199; the passage is excerpted in this book, p. 72.

2. The Center for Holistic Resource Management is an international nonprofit corporation based in Albuquerque, New Mexico. It was organized in 1984 to increase and diffuse knowledge of HRM.

3. Andre Voisin, *Grass Productivity* (London: Crosby, Lockwood & Son, Ltd., 1961).

4. M. E. Ensminger, known far and wide as "Doctor E.," drew crowds to stockmen's short-courses at Washington State University during his 21 years as chairman of the Department of Animal Science. He later developed those courses into the International Stockmen's School, under the auspices of his Agriservices Foundation headquartered at Clovis, California.

Allan Savory and his partner, Dr. Stan Parsons, delivered papers on short-duration grazing at the International Stockmen's School held at Phoenix in 1978, San Antonio in 1979, and Tucson in 1980.

7
Range Know-How

1. Savory no longer uses the term "short-duration grazing," although he did when he and Stan Parsons wrote papers that were published in M.E. Ensminger, ed., *Beef Cattle Science Handbook*, vol. 17 (Clovis, Calif.: Agriservices Foundation, Inc., 1980).

2. Kochia is a common annual weed of the goosefoot family: *Kochia scoparia l.* It comes in quickly where vegetation has been removed, by farming or otherwise.

3. Zero-tillage is not a new idea. Edward Faulkner wrote in *Plowman's Folly* (Norman: University of Oklahoma Press, 1943): "The truth is that no one has advanced a scientific reason for plowing"— words that profoundly influenced Ike Lanier.

4. These statements about the high percentage of residual nutrient value in prairie root systems is borne out in a variety of literature,

and is apparently accepted by the scientific community, if not yet understood by the general public in 1990. Scientists at the Lethbridge Research Station (C.A. Campbell, R.P. Ventner, H.A. Janzen, and K.E. Bowren) have compiled the long-term agronomic data relevant to this subject in a booklet from Supply and Services Canada, Publication 1841/E, entitled *Crop Rotation Studies on the Canadian Prairies*, (Ottawa: Canadian Government Publishing Centre, 1990); its data corroborates Lanier's following statement about moisture loss from summer-fallow land.

5. Roundup, a registered trademark of the Monsanto Company, is an organic herbicide that breaks down quickly into natural products: carbon dioxide, water, nitrogen, and phosphate. In soil, the active ingredient is not taken up by plants and is essentially immobile and non-persistent. Roundup normally has a half-life of less than sixty days.

6. The Q7 Ranche has for many years used high-energy, custom-built range cubes. About 3 inches long and 1½ inches thick, they are much larger than average "cakes" and don't easily get lost in the snow. Also, they must be chewed, which takes some time, so the strongest cows can't race in and scoop up more than their share. Elk, no doubt, get many leftovers.

7. Beefbooster is a registered trademark in the United States and Canada of Beefbooster Management Ltd. of Calgary, Alberta; it denotes a genetic process, not a breed. About twenty different breeds are used under license by seed-stock producers to produce five "synthetic" strains, each designed for a specific purpose. Neil Harvie founded the Glenbow M1 line, on an Angus base, selected for maternal characteristics.

8. Montana State University "peaked" in 1981 with 26 graduates in range science. In 1988, MSU had only eight range graduates; the University of Alberta, five.

8

Range Grasses

1. See U.S. Department of Agriculture, ARS Program Aid No. 1188, *The National Plant Germplasm System* (Washington, D.C.: Government Printing Office, 1977).

2. See Palliser, *Further Papers*, in which he refers to a grassy area (Palliser's Triangle) based on the 49th parallel and peaking southeast of Edmonton.

3. For a fascinating account of plant exploration in the early years of this century, see Isabel Shipley, *Frank N. Meyer: Plant Hunter in Asia* (Ames: Iowa State University Press, 1984).

4. See Howard E. Waterworth and George A. White, "Plant Introductions and Quarantine: The Need for Both," *Plant Disease* 66 (January 1982).

5. This happened before Dr. Lawrence's time. An older, longer-retired, plant scientist told me that "young Tom Lawrence" was mistaken: the solid-stemmed spring wheat was from Portugal, not China. In any case, Tom Lawrence—now recently retired, himself, after a long and distinguished career—makes a valid point.

6. The National Seed Storage Lab holds several thousand Canadian samples, including cultivars of Northern and Western wheatgrass bred by Alex Johnston and Sylvester Smoliak. Canada has its own Plant-Gene Resources Centre in Ottawa, where samples receive a plant-gene resources (PGR) number.

7. Of possible interest to many cattlemen is the fact that the National Seed Storage Lab switched to liquid nitrogen storage in 1988. The vats now storing grass seed were designed for preserving bull semen, identical to those found at artificial breeding centers.

8. See Johnson, *Plants and the Blackfoot*.

Bibliography

Breen, David H. *The Canadian Prairie West and the Ranching Frontier, 1874-1924.* Toronto: University of Toronto Press, 1983.

Brisbin, Gen. James S. *The Beef Bonanza, or, How to Get Rich on the Plains.* Philadelphia: Lippincott, 1881.

Campbell, C.A., R. P. Ventner, H. A. Janzen, and K. E. Bowren. *Crop Rotation Studies on the Canadian Prairies.* Supply and Services Canada, Publication 1841/E. Ottawa: Canadian Government Publishing Centre, 1990.

Cates, Jon. *The Story of the National Bison Range.* Helena, Montana: Falcon Press, 1986.

Chase, Alston. *Playing God in Yellowstone: The Destruction of America's First National Park.* New York: Harcourt Brace Jovanovich, Publishers, 1987.

Cunningham, Carolyn, comp. *Montana Weather.* Helena: Montana Magazine, Inc., 1982.

De Kruif, Paul. *The Hunger Fighters.* New York: Harcourt Brace & Co., 1928.

Dempsey, Hugh A., ed. "Simpson's Essay on the Blackfoot, 1841." *Alberta History* 38 (Winter 1990).

Ensminger, M.E., ed. *Beef Cattle Science Handbook.* Vol. 17. Clovis, California: Agriservices Foundation, Inc., 1980.

Ewers, John C. *The Blackfeet: Raiders on the Northwestern Plains.* Norman: University of Oklahoma Press, 1958.

Faulkner, Edward H. *Plowman's Folly.* Norman: University of Oklahoma Press, 1943.

Grey, Zane. *Wildfire.* New York: Grosset & Dunlop, 1922.

Guide to Common Montana Range Plants. Range Management Club. Bozeman: Montana State University, 1974.

Herr, Ronald J. "The Federal Rangeland Grazing Fee: A Study of the Subsidy Question and a Review of the Public Rangelands Improvement Act Fee Formula." Unpublished. Park Ridge, Illinois: American Farm Bureau Federation, Economic Research Division, September 12, 1986.

Hornaday, William T. *Extermination of the American Bison, With a Sketch of its Discovery and Life History*. Washington, D.C.: U.S. Government Printing Office, 1889.

Howard, Joseph Kinsey. *Montana: High, Wide, and Handsome*. New Haven: Yale University Press, 1943.

Johnston, Alex. *Plants and the Blackfoot*. Lethbridge, Alberta: Lethbridge Historical Society, 1987.

Journal of Range Management. Denver: Bimonthly publication of the Society for Range Management.

Kelly, L.V. *The Range Men*. 1913. Reprint. High River, Albrerta: Willow Creek Publishing, 1988.

Lacey, John R. and James B. Johnson. "Livestock Grazing on Federal Lands: A Boon to Montana's Economy." *Western Wildlands* 16 (Summer 1990).

Lavender, David. *History of The Great West*. New York: American Heritage Publishing Company, Inc., 1965.

MacKay, Donald. *The Asian Dream*. Vancouver, British Columbia: Douglas & McIntyre, 1986.

MacLaren, Sherrill. *Braehead*. Toronto: McLelland & Stewart, 1986.

McCracken, Harold. *The Charles M. Russell Book*. Garden City: Doubleday & Company, 1957.

Mosley, Jeffrey C., E. Lamar Smith, and Phil R. Ogden. *Seven Popular MYTHS About Grazing Livestock on Public Lands*. Moscow, Idaho, and Tucson, Arizona: University of Idaho Forest Wildlife and Range Experiment Station, and University of Arizona Agricultural Experiment Station, March 1990.

Neilsen, Darwin B. "Grazing Fees for Public Lands: What's Fair?" *Utah Science* 42, 1 (Spring 1982).

Pace, Dick. "Henry Sieben: Pioneer Montana Stockman." *Montana, The Magazine of Western History* 29 (January 1979).

Palliser, Capt. John. *Further Papers Relative to the Exploration Under Captain Palliser.* London: George Edward Eyre and William Spottiswoode, 1860.

Parsons, John E. *West on the 49th Parallel.* New York: William Morrow & Co., 1963.

Rangelands. Denver: Bimonthly publication of the Society for Range Management.

Ross, Alexander. *The Red River Settlement: Its Rise, Progress, and Present State.* London: Smith, Elder, 1856.

Savory, Allan. *Holistic Resource Management.* Washington, D.C.: Island Press, 1988.

Sharp, Paul F. *Whoop-up Country.* Minneapolis: University of Minnesota Press, 1955.

Shipley, Isabel. *Frank N. Meyer: Plant Hunter in Asia.* Ames: Iowa State University Press, 1984.

Spry, Irene M., ed. *The Papers of the Palliser Expedition.* Toronto: The Champlain Society, 1968.

Voisin, Andre. *Grass Productivity.* London: Crosby, Lockwood & Son, Ltd., 1961.

U.S. Congress. Senate. *Report on Western Range, Great But Neglected Natural Resource.* 74th Cong., 2d sess., 1936. S. Doc. 199. Serial 10005.

U.S. Department of Agriculture. *The National Plant Germplasm System.* ARS Program Aid No. 1188. Washington, D.C.: Government Printing Office, 1977.

Ward, Christopher. *The War of the Revolution.* New York: The Macmillan Co., 1952.

Waterworth, Howard E. and George A. White. "Plant Introductions and Quarantine: The Need for Both." *Plant Disease* 66 (January 1982).

West, Helen B. *Flood: The Story of the 1964 Blackfeet Disaster.* (Browning, Montana: Blackfeet Tribal Council, 1970)

Worster, Donald. *Dust Bowl: The Southern Plains in the 1930s.* New York: Oxford University Press, 1979.

Index

278

281

proper-use philosophy, 159
  science of, 160, 211-12
  seed-ripe treatment, 196, 210
Range soil,
  loss of organic matter, 93,
    152, 186-88
  pulverizing, 93, 187
  salinity, 6, 187, 222
  summer fallow, 93, 186-89
  wind erosion, 92, 93, 94, 174,
    187
Renner, Frederick, 132
Rest-rotation grazing, 158-61,
  179, 181
Rogers Pass, 119
Rogler, George, 223
Roskie, George F., 139-43, 257
Rosemary, Alberta, 80
Ross, Bob, 30-31, 100, 144-47, 143,
  257
Ross, Walter, 83
Russell, Charles M., 21, 22, 31,
  132
Russia, plant exploration, 224
Ryerson, Don, 148-149, 220-21,
  257

Sampson, A. W., 160
Saskatchewan, 47, 52, 54, 55, 58,
  59, 61-63, 83, 92
Saudi Arabia, grazing in, 148, 220
Savory, Allan, 167-73, 181, 182,
  257
Savory Grazing Method (SGM),
  182
Sears, Harold and Hal, 133
Sellars, A. R. "Porky", 174
Sheldon National Wildlife Refuge,
  163
Siberian grasses, 218
Sieben, Henry, 19, 20-23, 179
Smith, Maynard, 43, 91, 210, 258
Smith River, 59, 63
Smoliak, Sylvester, 191-93, 218-
  20, 258
Society for Range Management
  (SRM), 132, 155

Soil Conservation Service (SCS),
  144-46, 153, 155, 204, 206
Stanford, 96
Strip-farming, 2, 94, 95
Sun River, 6, 26, 123
Sweet Grass Hills, 3, 6, 26, 116,
  120, 132
Swift Current, Saskatchewan, 54
  Research Station, 94, 217,
    230-33
Swift Dam, 126-27

Taylor Grazing Act, 69, 71, 135-
  39, 148
Two Medicine River, 109, 125,
  127, 199

U.N. Food and Agriculture
  Organization, 234
U.S.D.A. plant seed classification
  system, 223
U.S.D.A. plant exploration
  program, 224
U.S. Fish & Wildlife Service, 163,
  164
U.S. Forest Service, 136, 139-44,
  203, 206
  commensurability rule, 138
U.S. Grazing Service, 138, 158
Utah, 20, 71, 219, 221, 226, 232

Vavilov, N. I. 229
Vavilov Institute, 230, 232
Voisin, Andre, 170

Walking-Coyote, Samuel, 12
Wallace, Henry, 72
Wallace, J.H., 83
Weeds,
  biological control, 166
  halogeton, 166
  knapweed, 228
  kochia, 184, 185
  Roundup herbicide, 190
  Tordon herbicide, 228
Western Stock Growers' Associa-
  tion, 88